Judith Butler and Politics

THINKING POLITICS
Series Editors: Geoff M. Boucher and Matthew Sharpe

JUDITH BUTLER AND POLITICS

Adriana Zaharijević

EDINBURGH
University Press

Edinburgh University Press is one of the leading university presses in the UK. We publish academic books and journals in our selected subject areas across the humanities and social sciences, combining cutting-edge scholarship with high editorial and production values to produce academic works of lasting importance. For more information visit our website: edinburghuniversitypress.com

Edinburgh University Press Ltd
13 Infirmary Street
Edinburgh EH1 1LT

First published in hardback by Edinburgh University Press 2023

Typeset in 11/13pt Adobe Sabon LT Pro
by Cheshire Typesetting Ltd, Cuddington, Cheshire
A CIP record for this book is available from the British Library

ISBN 978 1 3995 1708 9 (hardback)
ISBN 978 1 3995 1709 6 (paperback)
ISBN 978 1 3995 1710 2 (webready PDF)
ISBN 978 1 3995 1711 9 (epub)

Contents

Acknowledgements

This book has been written twice. It first appeared in Serbian as *Život tela. Politička filozofija Džudit Batler* (Belgrade: Akademska knjiga, 2020) and was then translated into English and heavily rewritten. I am most grateful to Bora Babić, my Serbian publisher, for allowing me to use the book as a template for this one.

I wish to sincerely thank Geoff Boucher for his continuous support during the entire process of (re)writing this book, as well as Ersev Ersoy and Sarah Foyle from Edinburgh University Press for making the publication process an enjoyable experience.

The manuscript benefited greatly from innumerable conversations with valuable interlocutors I was privileged to have in the last four years. I especially wish to thank those who helped me either advance my thoughts or shift them in the direction of being presented in English. Hana Ćopić, Mark Devenney, Éric Fassin, Clara Gallagher, Ben Gook, Sabine Hark, Emma Ingala, Biljana Kašić, Predrag Krstić, Hanna Meißner, Ana Miškovska Kajevska, Aleksandar Pavlović, Elisabeth Plate, Eva von Redecker and Nuria Sánchez Madrid all became, in different ways, fellow travellers, turning this into a truly exceptional journey. The chance to present parts of the manuscript in Belgrade, Brighton, Ljubljana, Madrid and Warsaw provided me with fulfilling discussions which, in some cases, significantly altered the text; nor would the text be what it is without Edward Djordjevic, with his careful reading and subtle feeling for languages.

Being acquainted not only with the work of Judith Butler but with her personally invited a sense of great humility, imposing an imperative not to attempt the most accurate interpretation, but to offer Butler's expansive thoughts through a frame of political imagination – a more than necessary requirement in the moment in which our world finds itself.

Finally, this book would never be without the loving companionship of Gert Röhrborn, his piercing mind and inexhaustible desire to always complicate the discussion.

Abbreviations of Butler's Works

AC – *Antigone's Claim*
BTM – *Bodies That Matter*
CF – 'Contingent Foundations'
CHU – *Contingency, Hegemony, Universality*
D – *Dispossession*
ES – *Excitable Speech*
FCR – 'For a Careful Reading'
FN – *The Force of Nonviolence*
FoW – *Frames of War*
GAO – *Giving an Account of Oneself*
GT – *Gender Trouble*
MC – 'Merely Cultural'
NT – *Notes Toward a Performative Theory of Assembly*
PL – *Precarious Life*
PLP – *The Psychic Life of Power*
PW – *Parting Ways*
SD – *Subjects of Desire*
SS – *Senses of the Subject*
UG – *Undoing Gender*

Introduction

It is not very often that reading a book leaves us with a feeling that something in us has changed. Yet, there are many testimonies to this experience when it comes to reading Judith Butler. Butler's texts seem to have the power to challenge us profoundly and coax us into thinking differently. The seemingly simple question that hovers over the pages of this book is: how is this possible? What do Butler's texts do to their readers? What do they perform on us? Moreover, what is it about these texts that incites us into thinking that there is something about the world that needs to be remade, done differently?

Given that Butler's thought is shaped by the registers, questions and frames largely taken from philosophy, its inherent political impetus is a continual source of puzzlement. All comprehensive studies of her work show full awareness of its entanglement with the political. Situating Butler's thought at the crossroads of gender and queer theory, Sara Salih (2002), Vicki Kirby (2006), Moya Lloyd (2007) and Gill Jagger (2008) all put strong emphasis on the political power of the performative. Elena Loizidou (2007) was the first to discuss Butler's work in the triad of ethics, politics and law, Samuel Chambers and Terrell Carver (2008) present Butler as a significant political thinker, while Birgit Schippers (2014) defines her work as belonging to an emerging field of international political philosophy. Butler, however, complicates straightforward definitions. She has adamantly claimed that she has not produced a specific conception of the political: 'I am sure I do not have "a conception of the political". I am not sure one needs to have such a conception in order to think about politics or even to engage politically' (Ingala 2017: 26). In addition, on many occasions she has insisted on important differences between theory and politics.

Taking these cues into account, this book aims to capture an almost paradoxical dynamic of philosophy and politics that gives shape to Butler's thought. Urging us to question even the most basic experiences, philosophy interrupts business as usual, arrests us midstream, forces us to stop and question, and to sometimes remain in question. Philosophy slows down. The political, on the other hand, impels us forward, coerces into action, speeds life up, always launching us in the midst of the multitude and amongst others. This double commitment in Butler's thought – to urgency and to the scrupulous labour of thinking – is a crucial part of its peculiar performativity.

'Insurrection at the level of ontology', possibly the leitmotif of this book, attempts to take stock of this double commitment. The phrase itself appears in one significant paragraph in *Precarious Life*, which spurs us to open up critical questions about reality (*Precarious Life*, 2004a [hereafter PL]: 33). The phrase as such is curious, combining hardly relatable nouns. Insurrections are paradigmatically political acts of open resistance against the established order and authority. One can rebel, of course, at various levels, but ontology is not usually considered one of them. Reading Butler, however, compels us to rise up at precisely that level, to rebel against what we thought was real. The insurrection is performed as a demand on the reader, challenging us, urging us to question what is given, and whether it can be thought differently – indeed, whether something can be done for reality to be remade. Thus, the political emerges out of the text itself; it appears and challenges *in medias res*. The text as such does not offer an account of an insurrection; it is neither description of it, nor does the text ever explicitly prescribe it. Still, caught by this textual insurrection at the level of the real, we are seized by an act that opens us up, initiates us into a change happening to us here and now.

Extricating politics from philosophy in Butler is not easy. Politics is about action; it is performative in the truest sense of the word. Philosophy does something as well, but these actions differ. Crucially, philosophy is not there to supply the vision that will redeem life ('For a Careful Reading', 1995b [hereafter FCR]: 131). Butler's politics of philosophy, to borrow a phrase from Tuija Pulkkinen, aims at something entirely different. 'The kind of politics of philosophy which we encounter in Butler's texts is doing rather than explaining or arguing' (Pulkkinen 2018: 142), let alone procuring axioms for action. Whenever she engages with philosophical textual traditions, and this book aims to shed light on some of those creative dialogues, she disentangles them from their omnitemporal foundations, intervening in the here and now, presenting those interventions as a direct performative engagement with the social and political reality. If we follow Mark Devenney, we could claim that Butler's 'insurrectionary ontology' entails an 'improper politics', which is in the end always about 'unpicking the violence intrinsic to proper ways of being'

(Devenney 2020: 3). The notion of violence here is crucial, and it is crucially political: ultimately, Butler's entire opus can be understood as a philosophical struggle to reduce violence.

This may seem too strong a statement. Certainly, there will be those who will claim that it does apply to the more recent work, but not to Butler's entire oeuvre. Indeed, some caution is in order, since from 2004 – which saw the publication of two significant books, *Undoing Gender* and *Precarious Life* – a certain redirection in her thought did take place. *Undoing Gender* brought the curtain down, at least temporarily, on debates about gender performativity. *Precarious Life*, on the other hand, was a response to US policy after September 11th, introducing various problems that would shape Butler's texts from then on: war, antimilitarism, precarity, dispossession, assembly and, finally, nonviolence. The new topics also carry with them a seemingly entirely new terminological arsenal, and this 'second phase' was described variously as her ethical turn, humanist turn, a shift from performativity to precarity. Given its utility for wading through Butler's fractal and layered work, the distinction between phases can be deployed, and is deployed in this book. However, I do not support the thesis of a clear and fundamental break – in which violence appears as an entirely new subject, where political gave way to the ethical, in which the human irrupted into a previously antihumanist discourse, with performativity abandoned for a different ontological axis.

Ordinarily, when there are perplexing distinctions between the phases of someone's oeuvre, interpreters tend to fall into one of two types: those seeking to emphasise the differences, and those seeking similarities and connections even when those are difficult to find. My endeavour belongs to the second group, even at the risk of ignoring Butler's own advice for reading her work. She once claimed that, in general, she does 'not try to connect the earlier work with the more recent work. . . it was never my intention to produce a systematic or internally coherent system of thought' (Zaharijević and Butler 2016: 106). At first glance, it is indeed difficult to construct intrinsic ties between debates about gender and those regarding interdependence, just as it is unusual to fit under one umbrella figures as diverse as Walter Benjamin, Joan Scott and Melanie Klein. The social ontology she professes to offer does not seem causally related to her theory of performativity. Butler's work does not have the features of a system, while some of the paths through the thicket of her concepts can only become visible by means of careful reconstruction. They reveal that

3

some initially small byways later become main roads (such was the case with the notions of grief and mourning, which alongside melancholy haphazardly appeared in early texts, only to flare up from the margins of the debate on Antigone, becoming a mainstay of the texts written after 2001); or else, that some notions that looked early on to carry a lot of weight, have receded from view in later work (such is the notion of subversion).

Despite there being no system, there is a fine thread in Butler's work connecting many diverse and non-overlapping problems. The thread can be briefly described by way of a formula-question that will be varied throughout this book: how is it possible that some lives do not count as lives? From this question issue a series of others that shape the political thought of Judith Butler: how is the differential value of lives produced and maintained? How does the counting itself effect violence? How can a (human) life be lived if not counted? Finally, how can we think life – life of the body, social life – such that all count? The main question, philosophical in kind, appears – in Butler's double commitment – also as a political demand. In *The Force of Nonviolence* (2020), it is articulated as the demand for radical equality.

In addition to the claim that Butler's philosophical endeavours revolve around the reduction of violence, this book proceeds from two important assumptions. The first one is that, throughout her work, Judith Butler tries to think *bodies* differently, such that all bodies count. The second one is that by doing this, she provides a peculiar social ontology guided by an ethico-political impulse.

Now, even those well acquainted with Butler's work would surely pause over the word 'body'. Has not a significant portion of criticism revolved around the charge that the body has not been given sufficient attention in her writing? Is there not well-nigh consensus that the theory of performativity and its specific shaping of gender and sex cuts across the usual ways of speaking about bodily matters? There will be indeed those who claim that, of late, Butler has begun to include bodies in her thinking with greater persistence: 'While Butler started off with a merely linguistic theory of (gender) performativity, in her recent works she broadens her approach and explicitly includes the bodily dimension' (Wehrle 2020: 120–1). Certainly, the books written after *Precarious Life* foregrounded the bodily dimension quite strongly. However, my assertion is that bodies were there all along. Once asked why she decided to put an emphasis on corporeality of public gatherings in her performative theory of assembly,

Butler responded: 'Well, I have always focused on corporeality, even in *Gender Trouble* some 23 years ago, so it is probably no surprise that this dimension of current demonstrations interests me' (Kania 2013: 38). This book tries to confirm this thesis, which goes against the grain of widely accepted interpretations. I argue, moreover, that the body binds seemingly disparate phases or divergent themes within her work. Social ontology – or the ontology of the body – developed especially in *Frames of War* (2009) only makes this bond tangible.

It seems fair to indicate what this book can and cannot do. First, it cannot retain the peculiar manner of Butler's writing. To write about Butler is to accept that one is writing against the performativity of her writing. Gathering, cross-reading and synthesising is far less performative, as it necessarily involves definitions or at least a quest for them. Second, Butler often wrote 'in concert' with others – sometimes quite literally.[1] She has been part of many and, content-wise, truly sundry joint writing projects, which Eirini Avramopolou (2014: 201) describes, referring to *Dispossession*, as 'a new strategy of writing that foregrounds the significance of speaking-with, co-thinking and creating alliances'. This book aims to look for and preserve this thinking with others: her philosophy is not a product of a heroic individual, but a truly joint enterprise. Third, a remark on language: the author of this book is not native to the language in which the book is written. In its current form, the book has been partially translated from Serbian, partially written anew. This bears mentioning not only because of the great importance of the notion of cultural translation in Butler's double commitment, but also because this walk back and forth between languages is a common experience for many of Butler's readers whose life has been changed by the encounter with her texts. If cultural translation and building cross-national alliances is essential to Butler's political project, then it must be that her philosophy only acquires its full shape in being transferred across various linguistic boundaries, as well as returning to the language in which it was originally conceived. Fourth, this book attempts to invoke a wide variety of women, many of whom spoke and speak in mother tongues other than English. In a way, my task was to heed Clare Hemmings's advice on how to tell feminist tales: that is, imagine 'the feminist past somewhat differently – as a series of ongoing contests and relationships rather than a process of imagined linear displacement' (Hemmings 2005: 131). Although one cannot – and should not – underestimate the influence of Hegel, Foucault and Freud, three of Butler's most consistent interlocutors, her story of a famous gender and queer theorist begins with an engagement with Simone de Beauvoir (Butler 1985, 1986). Through this engagement, Butler's double commitment also begins to gain shape. Butler read *The Second Sex* not as feminist primer, but as a book whose fundamental question – what *is* a woman? – is ontological, and can be further operationalised for political reasons. Developing her own framing of this ontological quandary, she indeed contested many of Beauvoir's ideas, but the question itself remained the true point of departure for the theory of performativity. Thus, whenever such acknowledgements were possible, this book tried to shed ample light on them.

The book systematically reads through Butler's texts written from the mid-1980s to the most recent articles, lectures, interviews and op-eds. Its aim is to supply readers with problems and frames peculiar to different phases of Butler's thinking, through various registers in which they were voiced. The book is structured as a trajectory of Butler's thought, which assumes a certain chronological order. The first part of the book, 'Performativity', focuses on texts written mainly before 2001, while the second, 'Liveable World', presents the ideas that followed thereupon. However, we need to tread lightly here, since chronologies can be misleading. For example, if we rely exclusively on text as a witness, we could say that 'the early' Butler developed her thought in the theoretical circle of so-called French feminists, perhaps crucially Beauvoir and Monique Wittig. Such company provided space for new understandings of feminism and first definitions of queer, and no one would reasonably expect to find Hannah Arendt in it. Rightly so. Arendt only becomes more prominent in Butler's work from 2007, that is, from *Who Sings the Nation-State?*, and further, *Parting Ways* (2011), in which she explores the possibility of Jewish thought opposed to Israeli Zionism. One could simply say, Arendt came later in Butler's career, she is part of a new set of problems. However, in 'Ethical Ambivalence', a text published in 2000, at the beginning of which Butler biographises this ambivalence, she mentions something that at that point in time must have sounded like a practical joke: 'I read since the age of fourteen a series of Jewish thinkers and writers [referring to Maimonides, Spinoza, Buber, Benjamin, Arendt and Scholem], and if I am to be honest, I probably know more about them than I know about anything written in queer theory today' (Butler 2000: 16). Such a statement complicates the seemingly neat division into 'before' and 'after'.

The book as a whole is organised 'in doubles' to reflect Butler's double commitment. The two parts, 'Performativity' and 'Liveable World', are further divided into two chapters each, which complement one another. The two-step architectonic is particularly reflected in the preceding first chapter, 'Ontology and Politics'. Shifting between philosophical and political stakes of Butler's endeavours, it plays out the paradox of slow thinking and acting *in medias res*. The chapter provides a kind of glossary of terms that function as pillars, or key motifs, giving shape to the *mise en scène* of the theory of performativity. It outlines the idea of the insurrection at the level of ontology, the purpose of which is to open up and produce possibilities, allowing something new to appear. Uprisings against restricted possibilities are enacted through collective struggles and the laborious work of cultural translation, both of which are political tools for producing a more liveable world.

Part I, 'Performativity', consists of two interrelated chapters, which describe performativity's double movement – the crucial idea that we act and are acted upon. The chapters 'Bodies and Norms' and 'Agency' aim to capture this dynamic. There are many accounts of Butler's understanding of performativity, and the one I am offering relies primarily on its relation to becoming. To this end, the second chapter reads early Butler, trying to reconstruct the influence of Simone de Beauvoir, along with Gayle Rubin, Wittig, Hegel and Foucault, on her conceptualisation of the relation between bodies and norms. The theory of performativity is about the reality in which we live, as embodied – and hence also always gendered – beings. Thus, performativity tells us something about how the real has been established for us, but also about our role in the constitution of such reality. Norms shape our social reality that we at the same time perform – under constraint. The second chapter presents Butler's understanding of sex, gender and performance, so to say, prior to the introduction of the complex notion of performativity. It thus ends with a host of unresolved questions, most important of which is why we do our genders – or, why we craft our bodies – the way we do.

Chapter 3 focuses on what it means to act. In various places, Butler claims that performativity is an account of agency. Agency, as this chapter endeavours to explain, is a mode of remaking the social reality in which we live as embodied beings. In that sense, it needs to be understood as Butler's political commitment to social transformation. However, agency is not only employed to transformative ends. It belongs to acting itself; it is part of our performative becoming in the world, it constitutes us into subjects. The third chapter therefore introduces a fully fledged understanding of performativity as citationality, and presents the notion of constrained and conditioned agency, offering, in addition, Butler's peculiar theory of the subject. It unpacks the transformative aspects of agency, attempting to define who is the agent of social transformation. The last part of this discussion involves various subjects – from drag queens and Antigone to the precarious assembled to performatively protest their disposability. It also prefigures the notion of the social, which is important for subsequent chapters.

In the years after 2001, Butler placed the issues of gender somewhat on hold, turning increasingly to equality and nonviolence. Instead of the subject of agency, the focus was now more on the conditions of life in which any agency becomes possible. Part II, 'Liveable World', consists of two, again interrelated, chapters, 'Liveable Life' and 'Nonviolence'. The world in the title refers to *our world*, the one in which we appear – or do not appear – as humans. The world is thus another name for social reality, the reality of norms that turn us into intelligible and, in a certain way, valuable beings, creatures worthy of being taken into account, protected and, in the final instance, grieved.

Chapter 4 focuses on liveable life, the curious concept engendered by the theory of performativity. The main thesis of the whole section is that not all lives are liveable. Some lives, varying historically and topographically, are unliveable because they are not qualified or counted as alive in the same way. The bodies in which such lives are lodged do not permit of capaciousness. However, the emphasis here shifts from the bodies to the world which fails to respond to the conditions required for a liveable life. Although ultimately undefined, the notion of life appears in Butler's work with many attributes, and this chapter functions as a comprehensive review of them. The section ends with the considerations of war, understood not only as a legitimised mode of manufacturing death, but also as a mode of enhancing ungrievability of lives. Crucially as well, war is the most apparent and the most destructive mode of violating the relation between the bodies and the world.

The fifth chapter delves into Butler's understanding of nonviolence, defined as a way of acknowledging social relation (*The Force of Nonviolence*, 2020 [hereafter FN]: 9). The first part of the chapter offers a trajectory of the notion of violence, tracing its appearances in Butler's thought from the very beginning, where one would probably not expect to find it, to the present where it has become fully recognised as the landmark theme of her work. The lives that do not count in the present configuration of the world are exposed to violence which both precedes and effectuates their not counting. Insurrection at the level of ontology is, conclusively, motivated by the urge to stop or at least reduce violence. In Butler, there are two main paths towards this goal. One is the active repudiation of our own violent and destructive impulses; the other refers to acknowledging interdependence between all lives on Earth. Interdependence appears as the pillar concept that describes our position in the world, by which we are all given relations that help us thrive or otherwise preclude us from possibility.

The conclusion, with the poetic title 'Our Place', is about our reclaiming the world – the only one we have, the one in which we craft ourselves *in medias res*. Our place is one in which we live as bodies, plural, occupying space together with unchosen others, vulnerable to relation or the lack thereof, responsible for the relation we build by our own acting, and interdependent by merely being there. Nonviolence thus appears as a performative perseverance in cohabitation, as 'an experiment to living otherwise' (Butler 2001b: 39) to the current configuration of continuous violation of social bonds. Far from being a mere absence of violence, a politics of nonviolence impels us to do something with the world, the only place we have, here and now.

Notes

1. In addition to *Dispossession*, Butler was in dialogue with Seyla Benhabib, Nancy Fraser and Drucilla Cornell in *Feminist Contentions*; she discussed radical democracy and philosophy with Slavoj Žižek and Ernesto Laclau (*Contingency, Hegemony, Universality*); she had an exchange regarding the necessity of opening feminism to plurality of all women's voices with Elizabeth Beck-Gernsheim and Lídia Puigvert (Beck-Gernsheim, Butler and Puigvert 2003); she commented on Axel Honneth's reading of the notion of reification together with Raymond Geuss and Jonathan Lear (Honneth 2008); she discussed a presumed secularism of critique with Wendy Brown, Talal Asad and Saba Mahmood (Asad et al. 2009), and had debates with Jürgen Habermas, Charles Taylor and Cornel West on the place of religion in the public sphere (Butler et al. 2011).

Chapter 1

Ontology and Politics

The Philosophy of Judith Butler

If there is any need to offer a more precise description of the philosophy Judith Butler produces, we may provisionally call it 'queer'. The use of mischievous vocabulary, concepts such as 'sex', 'jettisoned life' or 'parody', together with an emphatic, almost deliberate disrespect for strict boundaries between disciplines, their proper objects and language, fits well with the idea of queering. Butler weaves the ecstatic and improper movement of thought, to the point of sometimes questioning the standards of coherence, clarity and unity of text. Her writing is a performance in language, frequently spilling over into activist practices, which unintended ecstatic afterlife then gets woven back into the fold of following texts.

To write about Butler – to impose a sense of unity or coherence to her oeuvre – is to accept to write against the performativity of her thought. One can attempt to do a kind of bio-bibliographical inquiry, to collect data and trace textual trails that reveal the causal chains and intellectual influences on certain ideas. Any endeavour seeking to present large portions of an oeuvre must do precisely this kind of mining work, an excavation that of necessity straightens many of its curves. It seems that this straightening becomes particularly emphatic when the task is to present two transversal, deeply entangled sides of her thought: one belonging to philosophy, the other to politics. This chapter begins with a bold statement – Butler is a philosopher – and with an acknowledgement that some of the queerness in her philosophy must be lost in this process of mining and honing. Despite this, I hope to have preserved a double movement of philosophy and politics, organised as a two-step and sustained throughout the book – and specifically in this chapter, which is supposed to provide a kind of glossary of terms to help us move through the continual shifting of demands to think and act differently.

To insist on Butler's doing philosophy is also to go against her own somewhat ambivalent relationship towards it, which she has voiced on numerous occasions, but perhaps most prominently in a text with the suggestive title, 'Can the "Other" of Philosophy Speak?' (*Undoing Gender*, 2004b [hereafter UG]: 232–50) – where the 'Other of philosophy' seems to stand in for the subaltern. Or, consider how *Gender Trouble* begins with an avowal of the philosophical register – 'philosophy is the predominant disciplinary mechanism that currently mobilizes this author-subject' – only to be put into question a moment later with the claim that this 'inquiry seeks to affirm [. . .] positions on the critical boundaries of disciplinary life' (*Gender Trouble*, 1999 [hereafter GT]: xxxiv). This affirmation, which continues to take place at the nexus of thought and life, goes consistently against 'boundarying' (Sabsay 2016: 46). Resistance to boundarying is itself a mode of queering of language and definitions.

Before she became famous as a gender theorist, Butler wrote a book on Hegel, which was – judging from the topic, but also from the journals in which the book was reviewed at the time – a properly philosophical book. The properness of this endeavour needs to reflect its aim, since – although the book was on Hegel and his reception in twentieth-century France – the book in fact dealt with the life of desire, something that, strictly speaking, escapes thinking. Butler is careful to note that hers is not an attempt at an intellectual history or a sociology of knowledge (*Subjects of Desire*, 1987 [hereafter SD]: x–xi), but it might be added that her reading of Hegel was not a contribution to the history of philosophy either, because, as will be the case with numerous later encounters with philosophical texts, she never took the trouble to produce comprehensive interpretations of those she read. What *Subjects of Desire* grapples with is desire itself and its philosophical life – the refusal, contestation and discomfort of philosophy with life as a process, as change. Confronting the refusal to release possibilities, foreclosed by certain habitual and often violent presumptions, remains part of her work to this very day. This too may help us understand Butler's enduring defiance against definitions of the many concepts she uses: the language of philosophy often frames and forestalls the processuality and change so characteristic for the unfathomable life outside of the concept, delimiting and shoring it up, fixing and preventing it from spilling over.

Butler's thinking is characterised by continual, even constitutive open-endedness. In her first interview, she contends that 'the whole question of "What is a woman?" ought to be kept open as a question [. . .] To the extent that gender is a kind of psychic norm and cultural practice, it will always elude a fixed definition' (Kotz 1992: 86). This is a paradigmatic Butlerian claim, which has become a mainstay of queer and performative theory of gender. I suggest, however, that we also read it as an active engagement with the philosophical means of capturing life and desire – desire to be, to be recognised – something Butler admitted to still writing about in the midst of queer and gender troubles ('What I wrote on in Hegel was desire, and the relationship between desire and recognition [. . .] And I think I'm still writing about that' [ibid.: 89]). How, then, can language be deployed for the purposes of uncovering that which eludes fixing? How can philosophical means offer an entry into something that is fixed by thinking itself?

Butler's examination of *The Phenomenology of Spirit* begins with looking at Hegel's idiosyncratic and 'sometimes tortuous' language that defies the rules of grammar and tests the limits of ontological imagination (SD: 17). But there is something about this language that goes far beyond mere testing of one's intellectual endurance. The reader is required to accompany the subject on a convoluted and torturous journey, during which, moreover, the text *does* something to the reader. 'We do not merely witness the journey of some other philosophical agent, but we ourselves are invited on stage to perform the crucial scene changes' (SD: 20). The setting transforms rapidly and unexpectedly – the whole idea of phenomenology is, ultimately, about a continuous becoming something other than what the appearing subject thought it was at a previous point in the journey. The changes are necessary, functioning as the condition of possibility for the journey itself. It is they that propel the movement of the subject, who in its quest for a circumscribed identity endures innumerable tragic failures. The language untethers thought from unilinearity, exposing it to processuality and change; the changes that the text performs disclose – tragically or comically – that the apparent onto-logical givenness is in fact deceptive. Crucially, *The Phenomenology of Spirit* does not tell, but it enacts (SD: 18): it performs for and with us, entangling us with the arduous life of thinking.

We recognise some of these motifs in Butler's own texts written well after *Subjects of Desire*. They do things as well, implicating us in a performance, enacting something both transformative and not easily accessible. We are invited to join, to become part of the scene, to participate in the deception that we know ourselves and the world around us. The texts are sometimes equally tortuous – unruly, serpentine, dense, refusing to offer closures, evasive of definitions and clear conclusions. And yet, something transpires through them, something that bends and flexes thought, something living and pressing, with the power to carry us elsewhere. Thus, perhaps we may say that the hunt for desire, begun with the reading of Hegel's *Phenomenology*, continued as a quest for something alive and pulsating, which must be mediated, yet without being disjointed, by language.

Leszek Kołakowski (2010) offered a beautiful description of the history of philosophy as an everlasting antagonism between a multitude of priests and a handful of jesters. On the side of the jesters, Butler's philosophy sometimes goes against coherence and clarity, absolutes and common sense, against that which alleges it must be the way it is. Plunged into texts that have the capacity to turn language upside down, we are made to think about what can appear in language and what remains hidden by its use. Invited onto a stage where a philosophical performance – of the real and the possible – is taking place, we are sometimes literally inventing possibilities, and maintaining them as possibly real. Queer performances are of necessity improper, both in the sense of propriety and property.

Now, it may come as a surprise that Hegel, probably the greatest priest in the history of philosophy, appears in the role of midwife to a queer philosophy. No doubt, many of Butler's interlocutors who will appear in the pages of this book stand firmly on the side of jesters. One, who also egregiously disobeyed boundarying practices, Michel Foucault, can help us understand how Butler worked with the thought of others, including Hegel. Foucault once suggested that all his books are little toolboxes, welcoming those who decided 'to open them, use a particular sentence, idea, or analysis like a screwdriver or wrench in order to short-circuit, disqualify or break up the systems of power' (Foucault 1996a: 149). On another occasion, when asked to comment on the growing popularity of Nietzsche's thought, Foucault protested against the tide of the 'most accurate interpretations', saying that, for him, it is important to utilise the writers one likes. 'The only valid tribute to thought such as Nietzsche's is precisely to use it, to deform it, make it groan and protest' (Foucault 1980a: 53–4). No one understood those precepts better than Butler, who peruses texts meticulously for tools, sometimes used against their original authors.

For this reason, Butler's thought often weaves together those who would otherwise rarely meet, such as Hegel and Foucault, among many others. Strangely positioned next to one another, both are her true and long-standing interlocutors – although she remains neither entirely faithful nor interpretatively loyal to either. Take Hegel: the pilgrimage of the spirit, rising over high peaks and across deep valleys in its quest for dialectical harmony with the world, ends in absolute knowledge. In Butler's philosophical journeys, there are no happy dialectical endings that provide certainty; rather, she stays with the negative. Or, take Foucault: *Gender Trouble* deployed genealogy as a method; but not as we have come to know it in either Nietzsche or Foucault. Although historicity, context, contingency and discursivity all have a prominent place in her work, she does not follow Nietzsche's claim – which Foucault did – that for a genealogist, the most vital is 'what is documented, what can actually be confirmed and has actually existed, in short the entire long hieroglyphic record, so hard to decipher, of the moral past of mankind' (Nietzsche 1989: 7). There is no archival work in Butler, who, even when she claims to do genealogy, does genealogy at the crossroads of ontology and politics – mapping 'out the political parameters of [the "being" of gender's] construction in the mode of ontology' (GT: 45). She makes no inquiry into how, historically, 'certain cultural configurations of gender take the place of "the real"' (ibid.), although the fact that there is a history behind these configurations gives them changeable status, precisely making a different real possible. Butler's 'genealogy of gender ontology' draws on other texts as its archive, ranging from Plato to Mary Douglas, all treated as toolboxes and utilised in a singular way.

I dare claim that Butler's method, which has remained characteristic across her entire opus, was given in one unpresumptuous footnote, in which she defines her understanding of Foucault's notion of genealogy as a 'specifically philosophical exercise in exposing and tracing the installation and operation of false universals' (Butler 1993b: 30). This particularly philosophical exercise has two main motivations. The first belongs to 'queered philosophy', which aims to create a counter-imaginary to the dominant ontological claims, or, in Butler's own words, 'to produce ontology itself as a contested field' (Meijer and Prins 1998: 279). The second is political and relates to the opening up of possibilities.

Insurrection at the Level of Ontology

Among the various turns that characterise interpretations of Butler's philosophy, the ontological one has garnered only minor attention (for exceptions cf. White 1999; Mills 2007; Chambers and Carver 2008; Schippers 2014; Vogelman 2017; Charpentier 2019; Richard

2019). Continuing with bold statements, however, I wish to suggest that Butler's philosophy as such can be understood as an insurrection at the level of ontology.

Lisa Disch (1999: 547) once claimed, with a certain foresight, that politics of the performative is a politics of insurrection, while Athena Athanasiou has suggested that the trope of insurrection at the level of ontology should be read as a gesture of politicising ontology (*Dispossession*, 2013 [hereafter D]: 120). To justify the importance of this trope, I propose we take a careful look at a paragraph from *Precarious Life*, which will resurface at a number of different places in this book. Butler says:

> I am referring not only to humans not regarded as humans, and thus to a restrictive conception of the human that is based upon their exclusion. It is not a matter of a simple entry of the excluded into an established ontology, but an insurrection at the level of ontology, a critical opening up of the questions, What is real? Whose lives are real? How might reality be remade? Those who are unreal have, in a sense, already suffered the violence of derealization. What, then, is the relation between violence and those lives considered as 'unreal'? Does violence effect that unreality? Does violence take place on the condition of that unreality? (PL: 33)

What is real and how do we know it as such? These questions have probably propelled philosophy from its Greek roots until today. The question of the real – of what is – belongs to the realm of ontology. The second question in the quote tells us what kind of real interests Butler: one that has something to do with lives, and expressly human lives. Finally, the third question – how might reality be remade? – is crucial, as it suggests two important things: reality as it is could be different, it could be transformed by certain acts or actions.

We might expect that such engaging words would be accompanied by directions or prescriptions about how to do this remaking; but we would be mistaken. These are not to be found easily in Butler's texts: she offers no definite and precise formulas, she does not strictly enumerate 'good' actions, separating them from the 'bad'. Butler does not focus on how to include the excluded or widen the legally or culturally closed space to those not understood as properly human. What she demands from us is to take several steps back, return to the realm of ontology, and once again ask if what we think is real – is the only possible real. Her motives are political – she obviously wants this remaking to happen – but the first step needs to take place in thought. Such a demand is, of course, inexorably complex.

Yet, violence being an integral part of our reality demands rethinking that reality all the more. So long as there are some human lives to whom reality is refused and who are violently removed from it, such a demand must always be made. For that reason, Butler suggests an insurrection at the level of the real with a clear political aim: to demand equality in reality, such that certain lives are no longer more or less real, that the 'derealisation' of lives, violent as it is, ceases to be a viable option.

From *Precarious Life* onward, this demand has an increasing role in shaping Butler's work. But could we say that it was also present, at least at the level of motivation, in the texts written before? Consider this *locus classicus* in *Gender Trouble*:

> Within feminist political practice, a radical rethinking of the ontological constructions of identity appears to be necessary in order to formulate a representational politics that might revive feminism on other grounds. On the other hand, it may be time to entertain a radical critique that seeks to free feminist theory from the necessity of having to construct a single or abiding ground. (GT: 8)

We easily recognise this passage as typically Butlerian: identities are constructed, feminism as a political practice needs grounds less confining than those it operates with and feminist theory should stop investing all its powers into fortifying these incapacious grounds. What may be overlooked is that the ontological frames in which identity (of woman, which then serves as ground for feminism) appears in need of radical rethinking. Radical critique should unpack what it is 'to be' a woman (a man, a gender, a subject, a human), and what this 'being' reifies, turning something dynamic into a static, thing-like entity, ontologically deprived of change.

One could wonder about the relation between the standard ontological question of the real and its feminist articulation. As humans, we are born into reality that has existed before us, and we live in it as bodies, which very much contributes to the ontological imagination of reification. *Bodies That Matter* begins by signalling that, as a rule and almost vocationally, philosophers had trouble with bodies: 'they invariably miss the body or, worse, write against it. Sometimes they forget that "the" body comes in genders' (*Bodies That Matter*, 2011a [hereafter BTM]: viii). Such an omission seems strange, since gender is one of the most prominent ways in which bodies live and which makes the life of the body a social one. Declining to repeat the vocational difficulty, Butler does write about bodies, emphatically wanting to think bodies – not as such, not in binarised way, but as plural.

The body is always somehow gendered because it is entirely entangled in social relations. This entanglement is not temporary or of a kind that could be wished away: the reality in which lives of bodies take place, in which bodies become, is a social reality that equips us with intelligibility and situates us. The realities of concrete bodies are, to a large extent, defined by their capacity to conform and reiterate the norms that define what is intelligibly real. In that sense, bodies that are intelligible – which we can clearly define, categorise as woman or man – are those that we can understand and assess as real. Those, on the other hand, outside the sphere of intelligibility, remain less real (even unreal) because they do not qualify or count in the same way. It is bodies themselves that become differently and 'exceed the norm, rework the norm, and make us see how realities to which we thought we were confined are not written in stone' (UG: 29). Due to their fleshy exposure, bodies are always potentially exposed to violence, almost invariably preceded by violence of derealisation itself.

For a body to be considered real – having a material, tangible reality – it must matter, that is, it must have certain value and a certain ascribed (and later also self-ascribed) meaning. The question 'what is real?' could also be read as 'what matters?'. Applied to bodily lives, it can be further translated into 'who counts as a life?'. There are zones that remain in the suspended, shadowy regions of ontology, inhabited by material, but only ambivalently living beings – who do not matter and are therefore only ambivalently human. 'To be a body is to be exposed to social crafting and form', to be exposed to norms, 'and that is what makes the ontology of the body a social ontology' (*Frames of War*, 2009a [hereafter FoW]: 3). In other words, the reality that interests Butler is a reality of living and plural bodies that are figured as more or less human: that is, a social reality. In reality as it is, not all lives count the same, not all merit equal protection. This prompts us to think about how reality might be remade, which is directly related to the issue of social transformation.

To take part in the insurrection at the level of ontology is to ask what counts as real, in order to then possibly understand what changes we need, under what conditions and on which terms. For various minority realities to become included and acknowledged, in order for them to gain equal status, which would then be legally and institutionally acknowledged, it is necessary first to question the established ontology. Although we certainly need to struggle for changes and radical expansion of laws, social transformation begins with our struggle to think the real differently. For this reason, we must expose ourselves to the risk of a 'certain destabilization of [. . .] familiar language, become exposed to something new, and begin to imagine the world otherwise' (Blumenfeld and Breen 2005: 25).

Possibilities

It seems that philosophy, almost vocationally, urges one to go against urgency, to think first, to take time. Nietzsche used to caution against thinking impatiently, especially 'in the midst of an age of "work", that is to say, of hurry, of indecent and perspiring haste, which wants to "get everything done" at once' (Nietzsche 2006: 5). But when philosophy becomes entangled with action, with a certain kind of politics, especially with struggles for emancipation, then patience becomes difficult to demand. To stop and think takes precious time, which could, and should, be used for struggling against injustice. Yet, perhaps paradoxically, this too appears in Butler's texts. There is in Butler, so to say, a contradictory movement of demands: one that urges us to do slow philosophy – being 'a chance to pause together and reflect on the conditions and directions of acting, [which is] a form of reflecting that has its own value, and not merely an instrumental one' (*Notes Toward a Performative Theory of Assembly*, 2015b [hereafter NT]: 123–4) – and the other, prompting us to act now.

Let us consider this conundrum in the context of feminism. Stopping to ask what is a body, what is natural, what is (my) experience, what it means to say that I am a woman, what it means to consider myself human, slows down action in which I may wish to simply struggle on the basis of my sense of a disenfranchised self in this world. It prevents me from using language of universality without interrogating it, or making strong normative claims about what is good, desirable or right for all women out there. To stop and think about, for example, what is a body, means to come face to face with a knowledge we rarely if ever consider, which is something acquired, accumulated, belonging to historical time, contingent and changeable. Yet, when we do stop to think about the body, one that this feminist takes to the street to protest the precarious state of abortion laws or the violent and disrespectful practices in maternity wards, we are faced with a simple fact that all questions about that body take place in language. Being shared and, properly speaking, belonging to everyone and no one in particular, language carries many sediments of uses that are not my own, that is, are only ambivalently mine. Thus, stopping to think about what at first seemed very personal and most intimate now appears as a pattern with an impersonal history. The simplest truths about ourselves, which we barely ever question, seem to be part of norms that are there long before we grew conscious of their existence. They help us orient ourselves in the world by supplying definitions of what is a body, natural, woman, human and so on. To question our fundamental knowledge about the world, about what is real, to stop and consider the language used to think the world and ourselves as subjects, to ask what is particularly mine and what is shared, may, of course, cause different reactions. It can make us dizzy, even paralysed; instead of propelling us to action, it may produce certain discomfort and a sense that we do not know what to do, a feeling that all that was firm and reliable has now become destabilised.

Butler decisively states that theory is transformative. This does not mean, however, that social and political transformation can be reduced to theory. Something else surely needs to happen, 'such as interventions at social and political levels that involve actions, sustained labor, and institutionalized practice, which are not quite the same as the exercise of theory. I would add, however, that in all of these practices, theory is presupposed' (UG: 204–5). Slowing down to think not only confronts us with the complexity of what previously seemed simple, but it also makes us aware that any action driven by certain principles or ideals is somehow philosophically informed. Asked about the role of philosophy, which compared to warmongering and the military-industrial complex looks powerless indeed, and no more than a kind of solitary heroism, Butler warns us not to forget that they too have a philosophy: 'the contemporary cowboy also has, or exemplifies, a certain philosophical vision of power, masculinity, impermeability, and domination' (Schneider and Butler 2010). Whenever one strives for social transformation – war being one of its possible faces, if a deplorably horrific one – or becomes involved in the acts that should bring it about, however expedient and swift, one is already involved in and informed by a certain theory or philosophy, by a certain understanding of what is possible and what is real. In the act of social transformation, we are all 'lay philosophers' (UG: 205). Thus it becomes increasingly important to think about some of the most elementary notions that seem to be at the basis of our thinking and acting.

19

Very well – we may imagine someone saying – even if we concede the notion that haste is not the best mode of doing either philosophy or politics, it is still unclear why we should involve ourselves in an insurrection at the level of ontology. What are the practical outcomes of such involvement and how is it exactly related to social transformation? The answers to these questions belong to three different orders: the first is related to the idea of possible life, the second to the political materialisation of an insurrection, the third to a certain discontinuity between philosophy and politics.

'The thought of a possible life is only an indulgence for those who already know themselves to be possible. For those who are still looking to become possible, possibility is a necessity' (UG: 219). Looking to become possible may happen through local or global struggles, through reforms or revolutionary acts, in organised or anarchic ways, but it will always be preceded by an insurrection at the level of ontology, at the level of critical opening up of questions: does reality consist of only these possibilities, is the real necessarily thus, must it be violent against lives that are less possible, and is it violent precisely due to their lack of possibilities? Posing these questions, motivated as they are by the sheer unviability or unliveability of life, is a critical 'no' to reality as it is, and a critical 'yes' to a political rearticulation of possibilities thus produced. Insurrection produces possibilities: it engenders the possibility of possibilities, the possibility for something new to appear. 'The ontology of the excluded' (Butler and Connolly 2000), however, does not fit into a merely somewhat extended old reality, which otherwise stays the same. If new possibilities are to become viable, the boundaries of established ontology cannot simply remain in place. The seams of the established are un-seamed by the new.

The decision on how the new should be materialised may take place only when possibilities appear as possible:

> The idea of producing possibility is a precondition to deciding which possibility to realise; there must first be possibilities established, and this is a crucial task, hardly simple. If theory does this, then it can be absolutely exhilarating in so far as it opens up this world we thought was so closed to us. (Reddy and Butler 2004: 122)

The production of possibilities takes place at the level of thinking about what is real, what is (an intelligible) body, to whom the prerogative of reality belongs, and what kinds of violence remain with us if we take the established reality for granted. If there are minority realities whose lives are impossible – and what is a minority reality has changed in time and is unequally distributed across space – then their mere 'becoming possible' is a political achievement (Butler and Connolly 2000). Becoming possible introduces disorder into possibilities that have previously been enabled, sanctioned and maintained as the only viable ones, and demands their reordering in which the new will be a viable, liveable possibility. Thus, making room – in thinking, in language, in the wording of policies and laws – for a possible life, or a life not steeped in violence, is a legitimate, if not vital political aim that does not go against urgency. To the contrary, there is even more importunity to making room, demanding that in haste we do not lose sight of how established boundaries of the real themselves effect violence, and how this imperils the survival of various real, pulsating and living bodies.

In Medias Res

Again, we can imagine someone protesting – alright, but are all possibilities advantageous? What if the production of possibilities causes our reality to decompose, or become derealised, or unreal? Is the new good and desirable, simply by virtue of being new? For Butler, what waits ahead belongs to the sphere of the unknowable, and it can never be derived from a plan established ahead of time. In order to assume responsibility for the future, we do not have to know its direction fully in advance, 'since the future, especially the future with and for others, requires a certain openness and unknowingness; it implies becoming part of a process the outcome of which no one subject can surely predict' (UG: 39). Embracing unknowingness is an integral part of radically democratic life. While we will have to act and politically decide which possibilities are good and desirable once they are realised, we also need to accept that 'nothing good or desirable will arrive without a new' (Butler and Connolly 2000).

The question of materialisation or institutionalisation of possibilities belongs to the sphere of politics, which is for Butler always, to a certain extent, discontinuous with philosophy. Despite being an unambiguous call for change, for social transformation, Butler's philosophy seems never to have developed a politics proper – a kind of hidden political agenda that should instruct us about the goals of insurrection, how exactly to realise them and how to make them functional once insurrection is over. We are indeed told that 'no political revolution is possible without a radical shift in one's notion of the possible and the real' (GT: xxiv), and we may infer that something new is going to emerge with the destabilisation of the status quo. But, what will the frame of the new be and what will be the political shape of social transformation? We do not find this in Butler's thought; it is rather about the charting of possible worlds, schematising possibility, without precisely telling us which possibilities to realise or where to go with them (Reddy and Butler 2004: 122).

For a long time, this was described as an issue of normativity, most often placed in the context of Butler's poststructuralism, postmodernism, antifoundationalism or Foucauldianism. Early on, she claimed that her work had a normative direction, but no normative ground (Butler 1993a: 125). Even in the latest texts where the normative direction is much more overt, Butler does not abandon her long-standing belief that philosophy is not supposed to provide a political programme or 'rush to *decision-ism* and to strong normativity' (Olson and Worsham 2000: 763–4). This may surely justify some in their opinion that one such position can never move too far from subversion. Tied down to trouble-making, in a political sense it refers only to something transient, frivolous, even trivial, in line with the conclusion that trouble is inevitable and that the task is 'how best to make it, what best way to be in it' (GT: xxix).

Although there is certainly something poignantly trouble-making about Butler's philosophy, there is nothing trivial about the claim that to live politically is to live *in medias res*. Insurrection at the level of the real is politically motivated and has a clear normative direction: to rearticulate the terms in which inequality of possibility is real, to open up space for possibilities, to reduce violence that upholds certain possibilities' circumscription, to call for a more liveable world. That is, however, not all that politics is about. To act politically is to act within the given circumstances that demand action now. Butler always philosophically contested the closure of identity categories. However, she is also explicit that there are moments when demonstrations, legislative efforts and radical movements make claims and have to make claims, for example, in the name of women ('Contingent Foundations', 1995a [hereafter CF]: 49). Or, that there were 'political occasion[s]' where she would appear 'under the sign of lesbian', although theoretically 'to write or speak *as a lesbian* appears a paradoxical appearance of this "I"' (Butler 1991: 13–14).

What exactly does it mean that politics is about the now and the new? To answer this, we need to briefly revisit the

Habermas–Foucault debate (see Ashenden and Owen 1999), part of much broader disputes between radical theories and post-Enlightenment normativism. The same breach can be detected in the volume *Feminist Contentions*, which, significantly, was first published in 1993 in Frankfurt under the title *Der Streit um Differenz*. Although I pay more attention to this important exchange in the chapter on agency, for the time being some of its motifs can explain the idea of politics *in medias res*.

The normativist-inspired understanding (represented by Seyla Benhabib in the exchange in question) is that to have an interest in emancipation, that is, a strong political direction, (feminist) theory has to be founded on certain philosophical (or metaphysical) premises. These foundations are necessary for the definition of the emancipatory subject, but also to provide a critical basis or normative grounds for what is to be achieved through this emancipation. It must be guided by certain ideals or utopian visions without which 'not only morality but also radical transformation is unthinkable' (Benhabib 1995a: 30). The premises supply the action with legitimating principles and narratives that are not value-neutral and strive to be universally valid.

For Butler, on the other hand, we can assemble and protest, under the sign of women or lesbians or under some other sign, in concrete political efforts to effectuate certain changes, without assuming that these efforts have, or must have, necessary foundations. Theory is not there to furnish the struggle with either grounds for action or the subject of agency. The political subject emerges in and through collective struggle, which is concrete, possibly paradoxical, always potentially thwarted because its effects cannot be calculated in advance. The struggle is not normatively shaped before it begins to take place, and does not take place according to a philosophical rulebook that guarantees full implementation of its regulative ideals. Theory has no necessary political consequences, 'only a possible political deployment' (CF: 41). Thus, instead of positing premises, together with the acting subject that precedes action itself, one needs to ask what possibilities of mobilisation there are in the existing configurations of power, 'for what is at hand politically is a set of challenges that are historically provisional, but are not for that reason any less necessary to engage' (FCR: 128). When, for example, protesters gather at Wall Street to reclaim public space in a political struggle against late capitalism, they stand in the midst of it, encircled by its architectural signs, equipped with gadgets and engaged in social media actions

that would hardly be imaginable without the existence of transnational corporations, extractivism or neoliberal political rationality.
Then and there, they are physically and symbolically entangled
with what is historically provisional but must currently be engaged:
'towers [are] mocking us, as we call for a more radical dismantling
of [capitalism's] terms. There is no transcendental purity to be had.
Or if there is, it is reserved for those who refuse to act' (Seeliger and
Villa Braslavsky 2022).

Against the normativists' presumptions, Butler refuses that the
philosophical establishment of the normative foundations can possibly pull the political subject out of the unruliness, contingency and
contextuality of political life. Positing the necessary foundations of
politics in effect desires the 'decontamination' of politics, to provide
it with a clean slate, which is never to be had. The foundations, in the
words of Wendy Brown, act as refusals 'to allow history and contingency to contour the existing dimensions and possibilities of political
life. In this sense, they constitute repudiation of politics, even as they
masquerade as its source of redemption' (2001: 94). The laying down
of normative premises in the form of necessary foundations of politics is used to authorise and define a priori what is politically good or
desirable. This, however, forecloses and excludes certain possibilities
from the outset, and stands in the way of some others that might
open up in the course of the struggle. Furthermore, the foundations
position 'the idealist actor at a distance from politics, [who thus
becomes] inevitably disappointed by it and perhaps even prepared to
renounce politics because of its failures and compromises vis-à-vis his
or her ideals' (ibid.). Doing politics *in medias res* means precisely that
we open ourselves to the de-idealisation, which can make us realise
'that your own critical position may be an effect of the very power
regime that you seek to criticize, without being fully coopted by it'
(Kotz 1992: 89). This realisation may appear as 'the very precondition of a politically engaged critique' (CF: 39).

Understanding agency as being neither exempted from the field of
powers, nor one-directionally leading to the fulfilment of ideals set
beforehand, is to remain with the lived difficulty of political life. To
live politically *in medias res* means to 'become available to a transformation of who we are, a contestation which compels us to rethink
ourselves, a reconfiguration of our "place" and our "ground"' (FCR:
131). It means to quit territorialism, to give up on the foreclosure
of the future through transhistorical, universally valid premises prescribed in advance, to renounce grounds which will remain anchored

and uneroded, regardless of potentially transformative contestations posed to us by the democratic life itself (FCR: 131–2).

The New

This critical endeavour is not guided by the Habermasian 'why struggle?', but by the Foucauldian 'how to proceed?' (Foucault 2000: xii; see Allen and Goddard 2014). For Foucault, politics is to be used for a 'permanent opening of possibilities', a means of unconstituting what has been historically constituted (Foucault 2014: 267). In that sense, politically engaged critique begins by asking what possibilities are produced on the basis of existing configurations of power, how this matrix can be reworked, how the legacy of its constitution can be reconstituted and destabilised (CF: 47). Yet, to act politically means to act now, with resources we have, and not those predefined or left to be obtained at some future moment. The question how to proceed implies that, for the most part, some kind of situational and insurrectionary political analysis and strategies have to be invented along the way, in and through the very struggles (Foucault 1996b: 211).

Now, normativist philosophy champions the production of possibilities as well. However, it begins by defining the possibilities that ought to be realised. The new that is supposed to come is, in that sense, not particularly new. That which will happen in the future is already projected, philosophically strategised and thought through before the action that should take us there takes place. There is, in other words, a direct continuity between philosophy and politics.

For Butler, in contrast, politics is about the present. To be sure, we act with normative direction. However, we are not endowed with authoritative knowledge of where acting will take us. What lies ahead belongs to the sphere of the unknown, regardless of our projections of a desirable future. 'We are all unknowing and exposed to what may happen, and our not knowing is a sign that we do not, cannot, control all the conditions that constitute our lives' (NT: 21) – which is what ultimately makes us all precarious. Thus, instead of reaching out for something that (still) does not belong to the domain of the real, projecting in it some already defined 'new', we should take part in a political performativity in the present, because the reestablishment of established reality 'is fundamentally dependent for its maintenance on that contemporary instance' (*Contingency, Hegemony, Universality*, 2000 [hereafter CHU]: 41).

To act politically is to push the limits of the established, without the illusion of the possibility of its total escape.

It is important to note that Butler's insistence on unknowingness, which stands in the way of a direct continuity between philosophy and politics, comes to her though the peculiar reading of Hegel, and not only, as the early debates on normativity seem to have emphasised, through her overreliance on Foucault. In point of fact, her philosophical landscape is here much wider, comprising not only Hegel's journeying subject and Foucault's political ontology of the present, but also Ernesto Laclau and Chantal Mouffe's understanding of radical democracy, as well as Hannah Arendt's notion of acting in concert that would become particularly prominent in Butler's later work.

Let us for a moment turn to Butler's particular reading of Hegel's *The Phenomenology of Spirit* and its subject's journey that presents itself as a series of acts of cognition. Before becoming cognisant – a long process with many dialectical stages – the subject is set for the unknown. It surrenders to the world each time, giving itself over to it, open to whatever it encounters on its path to absolute knowledge. 'Hegel's own persistent references to "losing oneself" and "giving oneself over" only confirm the point that the knowing subject cannot be understood as one who imposes ready-made categories on a pregiven world' (CHU: 19). The subject is fundamentally unknowing because the world is not given to it in advance. The world becomes known only through the categories shaped by the subject's encounter with it. Desire, 'this subject's necessarily ambiguous movement toward the world', urges the subject to be consumed, externalised and dispersed through the world, and 'the "Life" of the subject is the constant consolidation and dissolution of itself' (SD: 42). Ecstatic and relational, the subject remains open to the transformations that encounters bring: 'We do not remain the same, and neither do our cognitive categories, as we enter into a knowing encounter with the world. Both the knowing subject and the world are undone and redone' by these encounters (CHU: 20). Hegel was, further, vital for an understanding that the possibilities which need to be produced are not in some temporal and spatial 'elsewhere', but already in the world, in established reality. However, as we already know, Butler reads Hegel without closure, without a dialectical happy ending, which brings her close to a Foucauldian critical 'no' that always halts us in the now.

At almost the same time that Habermas proposed his theory of communicative action in an attempt to 'upgrade' what little had been

left of critical theory – which, in his view, had become totally negative, directed against reason as the foundation of its own analysis, and
no longer able to operate in the realms of truth and validity claims
(Habermas 1982) – Foucault also began to show strong interest in
the critical enterprise, with a startling admiration for Adorno and
Horkheimer's project of unrelenting critical theory. Both Habermas
and Foucault wished to offer a positive notion of critique, but their
understanding of positivity differed fundamentally. For Foucault,
critique appears as a practice necessary for the philosophical ethos,
even philosophical life that consists of questioning things we say,
think and do. Departing from Kant's reflections of limits, the critical
question today, claims Foucault, is positive and practical, and makes
us ponder what is given to us as universal, necessary and obligatory,
although it is actually singular, contingent, a product of arbitrary
constraints (Foucault 2007b: 113). This is necessary for our understanding of who we are, how we came to be what we are, and under
which constraints, or for what he calls a critical ontology of ourselves
in the present. However, critique is not only about knowing, but
is also 'an experiment with the possibility of going beyond' these
limits (ibid.: 118). It is an experiment based on separating out 'from
the contingency that has made us what we are, the possibility of no
longer being, doing, or thinking what we are, do, or think' (ibid.:
114).

   In 2001, possibly also as a retrospective account on Foucauldian
normativity ingrained in her work, Butler published a text on
Foucault's notion of critique, which, she claimed, has strong normative commitments that appear in forms that would be difficult,
if not impossible, to read within grammars of normativity shaped
by the currently dominant version of critical theory. Critique is a
practice of questioning the limits of what we are most certain we
(think we) know. To question these limits is to push them because
'one has already run up against a crisis within the epistemological
field in which one lives' (Butler 2001a). The 'one' appearing in this
assertion is any one of us for whom the epistemological field, or the
world, is given. The 'one' is, in that sense, not a Hegelian subject
who only comes to grow cognisant of the world and, through acts
of cognition, creates categories shaped by its encounter with the
world. We appear in the world in which there are already categories that order our lives, which, being given, seem necessary and
unchangeable. Yet, some of these categories produce incoherences
that, pushed to their limit, open up entire realms that previously

seemed unthinkable and unutterable, that is, impossible in the existing categorial apparatus.

To act uncritically or, in Foucault's words, to let oneself be governed by the categorial apparatus that defines what is and what is
not possible, means to comply with the given conditions that delimit
possible existence, to remain within the established order of truth or
the real. By contrast, to open oneself up to a critical attitude, to an
'art of not being governed like that and at that cost' (Foucault 2007a:
45) – which assumes that one is still within this very order, because
another has not (yet) been found – means to potentially suspend the
ontological basis of the given order. Critique is a form of defiance
against what Foucault calls the politics of truth, which orders our
very basic ways of knowing and acting in the world, so basic that it
refers to questions like 'what counts as a person? What counts as a
coherent gender? What qualifies as a citizen? Whose world is legitimated as real?' (Butler 2001a).[1]

These questions take us back to the realm of the knowable, thinkable and sayable. They urge us to consider ways in which these
realms have historically been circumscribed by the unthinkable and
the unspeakable. Such consideration, however, can only appear by
breaking through the prohibitions that enable and structure the
established truth and real. This breaking through is endowed with an
insurrectionary force (*Excitable Speech*, 1997a [hereafter ES]: 142)
and can produce something new. The 'rogue viewpoint' – that which
is unsayable and must be cast away for the domain of the speakable
to be established – 'is not the one that can be spoken without doing
some damage to the idea of what is speakable' (Butler 2009c: 777).
This 'damage' opens up a possibility for something new to arrive.

Collective Struggle

Foucault believed that to do critical ontology of ourselves we need to
abandon all projects that claim to be global or radical. His distrust
of projective and universally applicable 'programs for a New Man'
was related to the notion that there is no escape from the present that
would allow us 'to produce the overall programs of another society,
of another way of thinking, another culture, another vision of the
world' (Foucault 2007b: 114). We have to act without an architectonic theory or a philosophical-political programme. This position left many readers uneasy, believing that this would encourage
only small battles with 'a single-issue orientation' or 'personalistic

flavor': 'without a program, the left has had difficulty devising or orchestrating strategies for change in general' (Wapner 1989: 88). The preference for partial and local transformations, organised around the question 'how to proceed', seems perfectly fitting to this view, advancing only fragmented, immediate, collective, moderately militant and antiutopian actions (Allen and Goddard 2014: 43–43). Now, even if Butler agreed with many of these points, she was at the same time always explicit about her feminist, queer, antiracist, leftist and radical democratic activism. Unlike Foucault, who was amused by a long list of contradictory political ascriptions, from crypto-Marxist to Gaullist technocrat, without ever avowing any, Butler always insisted on the importance of collective struggle with recognisable political affiliations.

As a matter of fact, collective struggle is one of the oldest notions in her work. The term itself is hard to pin down as it refers to various phenomena: assemblies, human rights activism and uprisings, coalitional actions that go against seamless identities or proper objects, and projects of cultural translation. The idea of collective struggle is embedded in the notion that to act politically is to act performatively, in a plurality of voices, in coalition and immersed in the present moment. Philosophy does not need to tell us why we have gathered together to protest and under what banner – that belongs to the contextual and contingent sphere of political life – but it may inform us of the importance of the plurality at the heart of a radically democratic life, and the performative aspect of acting in concert.

In that sense, collective struggle refers to joint action, which is notably performative, radically democratic, rearticulatory and resignificatory, plural and expressive of competing universalities. Through them, 'those who are deemed "unreal" nevertheless lay hold of the real, a laying hold that happens in concert, and a vital instability is produced by that performative surprise' (GT: xxxviii). Queer alliance, for instance, managed to grasp these dimensions. Fundamentally non-identitarian and non-communitarian, it refers to a gathering across gender, race, class, geopolitical situations, and around a common issue, such as the AIDS crisis that affected a variety of people. The crisis produced 'the necessity of a really broad range of coalitions and ideas of equality: equality to education, equality to health care [. . .] equal grievability of lives' (Danbolt 2015: 6). The idea of the queer served as a site, essentially incomplete in its referentiality, and available for contested meanings and their performatively surprising rearticulations. It was to an extent similar to Laclau and Mouffe's (2001) understanding of radically democratic practices: striving for pluralism, in contestation over legitimacy claims, open for future revisions, and creating a chain of equivalence among varying democratic struggles against different forms of subordination.

Collective struggle gained an equally strong expression in Butler's performative theory of assembly (see NT). Performative politics of the precarious built upon the idea of queer politics, and assembling became a form of rising up in opposition to an unendurable condition, a form of making an embodied 'bid for a livable life' (Butler 2016b: 25). Those who assemble may 'have been crossed, denied, degraded, but now, in the moment of uprising, they gather a certain strength or force from one another, from alliance itself, one formed by a shared rejection of the unlivable' (ibid.). Those who rise up together do not have to read Marx or actively participate in leftist disputes, nor to have a drafted programme that would, by its mere existence, turn assembled bodies into a revolutionary force. They could, however, like the proletariat, rise up to negate the very conditions that negate their capacity to subsist, thereby re-embodying and rearticulating the power of negation itself. This reincorporation of negative power appears as a moment of uprising, as part of the signifying chain of negation (Butler 2015a). It will involve a moment of *critique*, as a sort of collective and embodied political judgement, 'a visceral judgement incarnated in stance and action' (Butler 2016b: 28), and a moment of *ecstatic desire*, often resulting from 'a long simmering process of dawning and expanding recognition' (ibid.: 27). The political subject of an assembly may appear under various synecdochal names – such as 'Tahrir', 'Syntagma', 'Zuccotti Park'. 'Taksim', for instance, gave its name to an uprising that began when a group of people defending public water rights was joined by anarchists, Marxists, feminists, drag queens, Kurdish mothers, environmentalists, activists fighting for the preservation of the common good, football fans, those fighting state authoritarianism and those protesting the war in Syria (Butler 2015a). All of them became *çapulcu*, looters, reappropriating a state-imputed derogatory name and grounding themselves in the very movement they made together. There is no 'single collective subject. It is a judgement shared, passed between people, heterogeneous yet concerted, embodied differently and yet in common' (Butler 2016b: 29).

Although uprisings refer to the collective struggles that are happening now, against a pressing, negating injustice, they also help us understand that Butler is not arguing for permanent presentism. In line with her understanding of performativity (discussed in detail in subsequent chapters), each new form of collective struggle belongs to a citational chain: they rearticulate previous uprisings, 'as a memory embodied anew, in events episodic, cumulative, and partially unforeseeable' (ibid.: 36), and form a layer in an open chain of futural reiterations (Butler, Laclau and Laddaga 1997: 10). Collective struggles are synchronic and diachronic forms of linking, of creating bonds and binds, that call for setting aside

> all recourse to primary and secondary oppressions and focus more on translation as a political practice. The possibility of a transregional and multilingual solidarity depends on having one's settled epistemic frame upended by another and then reformulated for the purposes of expanding solidarity. (Seeliger and Villa Braslavsky 2022)

Performative Universality

The occupiers of Taksim or Wall Street, each momentarily becoming the name of the universal, form a translatable concatenation of demands. 'Whenever universal becomes possible – and it may be that universal only becomes possible for a time, "flashing up" in Benjamin's sense – will be the result of a difficult labour of translation' ('Merely Cultural', 1998 [hereafter MC]: 38), in which a multitude of insurgents or movements converge against the backdrop of ongoing social contestation.

The notion of the universal appears in two forms in Butler's work. In *Gender Trouble* there are open hesitations about it: if something is said to have universal validity, it is significant to know who says it, what such totalising speech act aims at, where its limits are and who is excluded from its scope. These early misgivings are grounded in Butler's refusal of a normativist type-universalism and totalising gestures in feminism. *Gender Trouble* was, among other things, a radical critique of the universal validity of categories of identity and identity-based oppression, that is, of the dominant feminist understanding of patriarchy and neat distinctions between sex, gender and desire (GT: 5, 18–19, 48; for a full complexity of 'sexual identity', see Sedgwick 1994: 6–7). Casting domination as universal becomes a colonising epistemological strategy that produces and performs new modes of domination, reification and exclusion, with the help of seemingly non-porous, circumscribed and universally valid categories. In its endeavour, *Gender Trouble* is not an isolated project, but rather a continuation of the critical work of women of colour, radical thinkers of sex and postcolonial feminists (hooks 1981; Ferguson et al. 1984; Mohanty 1988; Spivak 1988; Rubin 1992; Moraga and Anzaldúa 2015). In this critical corpus, the universal functions as a 'false universal', integrative by force, erasing experiential differences, imposing a fixed, only purportedly shared structure, stifling disharmonious voices. Butler's early work was in that sense part of the collective struggle against the cloaked violence of a singular common essence that claims to have universal validity.

In the Preface to the second edition of *Gender Trouble*, written ten years after the original, Butler confesses to having revised her earlier positions on the meaning and usefulness of universality, under the influence of her political engagements. It turns out that if taken as non-substantial and open-ended, universality can have important strategic and performative use, 'conjuring a reality that does not yet exist, and holding out the possibility for a convergence of cultural horizons that have not yet met' (GT: xviii). This 'future-oriented' universal does not come to be through the processes of abstraction and decontextualisation, meaning that it is not known in advance. To conjure a reality that is not yet, assumes the possibility of something emphatically new and that 'the universal is only partially articulated, and that we do not yet know what forms it may take' (Butler 1996: 46).

Consider a historical example. In nineteenth-century Britain the demand for 'universal suffrage' referred exclusively to a demand for the suffrage of men. The notion of 'universal' was meant to incorporate those not yet included, referring, before the Reform Acts of 1867 and 1884, to the vast majority of working-class men. When the demand for women's suffrage was articulated, in the second half of the same century, from the start it was emphatically particular, since the 'universal' was obviously not capacious enough to include women. This, in turn, produced a rearticulation of the earlier demand, turning it into 'universal manhood suffrage'. Another question would be why universal suffrage, when it was first articulated as *universal*, did not involve everyone who was, by then, excluded from the (exclusive and exclusionary) universal (see Zaharijević 2014). What this example makes clear, however, is that the universal of universality, either in the ontological or legal and political sense, assumes certain historically articulated standards: they may appear as universal, necessary and obligatory, but they are in fact singular, contingent and a product of arbitrary constraints (Foucault 2007b: 113).

A critical relation to the parochial and exclusionary character of a given historical articulation of the universal is part of its expanding into the not-yet-reached universal. This 'not yet', or the temporal zone of those still without a claim to universality, constitutes the universal itself:

> The universal begins to become articulated precisely through challenges to its existing formulation, and this challenge emerges from those who are not covered by it, who have no entitlement to occupy the place of the 'who', but who nevertheless demand that the universal as such ought to be inclusive of them. (Butler 1996: 48)

Butler speaks of a performative and insurgent universality that arises out of contention with what now assumes the position of the universal, as something potentially new of which we are, as yet, unknowing (Butler and Connolly 2000). The appearance of women's suffrage is one such insurgent universality (of a particularity, [all] women). It helped redefine the boundaries of what was up to that point conceived as universal, as universally human, unmasking it as exclusionary universal and exclusively male. 'Women' appeared as ontologically new in the midst of the notion of the human, tearing apart both the seams of the human and of the universal, and expanding both in directions theretofore unthinkable.

Whenever one lays claim to a position of universality, one does so from a historically formed position in the social world, as there is no 'place' that is socially shapeless, untouched by and exempt from power relations. The performative speech act 'I lay claim to the position of universality' is made only in the context of extant norms writing such a claim off, making it unthinkable or unsayable. The British women who demanded suffrage in the second half of the nineteenth century had been written off as 'unsexed', as creatures removed from their essence, women who were not women, some kind of, literally, embodied contradiction, as if the mere demand for suffrage had the power to transmute bodies and impair the 'normal' workings of sex (Zaharijević 2014). Butler provides us with another example, which in today's anti-gender furore gains entirely new currency (Butler 2019a; Graff and Korolczuk 2022). In the context of the large international, UN-sponsored meetings of the 1990s (see Oosterveld 2005; Rothschild 2005; Girard 2007; Antić and Radačić 2020), when LGBT (lesbian, gay, bisexual, transgender) rights were only beginning to enter the discursive code of universally recognised human rights, there were political and religious groups that questioned the possibility of gay and lesbian rights being treated as universal, as rights belonging to the human on the basis of their humanness. For Butler, there was no space for surprise that the Vatican referred to the possible inclusion of 'lesbian rights as "anti-human" [. . .] To admit the lesbian into the realm of the universal might be to undo the human, at least in its present form, but it might also be to imagine the human beyond its conventional limits' (UG: 190).

Whenever a position excluded from the universal demands inclusion, two parallel processes take place: first, the 'universal' becomes uncovered as non-universal, because some or many groups linked together announce themselves as excluded; second, the demand for inclusion dismantles the existing 'universal' – unmasking it as false, seeking a more encompassing and capacious one. Each form of appropriation of the universal occurs in a context of that universal appearing unthinkable. In its appropriation, it resists the extant norm, but also calls for it to be transformed in certain quite unexpected ways. Laying claim to a 'non-place' and a temporal modality of a 'not yet' (CHU: 37) is fundamentally performative and opens the possibility of convergence of cultural horizons.

Cultural Translation

> Rather than imagining that women automatically have something identifiable in common, why not say, humbly and practically, my first obligation in understanding solidarity is to learn her mother tongue [. . .] This is preparation for the intimacy of cultural translation [. . .] if you are interested in talking about the other, and/or in making a claim to be the other, it is crucial to learn other languages. (Spivak 1993: 192)

To take one's own linguistic horizon as the limit implies a conceited self-sufficiency that can always turn into a colonising epistemological strategy. Not only can there be no solidarity, a kind of political commonality that I seek from you in a joint struggle, but if you do not understand the language I speak – even less, if I too cannot decipher the words you utter and there is no third as intermediary – there is no translation and 'there is no ethical response to the claim that any other has upon us [. . .] we are [then] ethically bound only to those who already speak as we do, in the language we already know' (*Parting Ways*, 2012 [hereafter PW]: 17). Without translation, my words directed at you – 'pomozi mi, немој да ме повредиш, ne čini to!' – a cry for help and a plea against violence in my language, remain unintelligible to you, without any ethical weight, faceless. No transformative encounter happens without translation.

The idea of cultural translation is, in my understanding, one of the most important practical-political tools of Butler's thought, running parallel to the political *in medias res*. Although without an explicit definition, it appears as a thread through a large part of Butler's work, crossing philosophical and political registers. The crossing is enabled by separable and, at first glance, quite discontinuous sources of this idea. Butler certainly draws on Benjamin and post-colonial theory for her understanding of (cultural) translation; but another source is also her engaged activism. This includes practical encounters in the domain of international law, the struggle against contemporary forms of epistemological and political colonialism, and a resolute break with any communitarian discourse. Over time, Butler's engagement expanded from the interrogation of a narrow western universalist epistemology to go beyond 'first world' feminism,[2] and the left that dismisses non-class, 'merely cultural' struggles as divisive and insignificant (see MC).

Claiming that cultural translation belongs to the key practical-political tools of Butler's thought is, however, not easy to justify. Not only is the concept not defined, but it appears in myriad contexts, including conflicts that require action that cannot be performed in the present. At one level, it seems to refer to a real task of learning another language, practically and humbly, to be able to translate and thus preserve a relation between speakers and cultures, without mastery. At another level, it refers to a tool that preserves the collective nature of struggle, enabling an encounter between competing horizons of those involved. At yet another level, cultural translation seems to be embedded, as a normative demand, in the preservation of cohabitation in plurality: there needs to be a translation 'in the midst of converging and competing ethical claims' in order to remap and preserve social bonds (PW: 8).

Unlike action *in medias res*, translation requires patience. The slow-moving work of translating cultural horizons allows the possibility of communal life, that is, cohabiting, slow-weaving of encounters that will not end in domination or annihilation. It potentially opens a non-hegemonic view of existence and allows unspeakable languages to become utterable. No sociality and no politics – other than mute warfare – is possible without translation.

For her understanding of the power of translation, Butler is specifically indebted to Walter Benjamin. For him, each translation is in a certain sense a new original: the original reappears in the other (language) reiterated, derived, same but also new and different. Benjamin refers to a profound ambivalence of the process of translation. As there is always at least a trace of the untranslatable, the original retains something that can never be transferred or exhausted in the 'new original'; but the translated is also a crucial form of survival (*Überleben, Fortleben*, of a life that goes on). As Benjamin claims in 'The Task of the Translator', 'languages are no strangers to one another, but are, a priori and apart from all historical relationships, interrelated in what they want to express' (Benjamin 1977: 72). As long as a language is spoken, written and translated, it survives. Translation is, therefore, a survival, a re-living and re-turning of life, which in a very fundamental sense depends on living language 'derivatives'. Linguistic survival also allows social bonds to survive, since languages themselves offer a tool for continual exchange and negotiation. Translation is a reaction against the impossibility of encounter, of contact: it enhances and augments communicability (FN: 126). In another text, Benjamin claims that there is a sphere wholly inaccessible to violence, 'the proper sphere of "understanding", language' (Benjamin 2004: 245). It provides the mode of preservation of agonism, even conflict, but in a non-violent, non-eradicating way (FN: 128). To agree to enter into a situation of translation means to, at least temporarily, give up on force, the right of the stronger, of the first: translation creates a situation of commutation, transfer, active and reciprocal interference. What is especially important for Butler: it constitutes and maintains the social relation.

The idea of *cultural* translation seems to be borrowed from postcolonial theory. For example, Homi Bhabha claims that translation is the performative nature of cultural communication, language *in actu*, which desacralises 'the transparent assumptions of cultural supremacy, and in that very act, demands a contextual specificity, a historical differentiation *within* minority positions' (Bhabha 1994: 228). For Bhabha, who draws on Benjamin, in the context of translation, the subject of cultural difference appears as irresolutely liminal, untranslatable and forever culturally inassimilable (ibid.: 224). This is, for Butler, the residue that can only violently fit itself into the established category of the universal – through a colonial imposition of its own dominant version, through erasure of certain kinds of demands and the refusal to engage in their rearticulation. Butler here follows Bhabha, for whom this liminal, residual and inassimilable element – which he calls cultural difference – is precisely that which urges us to submit to a translation, a slow and demanding – or as Spivak says, a humble and practical – process. Quick and hasty resolutions most often end in domestification or assimilation of difference. Only by consenting to the demand of translation does one become resistant to them. Cultural translation assumes a willingness to undergo an unanticipated transformation and yield to an amendment of one's terms.

Cultural translation thus maintains the idea of the untranslatable, but it also insists on something specifically dynamic, even performative, in the very possibility of translation, which pushes the process of the translation/communication forward. Cultural translation is what conserves and renews the social bond, while at the same time having the power to transform it. There seems to be a paradox here, because transformation rarely coincides with preservation. However, if difference is not domesticated or assimilated, then 'difference' is given a chance to transform what has until then been understood as 'same', real or universal. When a certain particular demands to be included in the universal (women of the late nineteenth century or lesbians of the late twentieth), it is demanding to be translated, along with its untranslatable residuum, along the way also altering the meaning of the universal. This demand puts both the universal and the particular to the test, together with the norms that enable and maintain the exclusion of the given particular from universality.

In a radically democratic framework, everyone has a right to translation and equal participation in a contestation of universality. And only in the dynamic contestation of competing, overlapping universalities do new fields of possibilities possibly open. In a radically democratic framework, the process of translation has no predictable end. Universality that is 'not yet', universality-to-come (Lloyd 2009), 'would not be violent or totalizing; it would be an open-ended process, and the task of politics would be to keep it open, to keep it as a contested site of persistent crisis and not to let it be settled' (Olson and Worsham 2000: 747). This is how translation appears as a task of politics informed by ethics, and understood as a process of pluralisation and institutionalisation. It is a process that follows, and has to follow, the insurgent acts in which unthinkable and unsayable claims enter language and reality, demanding to become thinkable and sayable, indeed demanding a right to a translation.

Human, Never Too Human

This chapter functioned as a sort of glossary of the key ontological and political linkages in Butler's work. Among these, the notion of the human has a special place. It can be said that the search for new forms of thinking and uttering, what in established ontology and grammar has no expression and appears unthinkable, is an attempt to find forms in which the human would be thought beyond its current boundaries. It can also be said that the production of possibilities refers to creating conditions for a broader, more capacious and more encompassing understanding of humanness, and that the insurrection at the level of the real is only possible because there are various humans who are closed off from reality, despite the fact that they are present and corporeal. In an important passage, Butler claimed that

> perhaps, then, it should come as no surprise that I propose to start, and to end, with the question of the human (*as if there were any other way for us to start or end*!). We start here not because there is a human condition that is universally shared – this is surely not yet the case. The question that preoccupies me in the light of recent global violence is, Who count as human? Whose lives count as lives? (PL: 20, italics mine)

Those who firmly believe that Judith Butler is representative of some version of postmodern feminism must find it quite odd that she decides to begin and end anything with such a question. Is she not here repaving the way to humanism (see Kramer 2015), the grand narrative to which Foucault bid farewell when he declared 'that man would be erased, like a face drawn in sand at the edge of the sea' (Foucault 2002a: 422; cf. Ingala 2018a)? Has not feminist theory denounced humanism, showing that 'man' was male all along? Had not Butler herself showed clear reservations about this concept which simulates universality, at the same time excluding so many from the scope of its validity? Perhaps we should take this focus on the human as a sign that the previous premises have been abandoned? Or, maybe, one could read this as a way to smuggle in (normative) foundations, together with the doer behind the deed? It might be that this 'bootleg' humanism comes at the cost of the ethical, which presumably took over from *Precarious Life* onwards, accompanied by vulnerability, dispossession and precarity, new notions by virtue of which Butler finally parted with her contentious poststructuralist past.

It seems that we will have to settle the dispute with a split between the human and humanism, which, I would argue, marks Butler's entire work. In an interview from 2016, Butler says:

> I think we cannot give up on the idea of the human. At the same time, we cannot become 'humanists' in any of the conventional senses attached to that term [. . .] The human works not as foundation, but as a criterion for recognition, precisely because there are those who have not yet been recognised as human, or whose recognition would 'break' the category, we have to keep it in place precisely to understand its historical changes, and the vector of power that works through it. (Zaharijević and Butler 2016: 107)

The human simply appears every time when one asks 'what is a human?', or 'who counts as human?', with an implication that there are humans who are not quite that, who lack something vital to be subsumed into the term. The very possibility of this implication urges us to further consider what layers of meaning have been woven into the norm that we take for granted as universal. These layers have their own histories, some of which are surely humanist, based on the idea of an autonomous, wilful subject, capable of acting independently in and from the world. These meanings, as Joanna Bourke claims in her history of the term, are built around a very particular type of human. 'Humanism installed only *some* humans at the centre of the universe. It disparaged "the woman", "the subaltern" and "the non-European" even more than "the animal"' (Bourke 2013: 3). These histories constrain the human from within, and have been used to justify the explanation of who counts as (fully) human. Yet, perhaps even more importantly, such histories reveal the human as an unfinished form, that is, having undergone various social transformations.

Unlike some other crucial notions in Butler, that of the human functions only within social frames. For humans, reality is always social reality, and the ontology of the human is always social ontology. Moreover, the human appears as *the* social norm, possibly the one that in social reality gives meaning to all other norms. Thus, the answers to very basic questions – 'what counts as a person? What counts as a coherent gender? What qualifies as a citizen? Whose world is legitimated as real?' (Butler 2001a) – are defined, ontologically and legally, on the basis of the norm of the human.

The histories of law, gender and citizenship show that there is no single, necessary, transhistorical and transcultural answer to these questions. What appeared as the universal in the past has undergone sundry transformations and has been redefined alongside social norms that regulate the scope of the human. For that reason, the question of the human is tightly bound to the articulation of the universal. The human cannot act as a foundation, or as something that is prior, outside or beyond volatile, contingent social conditions. It rather emerges as a horizon of recognition of the reality of particular bodies that demand to coalesce under the sign of the human, keeping universality in the form of 'not yet'. Recall that insurrection at the level of ontology takes place because the notion of the human appears too restrictive (PL: 33). This insurrection is about unwavering repetition of the questions: how is it possible that there are humans for whom there is no space in the principally unrestricted idea of the human? Where is the place of those living bodies not considered real? How does this alleged unreality justify violence?

Notes

1. We should note a certain affinity between Butler's and Foucault's use of the notion of insurrection, and its relation to the notion of critique. Insurrection first appears in *Excitable Speech*, referring to the force of the unspeakable, censored speech surfacing in the conventional, official discourse, which has the potential to open 'the performative to an unpredictable future' (ES: 142). This idea of insurrection is associative of Foucault's use of the term at the beginning of *Society Must Be Defended* ('c'est ce qu'on pourrait appeler l'insurrection des "savoirs assujettis"'; 'Il s'agit de l'insurrection des savoirs' [Foucault 1997a: 10, 12; 2003: 6, 9]), where he discusses the local forms of critique, opposed to the effects of all-encompassing, global theories. Butler and Foucault do not speak about the same dimension of things. Foucault is primarily interested in a recent phenomenon which he calls the 'return of knowledges', and the insurrection refers to subjugated (*assujettis*) knowledges, which he defines in two ways: as 'historical contents that have been buried or masked in functional coherences or formal systematizations' (Foucault 2003: 7), and as a whole series of knowledges from below, unqualified or disqualified as non-conceptual (and thus unintelligible), naive and hierarchically inferior, local, regional, differential, incapable of unanimity (ibid.: 7–8). It is precisely the appearance of subjugated knowledges, unburied by genealogy, that made critique possible. Several years later, in lectures on critique, the idea *assujettissement* – subjectivation, becoming a subject and becoming subjected – acquires a central role. 'If governmentalization is indeed this movement through which individuals are subjugated [subjected, *assujettis*] in the reality of social practice through mechanisms of power that adhere to a truth', then critique appears as

a counter-movement of voluntary insubordination, insuring 'the des-
ubjugation [desubjectivation, *deassujettissement*] of the subject in the
context of what we could call, in a word, the politics of truth' (Foucault
2007a: 47). Insurrection of the minority realities that were historically
buried and masked by a seemingly coherent and systematic order of the
real, unqualified or disqualified as unintelligible, is related to the 'ontology of the excluded' which makes critique, or desubjectivation, possible.
Critique is an act, or a series of acts, that question what makes us into
subjects – intelligible, real, human – in the existing order of reality,
questioning thus not only the regimes of truth, but also the reality that
consolidates them.
2. I believe we should add to this the experience of encounters with activists and theorists from around the world. In an interview with Maja
   Uzelac (2000) for the Croatian magazine *Zarez*, Butler links the idea
   of cultural translation to her first experiences with 'East-European'
   feminisms (which can, no doubt, be expanded to include encounters
   with South American, African and other non-north/western forms of
   reading, writing and acting, which she touches upon in referencing
   Chandra Mohanty's 'Under Western Eyes' [PL: 47–8]). In the interview,
   she explicitly mentions her early experiences of Prague and Budapest,
   facing resistance to Americanisation of Eastern European theory, that
   is, its refusal to simply appropriate the existing (western) models. Being
   cautious not to impose such models as authoritative without knowing or
   understanding local contexts is part of the idea of cultural translation.

Part I

Performativity

Bodies and Norms

The Revolution of Simone de Beauvoir

Philosophy seldom revolved around the field today known under the name of gender studies, but the concepts from which the idea of gender is built are as old as thinking itself. The first musings on the cosmos (Diels 1960: 105), an ordered whole characterised by harmony and proportion, were based on the division of opposites. Pythagoreans were said to have determined the ten principles (Aristotle 1991a, 11 [986a23–986b3]) classified into two columns of cognates: limited/unlimited, odd/even, single/plural, right/left, male/female, resting/moving, straight/curved, light/darkness, good/bad, square/oblong. First principles are constitutive for the functioning of the cosmos: nature is ordered (*physei*) and the social world of norms is legislated (*nomoi*) in line with them.

Thus, from the very beginning of philosophical thinking, the male/female couple was given a particular position in thought itself. In that couple, the female was one half of the dyad which, although in absolute terms necessary for order and harmony, represented the 'dark side'. For the Greeks, this was confirmed not only by the nexus of badness and femaleness, but also by the link between the female and disconcerting indeterminacy (plurality, the absence of limit, purposeless movement without rest). Aristotle developed this distribution of being further, by allocating form and matter oppositionally: 'The body is from the female [. . .] the soul is from the male' (Aristotle 1991b, 45 [738b]). The female provides the material, the male fashions it; the male is characterised by activity, the female by passivity, its ontological function being a mere reception of form; the male is distinguished by the capacity to produce, to create something new out of itself, the female by non-productivity, incapacity, sluggishness. Both sides are necessary, for without them there would be no life, but in the order of things their positions are unequal, reflecting the asymmetry of form and matter, soul and body. On the basis of this, it is also possible to think and justify the 'natural' configuration of the political community, because it is supposed to reflect the harmonious configuration of the cosmos: 'for the soul rules the body with the rule of a master, whereas understanding rules desire with the rule of the statesman or with the rule of the king [. . .] Moreover, the relation of male to female is that of natural superior to natural inferior, and that of ruler to ruled' (Aristotle 1991c, 8 [1254b5–15]).

When, many centuries later, Freud, paraphrasing 'the great Napoleon' (Freud 1912: 189), declared that anatomy is destiny, his ruminations were no less anchored in a metaphysics strongly resembling the one devised by early cosmologists, despite his current subject being not the cosmos, but the universal state of the civilised man. The notion that anatomy is destiny came to be interpreted as if the whole lifeworld of an individual is defined and conditioned by an unchanging skeletal configuration of its body. The given arrangement of bones and organs determines one's position in the universe. For a woman, it is her uterus; and her entire existence is inscribed in the proportions of her pelvic structure. Although Freud himself never made this particular claim, it was readily available among his contemporaries, such as, for example, Patrick Geddes. This today largely forgotten Scottish polymath, biologist, geographer, sociologist and urban planner relied on the discoveries of the young science of biology to claim that the sexes were entirely different, but complementary and mutually dependent, such an arrangement being necessary for an evolutionary harmony of the human species. The physiology of the cell provided him with an explanation of the 'biological fact' that human females are more passive, conservative, sluggish and stable, while males are more active, energetic, eager, passionate and variable (Geddes and Thomson 1889: 270; see Laqueur 2003: 6). On second look, new kinds of knowledges (biology) and their new discoveries (the cell) only confirmed old 'facts', produced long ago through Aristotle's combination of rudimentary forms of observation and the first cosmological principles. Similarly, the value of these supposed facts went beyond science: they were used to order the sphere of social and political life. Thus, Geddes claimed that 'what was decided among the prehistoric Protozoa cannot be annulled by Act of Parliament' (Geddes and Thomson 1889: 267). The year of the proclamation was 1889, and the insight was very timely. While the suffragists were attempting to perform fundamental changes in the sexual political sphere, they were confronted with their supposed nature and essence that emanated from their plural, limitless, curved and dark body. The Victorians might have believed that they were beyond metaphysics – they were in no need of external warranty, an unmoved mover or God of Scripture, to confirm the structural difference: the physiological axiomatics of the cell did all the work.

The notion that anatomy or biology is destiny – that the givenness of the cellular life is the basis of social and political acts – invalidates the difference between nature and society, between what we are, as complex sets of physical, chemical and biological processes, and what we do (and what is done to us) within our communities into which we were born with particular bodies. Although the language of Victorian science sounds more contemporary to our ears, in its essence it is not far removed from the mystical Pythagorean opposites on which cosmic harmony rests. Men and women are different; the difference is fundamental in kind; one side contains a surplus, the other bears a lack; there is active form and passive matter. The gendered order of the universe is a natural, not a social issue.

In this sense, gender – the specific positioning of male and female in the functioning of the universe – was part of philosophical thought from the beginning. The gendered arrangement of the natural and social cosmos was different, and the main difference lay in the unyielding postulate pertaining to the side of the female: to paraphrase Beauvoir's famous line, a woman is simply born. Woman *is*: her anatomy, her sex cells. The essence of a woman is given in the destiny of her corporeity. From that point of view, the idea that one is not born but rather becomes a woman represented a true revolution in the way socio-sexual ontology is thought. Beauvoir famously claimed that 'no biological, psychological, or economic fate determines the figure that the human female presents in society; it is civilization as a whole that produces this creature [. . .] described as feminine' (Beauvoir 1956: 273).

Simone de Beauvoir confronted the whole history of thinking of embodied destinies by posing a question: what is a woman? (ibid.: 13). The question was not particularly new, but her answer to it was. She is resolute that woman is not the female, a being imprisoned in her sex (ibid.: 33), entirely wrapped by her organs, the grand female, an imaginary creature that feeds on 'shreds of the old philosophy of the Middle Ages which taught that the cosmos is an exact reflection of a microcosm – the egg imagined to be a little female, the woman a giant egg. These musings, generally abandoned since the days of alchemy' remain persistent despite the scientific precision with which they are demonstrated, so Simone de Beauvoir urges for a scrupulous admittance that 'it is a long way from the egg to woman' (ibid.: 42–3).

Laws regarding woman rest on a paradox: 'The married woman has full legal powers. These powers are limited only by the marriage contract and the law' (ibid.: 143). (At the time of writing *The Second Sex*, this logical incoherence cloaked in legal language was still in force!) Society created the conditions in which it would be very difficult for a woman to become human, that is, it created the conditions in which one part of humanity can be imagined as reducible to the womb. The world given to each woman is a world in which she is

> treasure, prey, sport and danger, nurse, guide, judge, mediatrix, mirror [. . .] the Other in whom the subject transcends himself without being limited [. . .] she is the Other who lets herself be taken without ceasing to be the Other, and therein she is so necessary to man's happiness and to his triumph that it can be said that if she did not exist, men would have invented her. (Ibid.: 201)

This gallery of (imagined) female figures, from treasure to mirror, is not a mere reflection of an enlarged uterus, but a product of social forces, multiplied over centuries, renewed in each woman and each man, in a social structure that left women living dispersed among males (ibid.: 18). This could be defined as the space of gender, of social reality that adheres to and subsists on the corporeal frame of the woman, who is, among mammals, 'the most individualized of females [and] the most fragile [. . .] she who most dramatically fulfils the call of destiny [of her extravagant fertility (ibid., 88)] and most profoundly differs from her male' (ibid.: 53).

Although Beauvoir is unambiguous in her refusal of the anatomical *fatum*, the female in Beauvoir (the body of the female sex) cannot be renounced. In that sense, biology provides one – definitely insufficient – answer to her fundamental question: what is a woman? However,

> I deny that they [the data of biology] establish for her a fixed and inevitable destiny. They are insufficient for setting up a hierarchy of the sexes; they fail to explain why a woman is the Other; they do not condemn her to remain in this subordinate role for ever. (Ibid.: 60)

Categorically refusing to blend vague naturalisms with even vaguer ethics, proclaiming such attempts to be pure nonsense, Beauvoir not only refutes the likes of Geddes, but confronts the whole philosophical tradition occupied with the essences that remain inherent in being, thinking and acting.

If a female is born, a woman becomes. Despite the fact that, for Beauvoir, a woman has a certain biological beginning, it is the process of becoming that provides the full answer to the ontological question about what a woman is and what she is now. In order to imagine a state in which subjection would cease to be the only available option in the process of becoming a woman, Beauvoir underlines the importance of possibilities. The possibilities refer to a potential future, to what a woman may be. Existence – dispersed, contingent, varied – exercised by actual women is opposed to the static imperishable, inevitable, changeless myth of the Eternal Feminine (ibid.: 260). Finally, the drama of woman consists in the fact that, through her projects, she seeks to expand her existence into an indefinitely open future, since a woman is 'a free and autonomous being like all human creatures' (ibid.: 27). However, in contrast to other human creatures, woman does this while at the same time being defined as the Other, as object or immanence.

The Project and the Body: Beauvoir via Hegel and Sartre

The notions of possibility, freedom and existence are fundamental for the conception of being as becoming. Man does not inhabit the kingdom of necessities – his is not the sphere of immanence; he is free – nor does he live a reified life of an object, predetermined by an inner essence. The man became what he is due to the possibility of free choice of his own existence. Therein lies the key difference between man and thing. A thing is such by way of necessity and belongs to the order of necessity: it cannot be other than it is. Being other than a thing, according to the philosophy of existence, a man is destined to have an unreified existence. However, to speak of fate or destiny here is to speak only metaphorically, because the fate of man is freedom, unpredetermination, a being unconditioned by essences: 'that I do not become an object, is for me a possibility of freedom' (Jaspers 1956: 175). Autonomous freedom, which Beauvoir also evokes, entails the absence of givenness of what one is, as one is only what one becomes. The being that becomes *'is not,* but *can be and ought to be'* (ibid.: 1) – 'indeed, our existence is nothing but a *could be'* (Abbagnano 2020: 267). That there is a field of autonomous freedom, of possibilities, means that a man – or his destiny – cannot be defined in advance: 'He will not be anything until later, and then he will be what he makes of himself' (Sartre 2007: 22). Man is only what he has become – existence precedes essence. The first principle of existentialism is, according to Sartre, that man is nothing other than what he makes of himself.

What does it mean to make something of oneself? What distinguishes man from moss, fungus or cauliflower, is that he consciously projects into the future: each man is 'nothing other than his own project. He exists only to the extent that he realizes himself, therefore he is nothing more than the sum of his actions' (ibid.: 37). The man is not only architect, but also the main construction worker, the maker and governor of his existence. His existence is becoming; his reality is incessant action. The process of becoming consists of an endless series of acts that are quintessentially chosen. Yet, although man appears as autonomous architect of his own project, each man is at the same time humanity itself: all of humanity reproduces itself in each and every man. Thus, every man has total responsibility, since every choice is an affirmation of the value of the chosen. To support this, Sartre offers a typically Beauvoirian example:

> If I decide to marry and have children – granted such a marriage proceeds solely from my own circumstances, my passion, or my desire – I am nonetheless committing not only myself, but all of humanity, to the practice of monogamy. I am therefore responsible for myself and for everyone else, and I am fashioning a certain image of man as I choose him to be. In choosing myself, I choose man. (Ibid.: 24–5)

Let us now return to *The Second Sex*. It seems that the figure of an independent woman with which Beauvoir concludes her book goes in the direction of Sartrean godlike freedom of action, at least in the form of a project for the future. But the story of the second sex is rather about something else. It tells us that not everyone is their own project – not everyone, not yet. Not everyone is a sum of their actions: a woman, who is a human, is at the same time defined as the Other, the object and immanency, rather than as the Absolute, the subject and transcendence. Simone de Beauvoir introduced gender in the naive existentialist universalism, fully exposing the fact that the human was interchangeable only with man/'he'.

What follows from here are several equally important quandaries. Either there is something wrong with the notion of humanity and its universal reach, or humanity appears under different guises, some of which are somewhat less human. Or, perhaps, since they are not men, women are human only to a certain extent, only partially.

The ontological question, what is a woman?, which *The Second Sex* attempts to answer, demanded rethinking what existence, possibility and freedom mean when applied to a certain portion of humanity. As a true existentialist, Beauvoir claimed that one is not born a woman, but becomes one. However, even if the female is not the essence of woman's existence, the process of becoming a woman – of existing humanity in the form of womanhood – is a process of becoming the Other, not a project in which she becomes solely what she makes of herself.[1]

The question that *The Second Sex* opened up is surely: is there a human freedom unconditioned by gender? In other words, to what extent is freedom defined as the very possibility of transcendence of the body, and how the embodiment of certain humans precludes them from attaining one such bodiless freedom? This is, however, not the only crucial question that *The Second Sex* made possible. We also have to consider whether a woman can become otherwise? Can she, in her process of becoming, become something other than a woman, that is, the Other? Can this lead to certain outcomes that are not given or known in advance? Can she – by way of non-becoming woman – perchance become something other than man, the emblematic autonomous freedom, not tied down by the body?

It seems that Judith Butler embarked upon her considerations of gender precisely with these questions in mind. The question – can one become differently? – is, I would argue, the cornerstone of what will gradually become the theory of performativity. This, in turn, is closely related to the question of the body. Contrary to a deep-seated assumption that the theory of performativity neglects the body (Duden 1993; Alamo and Hekman 2008), I argue that Butler sought to return the body to thought. But to make this possible, the 'body as such' – an abstraction, a genderless body or a body imprisoned in sex – needs to be dislodged from thought and replaced by bodies understood as lived and plural processes of becoming.

In order to grasp these processes to which Butler's entire oeuvre is devoted, the body is not to be equated with sex. The justification for their untying also originates from *The Second Sex*. Detached from sex understood as the immanence of life of the species, as well as from the Sartrean bodiless sum of actions, the body is given a chance to emancipate itself from its reified status in thought. In that sense, the question of becoming otherwise goes beyond the liberation of the female (body) from its path of otherness, from its imprisonment in sex. It equally demands emancipation of thought from the reduction of being to the duality of subject (as *res cogitans*) and the Other (as *res extensa*), where *res extensa* is lived either as *the* body or as the transcendence of the corporeal, that is, in which the body is, ultimately, the destiny of woman, whereas bodilessness is merely a possibility for man.

From here we should turn to one of the most epic episodes in the history of philosophy, to further clarify the nexus between the body and becoming. The episode concerns the struggle of two self-consciousnesses that ends with their transformation into lord and bondsman. Beauvoir drew her own understanding of otherness from Hegel's *The Phenomenology of Spirit* (Lloyd 1983: 2; Butler 1986: 43–4; Lundgren-Gothlin 1996; Purvis 2003), and *The Second Sex* could even be read as an extended elaboration of an embodied, and of course gender-marked, version of the lord and the bondsman. The same episode greatly influenced Butler's philosophical endeavours, as will be discussed at various places in this book. I will now focus on Butler's first reading of the struggle of self-consciousnesses in *Subjects of Desire*, in a chapter entitled 'Bodily Paradoxes: Lordship and Bondage', which strongly impacted the general direction of her thought.

At the moment of encounter, in Hegel's *The Phenomenology of Spirit*, neither of the two self-consciousnesses is primary: they meet as equals. Their equality in sameness is reflected in the way they approach one another – to both, the other consciousness appears as an inessential object, a pure other. They are the same so long as they need the other to affirm their respective independence from their respective alienation in the other (SD: 50–1). In other words, they both equally demand recognition of their substance. Their desire for recognition creates an unwilled bond between them, which turns into a ferocious struggle unto death where both self-consciousnesses desire to prove themselves as independent beings for themselves. However, the major consequence of this potentially absolute negation is in fact the creation of a sense of appreciation of life. The newly discovered desire for life (SD: 54) is what in the next step produces inequality, that is, domination of the lord over the bondsman, where recognition becomes one-sided and unequal. In Hegel's words, 'one is the independent consciousness whose essential nature is to be for itself, the other is the dependent consciousness whose essential nature is simply to live or to be for another. The former is lord, the other is bondsman' (Hegel 1977: 115).

Butler reads this episode in quite a peculiar way, introducing a surprising corporeal dimension, absent in Hegel's text. For Butler, at the very moment when the two self-consciousnesses appear to one another, each becomes conscious of itself and of the body as a limit: from now on, 'corporeality everywhere signifies limitation, and the body which once seemed to condition freedom's concrete determination now requires annihilation in order for that freedom to be retrieved' (SD: 51). Becoming a self-consciousness assumes a desire to transcend the immediacy of 'pure life', but the price of such a desire is a very probable death. Thus, a radical life-and-death struggle culminates either in a fully autonomous death, which has to remain empty and unrecognised because both self-consciousnesses perish, both willing to lay down their lives in the struggle against the immediacy of mere living; or, it leads to domination as a continuation of annihilation within the context of life. In both cases, the body is annihilated. In their struggle for recognition, whatever its ultimate result, 'each self-consciousness engages in an anti-corporeal erotic which endeavors to prove in vain that the body is the ultimate limit to freedom, rather than its necessary ground and mediation' (SD: 52). Becoming lord and bondsman introduces a dynamic in which the bondsman as 'the Other must now *live its own death*', appearing as an illusion of 'an unfree body, a lifeless instrument' (SD: 52), while the lord lives an illusion of having managed to overcome the immediacy of life in the form of a free disembodiment. 'The lord's identity is essentially beyond the body; he gains illusory confirmation for this view by requiring the Other to *be* the body that he endeavors *not* to be' (SD: 53; cf. *The Psychic Life of Power*, 1997b [hereafter PLP]: 34–52).

Unlike Hegel, whose travelling subject continues its journey on a thorny path to absolute knowledge, Butler stops at this episode (both in *Subjects of Desire* and, generally, in later writing). The episode, however, echoes in her first texts on gender, in which a bondsman, a living and embodied Other, intersects with a woman, a body imprisoned in its immanence, as read through Beauvoir. Their intersection ushers in a view on the body, since in Butler lord and bondsman appear, significantly, as figures of embodiment. The lord's mastery consists in defining the corporeal field – the lord is the one who defines the Other as the body, the body as the feature of the Other. Defined by another, the bondsman becomes the body in its very essence, bonded because enslaved to its essence. Similarly, the 'women become the Other; they come to embody corporeality itself. This redundancy becomes their essence, and existence as a woman becomes what Hegel termed "a motionless tautology"' (Butler 1986: 44).

However, the masculine detachment from the body – which seems to be also the basis of the grand project of becoming a sum of one's own acts (the acts performed, so to say, without a body) – re-emerges in the form of denial ('the denial of the body, as in Hegel's dialectic of master and slave, reveals itself as nothing other than the embodiment of denial' [Butler 1986: 44]). On the other hand, feminine essentialised embodiment, the complete imprisonment in and by the body, may end either in a reverse and total denial of embodiment (in striving to become a lord/a man), or in passive yielding to bondage which will never be resolved by a specifically female form of 'labour' (since, according to Hegel, it is labour that in the end emancipates the bondsman from subjection). Woman's path to autonomy is onerous, because she is required to relinquish the body in order to become a set of bodiless acts, or to remain enslaved by her body as destiny, which is her fate regardless of any possible acts. The answer to the question 'can one become otherwise?' must then offer a way to overcome the dualist division into unfree, non-acting bodies, and free, acting disembodiments. In that sense, we can claim that the theory of performativity sprang from Butler's early commitment to the notion that the body is the necessary ground for freedom and a point of its mediation (SD: 52).

Could One Not Become Woman?

For Butler, the body is never bodiless. It is neither an abstractable body as such, a generalisable entity outside living processes, nor a destined given, reducible to a hidden essence emanating through its changing appearances (this kind of 'body' is just another, so to say 'female' side of the abstraction). The rejection of a bodiless body implies the need to grasp bodies differently – as lived, plural, changing, vulnerable, capable of pleasure, exposed to violence, and yet also as the ground for freedom, not its limit. The body is material, but its materiality is not a grave to possibilities, either in the old Platonic sense, or in certain feminist sentencing of women to sex,[2] and thus also to otherness radiating from female bodies. The body is mine, inextricably bound to this individual that I am, but its life is at the same time mine and not mine. We become social beings precisely by virtue of our bodies.

Thus, somewhat in contrast with the generally accepted view, I argue that Judith Butler began to develop her theory of performativity out of the imperative to think bodies differently, in order to make the life of bodies more capacious. The idea of the body as the locus of sociality would become central for Butler's later work, but its rhizomes can already be found in the early interpretations of gender, drawn from her readings of Beauvoir, through Hegel, Wittig, Rubin and Foucault. Here is a representative quote:

> As a locus of cultural interpretations, the body is a material reality which has already been located and defined within a social context. The body is also the situation of having to take up and interpret that set of received interpretations. No longer understood in its traditional philosophical senses of 'limit' or 'essence', the body is a field of interpretive possibilities, the locus of a dialectical process of interpreting anew a historical set of interpretations which have become imprinted in the flesh. (Butler 1986: 46)

The body functions as the junction of cultural interpretations, as a site of socially mediated interactions. My body – the configuration of materiality in this very concrete form – is at the same time given over to others, who see, understand and interpret it in this way or that, according to available social tools of interpretation. This is, however, not only done by others around me. I myself also acquire and appropriate the interpretations that are at my disposal, which I receive from the social and cultural context to which I belong. My body is the field in which I become who I am by virtue of others and together with them. But as bodies are always gendered in some way, I do not become an I in some abstract sense; rather, the I is gendered, and gendered according to the interpretative possibilities available to it. As cultural and social, the interpretations can never be axiomatic; they also always contain the possibility to be different. Which is why, quite in line with Beauvoir, there is freedom and there are fundamental limitations at play, there are both possibilities and constraints.

Butler's aim in her early texts is not to demonstrate which side prevails in this either/or situation. She remains primarily interested in what possibilities open for bodies in their processes of becoming. It comes as no surprise that the most promising conclusion she drew from Beauvoir is that 'women have no essence at all, and hence, no natural necessity, and that, indeed, what we call essence or a material fact is simply an enforced cultural option which has disguised itself as natural truth' (Butler 1985: 516). Butler's answer to the question – how one lives this cultural option, that is, how one interprets bodily available possibilities – takes us to the core of the theory of performativity. Let us, however, dwell for a moment on the 'most promising suggestion of Simone de Beauvoir, namely, that women have no essence at all' (ibid.). If one is not born a woman, perhaps one also need not become one? If the essence is absent and there is, in fact, no ultimate answer to the question what a woman *is*, would it then be possible for a 'cultural option', regardless of the body it happens to inhabit, to transform into something which is neither Other, nor the Sartrean godlike subject making himself into what he is? Is becoming otherwise possible and how? For that, we need to see how Rubin liberated the body from gender, and then also how Wittig liberated gender from nature.

Butler openly acknowledged the great significance of Gayle Rubin's 'The Traffic in Women' for her own approach to gender (Rubin and Butler 1994: 68; GT: xi). Rubin began this enormously important text with a question that paraphrases Marx and echoes Beauvoir: what is a woman? Without much hesitation, she declares that a woman is a woman, but she 'only becomes a domestic, a wife, a chattel, a playboy bunny, a prostitute, or a human dictaphone in certain relations' (Rubin 1997: 28). The implication is that outside these relations, she might play some other role or become something else. Rubin calls the shaping of the raw material of human sex and procreation the 'sex/gender system'. This arrangement is a product of specific social relations, which are, moreover, also productive of sociality itself. On Rubin's expanded map of the social world, humans are labourers, peasants and capitalists, but they are also wives, domestics and prostitutes. Political economy, so rarely interested in the sphere of gender identity, sexual desire and fantasy, or the conceptions of childhood and family, needs to understand and formulate a human productive activity in which we do not appear essentially as labourers and capitalists, and only accidentally as women and men. For this reason, Rubin adds Lévi-Strauss and Freud to Marx and Engels, trying to show how the structures of kinship and incest taboo enforce the specific production of relations through which we become men and women.

Sex is, for Rubin, not a (biological) condition of possibility for gender. Rather, gender, as the arrangement that makes sex socially productive, limits the possibilities of the body (not only female, but all bodies). 'The social organization of sex rests upon gender, obligatory heterosexuality, and the constraint of female sexuality', where gender functions as a 'socially imposed division of the sexes' (ibid.: 40). What becomes of great importance to Butler are Rubin's insights of this peculiar reversal of sex ('body') and gender (the socially productive uses of bodies), their unfixed nature, a certain system of social meanings, and the cultural positioning of practices, desires and anatomies. The cultural interpretations of our supposedly speechless anatomies are not so much reflection of our primary sex characteristics, as much as they are the reiterations of the elementary positions in a system of exchange constitutive of social relations. A cultural interpretation of bodies is enabled by replicating a system in which women function as gifts and tokens of peace between military units, change households, take other names as their own, act as someone else's property; while men, on the other hand, organise this exchange to expand the circles of kinships, imposing 'social ends upon a part of natural world' (ibid.: 38). What is socially sanctioned as natural is the exchange of sexual access, genealogical status, lineage, property, rights and the movement of people. Bodies become male and female through these social relations, becoming legitimate (or illegitimate) actors of social exchange.

The path from being born to becoming a woman is, in Rubin's rendering, a process of continual cultural inscription of gender identity onto the body, produced for the sake of the production of sociality itself. Thus, it seems that women are not at all oppressed by their bodies. What is oppressive is the specific gender configuration of the female body as something susceptible to oppression, a configuration in which penis and vagina seem indissoluble from the symbolic position of lord and bondsman. 'Far from being an expression of natural differences, exclusive gender identity [being either man *or* woman] is the suppression of natural similarities' (ibid.: 40). Through her reversal of the positions of sex and gender, Rubin seems to have opened up the possibility of liberating bodies from the binary division imposed on them by gender.

The liberation, however, cannot happen on its own; a 'cultural evolution' is as necessary as economic revolution, because it provides us

> with the opportunity to seize control of the means of sexuality, reproduction, and socialization, and to make conscious decisions to liberate human sexual life from the archaic relationships which deform it [. . .] [Feminist revolution] would liberate forms of sexual expression, and it would liberate human personality from the straightjacket of gender. (Ibid.: 52)

In the spirit of the revolutionary 1970s, Rubin believed that the archaic sex/gender systems could be eliminated, because they are

not 'an ahistorical emanation of the human mind; they are prod-
ucts of historical human activity' (ibid.: 55). After their elimination,
there would be no obligatory sexualities and sex roles: 'the dream
I find most compelling is one of [. . .] society in which one's sexual
anatomy is irrelevant to who one is, what one does, and with whom
one makes love' (ibid.: 54). The anatomy of sex becomes irrelevant,
since a female need not become a woman. Beyond the binary configuration of gender, bodies can become differently.

The way Monique Wittig expanded the idea that one is not born
a woman can be marked as the point of departure for the theory of
performativity. Wittig's text 'One is Not Born a Woman' represents a
fierce attack on those who believe that Simone de Beauvoir's dictum
allows for a conclusion that the basis of women's oppression is both
biological and historical. For Wittig, there is nothing 'biological' or
natural that would have any substantial role in constituting the categories of woman and man. Both categories are exclusively political
and economic (Wittig 2002: 15). Those who cling to the bond of
nature and history consent to a myth. They return to the same mythical female disclosed and denounced by Beauvoir: '"woman" does
not exist for us: it is only an imaginary formation, while "women"
is the product of a social relationship' (ibid.). The mythical 'Woman'
that remains forever rooted in her sex, socially natural and naturally
oppressed, helps naturalise the historical phenomena, which, in the
final instance, stands in the way of any possible change. Since this
oppression, although social in origin, cannot be dissociated from
nature, anatomy, one way or another, remains the destiny of women.
For Wittig, however, there is a 'living proof' that this is not so: 'by
its very existence, lesbian society destroys the artificial (social) fact
constituting women as a "natural group"' (ibid.: 9). The lesbian
is a woman that is not Woman; she is, however, not a man either.
Although born in the female body, she never becomes a woman, if
becoming a woman means to be in relation to a man, one that implies
the subjection of Other to the Absolute. The lesbian is the locus in
which sex and gender collapse. Regardless of her being born female,
she stands outside the relations that predispose those born female
to become 'a domestic, a wife, a chattel, a playboy bunny, a prostitute, or a human dictaphone' (Rubin 1997: 28). And while Rubin
dreamt of the feminist revolution that would forever disarrange the
links between gender, compulsory heterosexuality and limitations
to female sexuality, Wittig demanded a guerrilla 'destruction of heterosexuality as a social system which is based on the oppression of

women by men and which produces the doctrine of the difference between the sexes to justify this oppression' (Wittig 2002: 20).

Now, even if Butler may have had some sympathy for Rubin's dream of androgynous society, she turned away from both Wittig's and Rubin's revolutionary conclusions. This shift is the nucleus of her specific understanding of performativity and, a fortiori, agency. Butler neither endorsed their ideas of destruction (of sex/gender system, of heterosexuality), nor did she accept their utopias in which the power relations are no more, that is, in which sex (Wittig) or gender (Rubin) is transcended. It could be argued that the whole project of *Gender Trouble* is one extended polemic against a desire for transcendence and its attendant political meaning. Abandoning the desire for transcendence helps her remain complicit with a body lived now, rather than in some indeterminate (unlived) future, as well as to accept whatever agency there is at the moment, *before utopia*, in this body and in this life. However, while rejecting their political projects, Butler uses Wittig and Rubin to read Beauvoir in a performative way: the link between sex and gender is not fixed and can be brought into question; one could become in various ways, despite becoming being culturally delimited; the very presence of various 'cultural options' shows that becoming is not grounded in anatomy, biology or nature, but that it follows some other patterns that are part of the social/historical organisation of reality; finally, binarity in the sphere of gender stands in the way of the possibilities of liberation of the body. Since gender is not fixed (in sex), Butler will conclude that the possibilities for unmaking binary oppositions lie in gender itself. As performative, gender appears more capacious and open for social lives of various bodies, that may have the capacity to change the society and power relations it rests upon.

Bodies and Norms

To say that gender is performative is to say that it is a certain kind of enactment; the 'appearance' of gender is often mistaken as a sign of its internal or inherent truth; gender is prompted by obligatory norms that demand that we become one gender or the other (usually within a strictly binary frame); the reproduction of gender is thus always a negotiation with power; and finally, there is no gender without this reproduction of norms that in the course of its repeated enactments risks undoing or redoing the norms in unexpected ways, opening up the possibility of remaking gendered reality along new lines. The political aspiration of this analysis, perhaps its normative aim, is to let the lives of gender and sexual minorities become more possible and more livable. (NT: 32)

This paragraph from *Notes Toward a Performative Theory of Assembly* summarises the main points of Butler's understanding of performativity of gender, which will be examined at length in the remainder of this and the next chapter. The passage signals that the 'keywords' around gender are performance, enactment and appearance. The reality of performance, enactment and appearance is not a given one, but depends on certain actions, which at the same time function as the space of negotiation with the extant power relations (and this is why reality can be remade). The passage also states clearly the normative aspirations that spurred such analysis of reality; however, the very central position in it belongs to the concept of the norm.

This chapter is, however, called 'Bodies and Norms' for a reason. Namely, my claim is that bodies and norms are the two pillars of Butler's theory of performativity. Bodies perform, and the performance is guided by norms. Agency, which I discuss in the next chapter, provides the link between bodies and norms, that is, between the performance itself and the constraints that channel it.

Now, the concept of norm entered Butler's philosophy via Foucault. The obligatory relations through which we become recognised as women and men, in which our bodies 'speak' (in our name, and instead of us), delineating our life paths in socially acceptable and intelligible ways, are most frequently referred to as norms. In addition to norms, Butler also borrowed from Foucault the notion that reality is saturated with power relations, that norms are constantly reproduced in the most mundane circumstances, that it is impossible to reach some stable ground of utopia where there would be no power relations (or where 'good power' reigns), that agency is tied to its exercise, here and now, within power relations.

What is the norm for Foucault, and why is it, as a rule, discursive? As is well known, Foucault never dealt with sex/gender distinction. His 'political economy of a will to knowledge' (Foucault 1978: 73) revolves around sex, and sex for Foucault denotes far more than anatomy fixed onto the body: it is about practices, sensations, prohibitions, incitements, proper and improper appetites, desirable and undesirable thoughts, about desire that is manageable and should be managed politically. Sex is, above all, constituted as a problem of truth (ibid.: 56) – not something residing within us, not even something we do or indulge in, but something discursive through which we become aware of ourselves as sexual, through which we come to learn the truth about sexuality (Mort and Peters 2005: 13). This 'problem' does not manifest itself through risqué stories only. It refracts through the enormous variety of the forms of speech: social, political, economic, medical, moral hygienic and legislative. 'Between the state and the individual, sex became an issue, and a public issue no less; a whole web of discourses, special knowledges, analyses, and injunctions settled upon it' (Foucault 1978: 26). It is a web of discourses that has the power to govern bodies in myriad ways.

This discursive web – a dispositive of sexuality – accounts for economic relations, systemic exchange and transfer of name and property, work of drives, for having and being a sex, yet it is, on the whole, irreducible to any of them. This historically newer formation began to emerge when it became socially expedient to develop and multiply new techniques for maximising life, and politically opportune to institute an order of life of a new class that affirmed itself through care for the 'body, vigor, longevity, progeniture, and descent' (ibid.: 123). The dispositive of sexuality was first established for a purpose other than kinship arrangements as described by Rubin. In order to show that sexuality is a new thing, Foucault elaborated on the differences between the deployment of sex from the seventeenth century onwards and what he calls the dispositive of alliance (ibid.: 106). The latter refers to a complex system that defines the rules of conjugality, legislates certain transfers, supports certain statuses and specific forms of wealth circulation. Sexuality, on the other hand, is tied to historically more recent devices of power, is not primarily governed by reproduction, provides means of population control, and is relayed through the body and its various intensifications. The history of the political dispositive of sexuality is a history of bodies of sorts, focused on the direct connections between power and the body – its functions, physiological processes, sensations and pleasures (ibid.: 152). Only with the dispositive of sexuality does power penetrate deep into the body, into the most material and vital. This is how sex emerged – as something discrete and corporeal, separate from other organs, bodily functions and sensations, enabling, however, their specific groupings into an artificial, fictitious unity, which from now on functions as a causal principle – becoming at the same time the most material and the most speculative bodily element (ibid.: 152–6).

The historically new formation of sex seems not to belong to the body, but it also does not seem to function as a 'gender supplement': something belonging to the social sphere simply grafted onto the body. For Foucault, and later also Butler, sex lives through discourses, through knowledges that produce and maintain its truth, asserting that it is indeed something and what that something is ('anatomy is destiny' is one such authoritative assertion), imprisoning the body in the truth of sex, in a fictitious aggregation of axiomatic meanings – that is, the norm. The norm is at the same time restrictive and productive. Truths about the body inform it, put the body in motion, produce, conduct and govern it. The body becomes, incomparably more than in the dispositive of alliance, a locus through which power prismatically refracts.

Foucault's insistence on the engendered character and the historical novelty of this formation is of the utmost importance, as it invites us to imagine a possibility of an emergence of yet another, hitherto unknown dispositive. Foucault is certainly interested in such a possibility, as would Butler be later. They also share an interest in breaking away from sex, foregrounding the 'claims of bodies, pleasures and knowledges in their multiplicity and their possibility of resistance' (ibid.: 157), crucially, through tactical reversals of the mechanisms of power, through the invention of a different set of norms. Butler remains Foucauldian whenever she insists that there is no point outside, prior to or beyond power, no site free from power, which is one of the main claims of *Gender Trouble*. Power can be redirected, bent, transformed, multiplied, because the discourse through which it works 'transmits and produces power; it reinforces it, but also undermines and exposes it, renders it fragile and makes it possible to thwart it' (ibid.: 101); but it can never be abolished once and for all. Lastly, Butler's first mentioning of subversion is related to Foucault's rejection of a possibility to transcend the binary opposites: to subvert them is to have them proliferate to a point where binarity itself becomes meaningless. 'His tactic, if that is what it can be called, is not to transcend power relations, but to multiply their various configurations, so that the juridical model of power as oppression and regulation is no longer hegemonic' (Butler 1985: 514). Subversion, it seems, may function as a passageway to a new dispositive not based on binaries. Their relentless multiplication, brought to life by subversive practices, may derange the hegemony of the current system of norms.

Bodies and Acts: Doing, Crafting

Thus far I have presented the frames Butler combines in forming her early understanding of sex and gender, with the main emphasis on the body.[3] My claim – with which I am consciously departing from common interpretations – is that gender is a posterior, subsequential concept, serving as an explanatory tool for a more primary object of Butler's consideration. Although she is a world-renowned gender theorist, and her concept of performativity is as a rule tied to gender, at the core of her earlier, and I would argue also later, considerations on gender are, in fact, *bodies and acts* – that is, what one does with one's body. I emphasise this not only because of the obstinate accusations of a certain somatophobia (Butler 1993a: 110; BTM: xix), but also because the body provides significant links between the phases of Butler's work which this book aims to sew together.

Butler's text that introduces the notion of the performative, 'Performative Acts and Gender Constitution: An Essay in Phenomenology and Feminist Theory', also provides us with the definition of *becoming* as a stylised repetition of acts. It is the body that is stylised, although what is constituted in the process is an illusion of an abiding gendered self (Butler 1988: 519). Gender happens in time – and its temporality is emphatically social. Here Butler defines her task as an examination of the 'ways gender is constructed through specific corporeal acts, and what possibilities exist for the cultural transformation of gender through such acts' (ibid.: 521). The corporeality that acts is not the carrier of culture, or a material facticity, or a *res extensa* onto which cultural meanings are plastered. The body is not a piece of matter, but 'a continual and incessant *materializing* of possibilities': meanings are materialised with, through and in the bodies, and so one is not a body, 'but, in some very key sense, one does one's body' (ibid.).

Our bodies are active loci of cultural interpretation; they do the interpretations. Doing oneself is a certain dramatisation in the form of reproduction of available conventions and through available rituals that in the given circumstances have some socially relevant meaning. But we do not do ourselves from time to time, occasionally, when we are particularly inclined to interpret the social script. One does one's body daily, again and again, in an endless repetition of acts. What we repeat or re-enact by our own corporeal stylisations are certain possibilities that are at our disposal, certain norms that

are there for us as historically conditioned beings. The body, therefore, materialises possibilities – those present, available, allowed,
socially given to us.

To explain this further, let us take an example from the history of
clothing. At the beginning of the nineteenth century, women in the
west wore long gowns that always covered their ankles in public. This
social rule, today seeming perfectly contingent and quite Victorian,
was observed indiscriminately, even in some very odd circumstances,
such as horse-riding. At the beginning of the nineteenth century, it
was unimaginable for a woman to ride dressed as a man, that is, in
breeches. Instead, women riders were supposed to sit side-saddle,
to accommodate their impracticable dresses and the strict dressing/
moral codes of the time. In the mid-nineteenth century, the first form
of trousers for women appeared in the United States. Bloomers, as
they were known, were gathered around the ankles and worn under
a slightly shorter skirt, heralding dress reform, if somewhat unsuc-
cessful at first (Tortora and Keiser 2013: 26). Their name came from
Amelia Bloomer, the first US woman to own, operate and edit a news-
paper for women, *The Lily*. She wore and unabashedly promoted the
garment in her journal as a form of women's emancipation. Although
we are speaking about a mere hundred years, it would be a long path
from the crinoline, a whalebone-hooped petticoat that rapidly came
to replace the short-lived and ridiculed bloomers, to Mary Quant's
miniskirt, with sleeveless dresses worn under the knee in the Roaring
Twenties and the factory overalls of Rosie the Riveter in between.
From today's point of view, it feels incomprehensible that until very
recently women were forbidden from wearing trousers. Conversely,
Scottish kilts and priestly robes notwithstanding, men wearing skirts
still represents an almost improbable social transgression.

Of course, we should be always careful with examples. Doing or
crafting one's gender is not about apparel or, to what the perplexing
word 'stylisation' might lead, about fashioning one's appearance in
line with cultural commodities. Butler explicitly links it to the late
Foucault's understanding of the stylistics of existence (Butler 1988:
521; GT: 190), which in this context can be misleading too (cf. Butler
2001a; Boucher 2006: 137; Käll 2015). However, the example of
trousers tells us something about the social world, or the world of
norms, within which we do our bodies. Our existence, embodied
and therefore gendered, is manifested – appears, has its phenomenal
form – in certain ways, or styles. The birth of a girl is the birth of a
body that will throughout its life be stylised as feminine in an attempt

to affirm its femaleness: the existence of a woman is a continuous process of becoming one. Stylised affirmation involves the active crafting of certain models or ideals to embody certain social standards or patterns. This engagement is by no means deliberate; we do not knowingly calculate what and when to perform, with intention and specific results in mind. It is not a project in the existentialist sense, nor a set of premeditated, intentional acts. The affirmation refers to the adoption, appropriation and internalisation of models that are already everywhere around us (but also inside us, which Butler describes as the 'psychic life of power'), such that they appear as our own, an integral part of our will and self-understanding.

In that sense, when a Victorian woman wore a long, heavy and utterly impractical riding habit, this she did not do for its convenience, nor indeed because she consciously refused to deviate from the fashion of the day, but because the norms of the time prescribed only this particular behavioural pattern. There was no alternative available to horse-riding women; trousers were not a 'cultural option' that could have been interpreted by female bodies. Around her were other women who also wore comparable garments. The 'morals' that spoke through petticoats and riding breeches reflected a gender difference, which then impacted the agility of a rider. From here, it is a short step to Geddes' 'biological fact' of passivity, sluggishness and stability in the human female, and activity, spiritedness, eagerness and passionateness in the males. The 'biological fact' was further confirmed by the invisible physiological life of the sex cells. However, on a more mundane level, one accessible to those not versed in the mysteries of a new science, it spoke through gowns that made not only horse-riding extremely inconvenient, but prevented any kind of rapid movement, jumping, bending or running. This continual physical restraint, supposedly caused by cells, but safeguarded by garb, was then translated into mannerliness, and from there into distinctive traits of the entire gentler sex: meekness, timidity, decency and other similar qualities that outline the field of Victorian femininity.

Femininity/masculinity is thus about the stylisation of the body, but it also entails a certain stylisation of the will, of manners and modes of comportment, ways of apprehending our place in the order of social relations and adopting, not necessarily consciously, ideas of what that particular place implies. We are born bodies that throughout their lives 'get crafted into genders' (Butler 1988: 525) through a bodily adoption of the normative standards. In that sense, Woman does not refer to this or that woman, but to a set of norms to which every body born with recognisably female sex characteristics must seek to conform. This is an active crafting, a series of innumerable achievements, lasting continuously throughout one's life.

Each and every one of us strives to embody the gender norm. The norm is a rule, a standard of what is valued and valid; but it is also that which is normal, according to the norm, normalised – desirable through the workings of the norm, that from which one is not supposed to refrain. The norm operates as an implicit standard of normalisation (UG: 42). The norm imposes, organises and sustains patterns of sociality, against which we orient ourselves when reading others and assessing the extent and ways they too observe, or deviate from, the norm. As a standard of normalisation, it allows certain types of acts and practices to become acknowledged as valued and valid, and accords them social recognition (as well as protection, for example, through legislation and other forms of institutionalisation). As both prohibitive and productive, the norm provides the parameters for something or someone to appear within the field of social intelligibility. Thus, the norm works as a divider: it helps operationalise the (historically volatile) boundary between the knowable and legible, and the rest, that which remains (and should remain) non-appearing, unknown, unknowable and illegible. If one performs their social existence, not to appear means to socially disappear: their becoming is a becoming unreal. 'Having or bearing "truth" and "reality" is an enormously powerful prerogative within the social world, one way in which power dissimulates as ontology' (UG: 215).

What does 'having truth, bearing reality' mean? The world in which our bodies become crafted into gender is a social world. If bodies are thought as living and plural, then even those fundamental physical features – extension, mass, matter – have a social reality. They appear only in the space of the social world, not as static physical entities or, in another register, a motionless mass of bones swathed in tissue, but as dynamic modes of becoming, co-defined by the world. Within a given social reality, bodies appear as the processes of embodying. The truth of these processes can be confirmed only within social reality, in which bodies 'speak' themselves and are given meanings as they occupy space contiguous with other bodies, having a certain shape of pelvis or bosom, being underfed or old, having this or that skin colour. Materiality of the body materialises too: the material is not simply there, but becomes through the materialisation of available meanings, becoming real through the materialisation of possibilities, possible 'cultural options'.

Apart from spatiality, the embodying process is also characterised by a certain duration. As Butler often underlined, the temporality of our becoming embodied is markedly social and essentially repetitive. The norm, or set of norms, that precede us in time, impress on us, form and condition us, act on us from all sides, often in contradictory ways. This continues 'with a tenacity that is quite indifferent to our finitude' (*Senses of the Subject*, 2015c [hereafter SS]: 5). The acts of embodying these norms provide us with reality and truth. There is, however, no specific point in time when the acting stops, because the norm is embodied in full and is from then on lived as the model itself. Quite the contrary, the conformation to the norm and the confirmation of its truth is a continual, repetitive process. One never becomes one's gender once and for all.

This is where the idea of performative begins to emerge, providing the nexus between bodies and norms. The reality of gender as a norm depends on its embodying, on performing gender. 'Gender reality is performative which means, quite simply, that it is real to the extent that it is performed' (Butler 1988: 527). There is no reality of gender that would be outside of its performance; but also, bodies have no reality apart from the one they perform.

The notion of performance, although obviously belonging to a register of a certain social ontology, invites us to think in theatrical metaphors. Reality could be figured as a grand stage on which the life of bodies takes place. Somewhat like professional actors who embody characters, supplying voice and gesture to a script, we too embody our genders by reading the script of the norms that surround and inhabit us. And, like professional actors who excel in portraying Medeas, Cassandras or Lysistratas, or else remain pale copies of more talented colleagues, we too perform the script to varying degrees of success. As is the case with the performances repeated many times, some will be better than others. Some may seem quite bland and unpersuasive, sometimes to the point of being comic, even farcical. And while we watch, we may start to feel deceived, irate, develop an urge to yell or throw something at the actors. Likewise, our own embodying of the gender ideal can border on parody, especially as the text we get to interpret is never unambiguous. Public condemnation can and does ensue when we have 'bad' performances. In the process of constant repetition, failures, misinterpretation of the script, but also exaggerations and caricatures, are always possible. Of course, the theatrical metaphor has its limits. Once the curtain drops, professional actors leave the stage, lauded or panned, and their performance stops (at least the professional performance they freely and consciously chose). No such break appears in the labour of embodying one's gender: the stage lights never dim, as our performance is not a matter of decision. We literally perform our gender in order to live.

The assertion that the life of the body is a performance means that the body does something, that it performs, in a continuous and repetitive manner, countless series of actions that enable it to live, on a 'stage' – which can be variously termed as (social) reality, the (social) world (of norms), or sociality – where bodies are given meanings, where they become intelligible, legible, recognisable. Gender is one such intricate web of meanings or power relations. It is neither the exclusive nor the most substantial one, but it has an enormous influence on how the reality of the bodies is shaped. Appropriating the norms through their repetitive performance, and thus continually re-establishing them is a complex form of the life in the body, which, failing to perform properly, puts to risk the life itself. Because, 'if existence is always gendered existence, then to stray outside of the established gender is in some sense to put one's very existence into question' (Butler 1986: 41–2).

Early on, Butler set herself the task of examining simultaneously how gender is established through specific bodily acts and what are the possibilities for the transformation of gender through those very acts (Butler 1988: 521). Performativity is, in that sense, always already an 'account of agency' (Butler 2009b: i). In other words, performativity is about the question how bodies live in a social world in which they perform the very norms that enable them to live: what is it that they do; but also, what is it that they can do, in order to perhaps live otherwise, in a world in which no body would be unreal and untrue? By the end of this chapter, I will have further elaborated the nexus between norms and bodies, focusing on why we craft our bodies the way we do, and why – if we could become otherwise – we become men and women.

Gender and Sex: De-essentialised Body

From what has been already said, we may claim that gender is the norm enacted and materialised through our daily performances of our bodily existence. Our performances take place in the world, which recognises us as real or, in the absence of this recognition, makes us unreal. However, what happens with sex, if bodily enactments take place in the sphere of gender? In other words, if in the social sphere everything is reducible to our repetitive crafting, what happens with the 'non-social' sphere, to the domain of nature in which we are born before we begin to embody the norm? Is there, in fact, any reason to keep these 'spheres' apart, if the life of the body never really ceases to be performative, or, in a Beauvoirian register, a becoming?

The debates on sex and gender that began in the 1950s appeared first in relation to sexology and those 'otherly sexed' (Germon 2009). The distinction was further taken up by second wave feminism (Millet 1970), becoming a staple of feminist theory to this day, surviving through numerous policy documents that attempted to mainstream gender equality on national and international levels. According to the standard definition, sex is a natural or a material or a biological basis upon which gender is overlaid. That basis 'belongs to' the body, and it is, so to speak, determined by the body – by its anatomy, hormones, chromosomes, genes, depending on the level of the refinement of the scientific knowledge that describes it at a given moment in time. Being 'in' the body, sex is prediscursive, similar in its somatic muteness to bones and blood. Gender, on the other hand, is a social or cultural effect of sex: since I was born female, I acquire feminine traits and become a woman. It is a discursive superstructure built on a prediscursive base, or a cultural construction drawn from the fixed natural substrate, becoming imbued with specific values through the action of various social forces. Without a gender superstructure, the uterus and testicles are just another natural form of pistil and anthers. However, value categories, entirely absent from the world of gladioli, redwoods and sunflowers, turn nature into culture.

The feminist discovery of gender was emancipatory, as it was largely assumed that what is constructed and learned could be deconstructed and unlearned. The existing framework of values, nested in the social and cultural sphere, could be dismantled, expanded and prospectively equalised – almost despite the materially immutable nature of sex (taken as a given at the time when the idea of gender first appears), which still retained many aspects of destiny. The dismantling was supposed to be done by women, who – being the subject of change, of the political action – functioned as an identity around which the feminist demands were grouped and in whose name they were articulated.

Undoubtedly, Butler was impacted by Joan Scott's definition of gender as the 'primary way of signifying relationships of power'

(Scott 1986: 1067). As she claimed much later, Scott showed that gender always needs to be contextualised and seen as producing 'apparently unrelated domains, such as class, power, politics, and history itself' (Butler and Weed 2011: 3). It is not possible to know what a category of gender 'is' apart from the way it is produced, mobilised and deployed. When it comes to sex, Butler is very close to an understanding that sex is a 'somatic fact' created by a cultural effect (see Fausto-Sterling 2000: 21). However, what seemed to have incited the particular gender trouble Butler became renowned for was the emancipation in the sphere of gender that was supposed to be brought about by women as subjects of feminist politics. *Gender Trouble* begins with a quandary: 'Is the construction of the category of women as a coherent and stable subject an unwitting regulation and reification of gender relations? And is not such a reification precisely contrary to feminist aims' (GT: 7)?

The complex story of sex and gender, identities, subjects, coherences and foundations – forged in the dense language of *Gender Trouble* that veers between disciplines, but still heavily relies on profoundly philosophical tools,[4] and promises to think politics but then thinks ontology – seems to be premised on the following question: what is the life of the bodies for which sex, gender and desire are not causally related (as would be in the case of one born female, therefore become a woman, therefore desiring men) – and do these bodies matter? As we already know, Butler's motivation to pose such a question is political, as she wanted to imagine the lives of gender and sexual minorities as more possible and more liveable (NT: 32). However, the question is also unrelentingly philosophical, as it further complicates the idea of the body. With it, the body forever ceases to be thinkable as a kind of derivative of the 'body as such', as bodies always come in genders. But if gender remains defined as the expression of sex, a social or cultural effect of a natural cause, then this definition also goes against the lived bodies that diverge from such causality. The lives of these bodies seem not to fit their designations, even those – or precisely those – that were supposed to work for their emancipation (and Butler does think that gender can be such a designation[5]). For that reason, the question 'do all bodies matter?' is equally relevant for feminism as emancipatory politics. Feminism ought to take into account a 'moral and empirical problem', articulated by the end of Butler's first text on gender:

What happens when individual women do not recognize themselves in the theories which explain their insurpassable essences to them? When the essential feminine is finally articulated, and what we have been calling 'women' cannot see themselves in its terms, what are we then to conclude? That these women were deluded, or that they are not women at all? (Butler 1985: 516)

Lastly, this question has important ramifications related to the understanding of the social reality of bodies. If within established reality certain bodies have no available possibilities to embody, they would remain not only unequal, but also, significantly, less human, and so always exposed to some form of violence. The theoretical struggle for the emancipation of the possibilities should thus also be understood as a struggle against violence.

The emancipation of the body Butler was after, when putting gender into trouble, rests upon the expansion of the sphere of gender and on its permanent untying from sex. The latter is in fact the condition of the former. And although it may seem that Butler ventured to undo the tie only in *Bodies that Matter*, which figures sex in its subtitle, this had already taken place in *Gender Trouble*: 'If the immutable character of sex is contested, perhaps this construct called "sex" is as culturally constructed as gender; indeed, perhaps it was always already gender, with the consequence that the distinction between sex and gender turns out to be no distinction at all' (GT: 9–10; cf. earlier in Butler 1986: 45).

How are we to understand such a claim? The conflation of sex and gender does not only put in question the mainstay of feminist theory, but it seems to fall back on theses one would ascribe to the likes of Patrick Geddes. In fact, Butler does the former, without doing the latter. The statement 'anatomy is destiny' (or the like) does indeed reify destiny through anatomy. No distinction between sex and gender is possible, because *sex is* gender: the essence conditions existence. With their doubling, the domain of gender was seen, at least potentially, as liberated; but sex remained a metaphysical given: although the sphere of gender can be changed and is about becoming, sex *is*. What Butler suggests – that sex *is gender* – de-essentialises the body that was supposed to 'carry' sex. The assumption of the causal, expressive or mimetic relation between a mute sex and a chattering gender did not manage to emancipate the body from its fixed place in the established ontology.

So far, the body has been referred to as the locus of materialisation of norms, the point where power relations refract in each individual, a cultural situation. Does this mean then that the de-essentialisation of the body assumes that nothing of its materiality or naturalness is there to stay? What happens with the natural body, and its natural accompaniment, sex, after its de-essentialisation? What happens with the matter that the body is, so to say, regardless of its performative actions?

Butler was at various times accused of idealism, postmodernism, discursive essentialism, linguistic monism, for the erasure of the reality of bodies or of propagating the disembodiedness of women. These notions were so powerful that in some places, such as Germany, they provided the framework for feminist debates for years (Hark 2001). It is, of course, hard to disentangle these accusations from various related or unrelated phenomena: the so-called theory wars, revolving around the professed detachment of the language of theory from real life and material hardships, decried as the pretentious nonsense of the 'Pomo Left' (Duggan 1998: 13); the insistence on the 'ludic postmodern erasure of the political in the name of discursive difference' (Ebert 1993: 10), in which the operations of socioeconomic arrangements become obscured by the play of disembodied signifiers; reframing of the polemical gap between gender and sexual difference, where the latter supposedly more truly represents bodily existence and experience of women (Braidotti 1994); the appearance of queers and their continual pressure on the coherence of categories of sexual identities, in whose 'fantasy world of ambiguity, indeterminacy and charade, the material realities of oppression and the feminist politics of resistance are forgotten' (Kitzinger and Wilkinson 1994: 465); the institutionalisation of gender studies and their tentative removal from politics or activism, etc., etc. All this notwithstanding, Butler *is* wary of the naturalness of the body as the mute foundation of gender. She does question the natural that should be beyond discursive reach, that is, the material boundary and interior into which one supposedly cannot penetrate.

Responding to Braidotti's criticisms once, Butler 'confessed' that she is not a very good materialist, because whenever she tries to write about the body, she ends up writing about language (UG: 198). This is, however, insufficient to separate good from bad materialists. Although the body is a physical object as described by physics, a complex set of organs as described by anatomy, and a complex set of tissue functions as analysed by physiology, each of these 'appearances' of the body is always and primarily given in language, setting apart certain corporeal aspects from others. Bodies are in language whenever we think or speak (about) them, regardless of jargon or register, and notwithstanding the various scientific fields' pretensions to accurately reach a non-linguistic, material understanding of them. Whatever this 'natural' body is, it comes to us through a linguistic mould: language fabricates, produces and constructs the body. The natural is always already said or thought as social.

We can imagine someone protesting: does this mean that this body of mine is, in fact, not bodily, that it has no reality outside language, no matter, no natural residuum that remains forever prediscursive, unutterable? Is my volume, my mass, the texture and the firmness of my tissue just a series of illusions? Is there nothing material in me capable of resisting the invasive reduction of social construction? Are there no bodily processes, such as fluid discharge or gravidity, that are part of the corporeity beyond its sociality? A response to such questions would be that the body depends on language to be known, but also exceeds linguistic capture. For Butler, 'the body is not known or identifiable apart from the linguistic coordinates that establish the boundaries of the body – *without* thereby claiming that the body is nothing other than the language by which it is known' (SS: 20). Yet, the search for the separate, pure, extralinguistic bodily ontology does nothing but underscore the chasm between language and body (SS: 21).

So, we may rest assured that the body is corporeal and material, that it has surfaces that are firm and impermeable, and that it is characterised by the processes that belong to corporeity itself. But, when the bodily discharges turn into sweating, when bleeding is termed to be menstruation, and gravidity translates into pregnancy, these corporeal processes become socially encoded and saturated with meanings that do not spring out of corporeity itself. Whatever the matter of our interiors, we materialise the possibilities according to what is available to us in the social world. Karen Barad is right when she claims that the crucial limitation of Butler's theory of materiality – if it is indeed a limitation – is that it concerns the materialisation of human bodies, or more precisely, only their surfaces, 'through the regulatory action of social forces (which are not the only forces relevant to the production of bodies)' (Barad 2007: 209), without exactly explaining how the norms materialise the very substance of the human body. Butler is not interested in the substance of the flesh or matter or nature 'as such'. She is after a lived body, a body that lives in a social reality, a body that comes to us – appears as knowable, intelligible and legible – only through language, or cultural articulations (Blumenfeld and Breen 2005: 14). This does not necessarily mean that there is no 'matter' or 'nature' – that they do not exist. It only means that what we seek to grasp as natural reaches us as already naturalised, linguified, culturally articulated – social.

This takes us back to sex, the supposedly most material, natural and corporeal foundation of gender. Each time when we attempt to say something about sex, which supposedly resides in the sphere of non-discursivity, it reaches us 'as gender'. It comes to us in the form of Geddes' sluggish cells and Freud's anatomy, both of which point to something 'in' the body, ushering both the historical idiom and its tacit ontological assumptions disguised as scientific truths. If we wish to, for example, reject Geddes' or Freud's stylisation of sex, but still persist in holding on to it as a natural prediscursive foundation, then '"sex" becomes something like a fiction, perhaps a fantasy, retroactively installed at a prelinguistic site to which there is no direct access' (BTM: xv). Sex thus comes to us either as already absorbed by gender, or as a fictional entity, somewhat like the mythical wandering womb.

Butler's interest in sex is, however, not only epistemological, restricted to the question 'what can we know about the true nature of our bodies?'. It is, from the start, also emphatically political. The detachment of the body from sex as its natural anchor opens up possibilities for bodies in the sphere in which transformation *is* possible, the sphere of gender. Retaining the causal or mimetic relationship between sex and gender not only leaves us with biological determinism, but it extends biology to the sphere which, presumably, ought not to be determined by destiny. That is why Butler asks: 'If gender is constructed, could it be constructed differently, or does its constructedness imply some form of social determinism, foreclosing the possibility of agency and transformation?' (GT: 10–11). If social construction of gender is possible in one way only, if even in the sphere of gender there are no other possibilities than those naturally imposed by the sex-substrate, 'then it seems that gender is as determined and fixed as it was under the biology-is-destiny formulation. In such a case, not biology, but culture, becomes destiny' (GT: 11).

Thus, if we are not born but become women, our becoming is not determined by a facticity, an invariant, unchangeable pattern from within. 'Indeed, it becomes unclear when one takes Simone de Beauvoir's formulation to its unstated consequences, whether gender need be in any way linked with sex, or whether this conventional linkage is itself culturally bound' (Butler 1986: 45; GT: 152). The

unstated, implied radical consequences of this are that the boundaries of gender are not prescribed by the assumed boundaries of sex,
that there is no single way of becoming a man or a woman, and that
bodies could materialise possibilities that may be unavailable to them
in the social reality shaped by determinism of biology *or* culture.

Repetition under Constraint

'Gender is the repeated stylization of the body, a set of repeated
acts within a highly rigid regulatory frame that congeal over time to
produce the appearance of the substance, of a natural sort of being'
(GT: 45), while sex is this 'natural sort of being'. Like gender, sex
neither belongs to us, nor is it 'a static description of what one is: it
will be one of the norms by which the "one" becomes viable at all,
that which qualifies a body for life within the domain of cultural
intelligibility' (BTM: xii).

Gender is something that one becomes, stylising one's body for
the sake of being viable. No essence directs this becoming, which
in Butler's radical way of reading Beauvoir also never stops, never
fully comes to be. Instead, it is 'an incessant and repeated action of
some sort' (GT: 152), a repeated process of materialising the norm
that qualifies a body for life. The time of this action is not just the
present time of my acts. Its time encompasses the past and the possible futures of my own performances and the performances of others,
to whom I am directly or very indirectly exposed. The temporality of
gender is social, and it is mine only to the extent that I, in my own
time, reiterate and reproduce what is already there for me in the form
of possibilities. The space where gender is crafted is not interior,
but public: even when no one else is around, others are constitutive
for the enactment of my own bodily stylisations. Gender as a norm
requires my repetitions, which is 'at once a re-enactment and re-
experiencing of a set of meanings already socially established; and it
is the mundane and ritualized form of their legitimation' (GT: 191).
Endlessly repeated acts by an endless number of actors who do their
gender, appear as socially available possibilities for all subsequent
stylisations of bodies. Over time, they sediment: the acts begin to
appear as something one is or has.

Sex is thus not an essence, but an appearance of something essential, of a natural being, of substance. Gender as performance '*produces* the illusion of an inner sex or essence or psychic gender core;
it *produces* on the skin, through the gesture, the move, the gait (that

array of corporeal theatrics understood as gender presentation), the illusion of an inner depth' (Butler 1991: 28). Incessantly repeated acts through which social reality is constituted produce an effect that there is something 'behind' the performance, something more real, more permanent, more lasting, more substantial that conditions the performance itself – as its internal schema, essence, cause, original. But there is nothing in the background of the acts. My gender is my imitation of the gender norm, which gets reproduced by my attempts to approximate and embody the norm.

If there is no internal truth of gender, the question is then – and this seems to be the central question of the theory of performativity – what makes us repeat, both in general and in specific ways? If gender is only an incessant and repeated action, why does it not take place in a variety of ways? Why is it that we (generally) act in a binary way, becoming either women or men? We might conjecture that it was precisely this question that motivated Butler's radical rereading of the notion of becoming, remodelled after Rubin, Wittig and Foucault. The notion of the performative was necessary to help further develop the unstated consequences of the idea that one is not born, but becomes, a woman. One indeed becomes, performatively, but not in an unconditioned way, choosing what, when and how to become. In a way, Butler rearticulated Sartre's idea that an existence is a sum of the realisations of possibilities, a sum of one's actions, but with an important – Beauvoirian – caveat: the realisation of possibilities takes place in a world that was there before any individual actor began to make any conscious choices; the possibilities we realise take place within an unchosen, rigid regulatory framework; we act within a framework of norms that qualify the body for an intelligible life. We become a sum of our actions under constraint, and act ourselves into men or women by the force of compulsory heterosexuality.

The constraint is rearticulated and renewed with every repetition, with every new approximation of the norm – either outwardly, or on the inside, as 'there are workings of gender that do not "show" in what is performed as gender' (PLP: 145). Psychoanalysis would need to meet Foucault to explain the psychic life of power, to show how what plays out or is exteriorised also stands in relation to what is repudiated, disavowed or barred from performance. It also helps Butler work through the double life of the norm, its attachment to our stubborn attachments to it. Lastly, the constraint plays out not only through the corporeal theatrics, the way we talk, the way we walk, or our passionate psychic attachment to our subordination to

the norm (PLP: 6); it is also very much part of the material organisation of life, which voices itself through a 'specific mode of sexual production and exchange that works to maintain the stability of gender,
the heterosexuality of desire, and the naturalization of family'
(MC: 42). Under constraint, we repeat our gender not only because
we desire recognition that qualifies a body for life within the domain
of cultural intelligibility, but also in order to be socially reproduced
as persons.

Bodies materialise possibilities, those that are available to them in
the established social reality. Their availability is organised according to norms of intelligibility that are socially productive, and on the
basis of which we become acknowledged as true and real. Life in
which 'one' embodies the norm qualifies the body as human. Those
'bodily figures who do not fit into either gender fall outside of the
human, indeed, constitute the domain of the dehumanized and the
abject against which the human itself is constituted' (GT: 151). To
'be' human is to be socially intelligible as one.

It has already been argued that Butler's main object of thought
was the lived body. There are bodies that are lived differently to
the prescribed norm, that have fewer (or even no) possibilities to
embody the norm(s) in a social reality that is nevertheless also theirs.
Knowing these bodies, making them appear in the register of knowa-
bility or intelligibility, particularly within feminist emancipatory
politics, was one part of Butler's aim. Understanding the norms that
organise the field of intelligibility was, however, never solely a philosophical enterprise. As Butler claims in an important interview with
Irene Meijer and Baukje Prins:

> My work has always been undertaken with the aim to expand and
> enhance a field of possibilities for bodily life. My earlier emphasis on
> denaturalization was not so much an opposition to nature as it was an
> opposition to the invocation of nature as a way of setting necessary limits
> on gendered life. To conceive of bodies differently seems to me part of
> the conceptual and philosophical struggle that feminism involves, and it
> can relate to questions of survival as well. The abjection of certain kinds
> of bodies, their inadmissibility to codes of intelligibility, does make itself
> known in policy and politics, and to live as such a body in the world is
> to live in the shadowy regions of ontology. (Meijer and Prins 1998: 277)

Being unintelligible means being deprived of the resources that can be
life sustaining. It means being exposed to violence (more) and barred
from equality in a more profound sense, as someone who lives, but

not quite equally to others; as someone who is real, but not entirely thinkable in reality mottled with shadowy regions. Embodying the norm *improperly* leads to various kinds of derealisation and dehumanisation. Embodying the norm *improperly* amounts to becoming (gendered as) monstrous, 'unthinkable, abject, unlivable', not mattering in the same way (BTM: x). The critical question – might such a reality be made differently (GT: xxiv), or might it be remade (PL: 33) – is what invites an insurrection at the level on ontology. Instead of bodies changing, making them conform to what they are not – a strategy employed for centuries – in order not to be condemned to death within life (GT: xxi; AC), it is established norms that need to be transformed.

This chapter focused on the first part of Butler's early stated task (Butler 1988: 521). It sought to show the relation between bodies and norms, or how gender is constituted through specific corporeal acts. The following chapter concentrates on the second part of that task: to examine what possibilities exist for the transformation of gender through such acts. In Butler's philosophical endeavour, the ontological and political lines of inquiry are rarely separated, even for heuristic purposes. This is why the theory of performativity needs to be understood as a theory of agency.

Performance/Performativity

The books written immediately after *Gender Trouble* sought to elucidate the theory of performativity and expand it in various directions. The Preface to its second edition is categorical: 'Much of my work in recent years has been devoted to clarifying and revising the theory of performativity that is outlined in *Gender Trouble*' (GT: xv). The term used here – 'outline' – is quite appropriate, since *Gender Trouble* is not a book *on* performativity. To complicate things further, this book (which also largely applies to Butler's entire opus, even to texts written as 'compendiums') does not seek to lay the foundations, to offer a firm frame with precisely defined theoretical levers. Quite the contrary, performativity there only emerges as a possible frame that would have to be filled in by way of other texts elaborating points that *Gender Trouble* only touches upon. Crudely speaking, *Bodies That Matter* elaborated on the workings of power in the sphere of materiality, introducing the key notion of citational politics; *The Psychic Life of Power* turned from matter to interiority, delving into the psychic effects of social power; and *Excitable Speech* worked out the link between performativity and language, bodily and speech acts, and offered an important account of vulnerability, which would become paramount for her later work.

The theory of performativity outlined in *Gender Trouble* has bodies and norms at its centre. It looks into those that perform, act or do ('their' gender), and into how gender regulates bodily acts by discursive means. Widening the sphere of discursivity, which remains a deep Foucauldian trace in Butler's work, to make room for the psychic, and later institutional and infrastructural dimensions as well, should be understood both as an attempt to expand the theory of performativity, but also to go beyond it.

At this level, the meaning of performativity could be drawn entirely from the famous Nietzschean postulate: there is no essence, being, inner core, subject or self behind (or prior to) the act, 'there is no such substratum; there is no "being" behind doing, effecting, becoming; "the doer" is merely a fiction added to the deed – the deed is everything' (Nietzsche 1989: 45). Although Butler reserved the notion of fiction for sex as an inner core of the woman-subject, and was less sceptical about the misleading influence of language and less disparaging about the subject than Nietzsche (who called it 'a changeling' [ibid.]), for her theory of performativity, the absence of substratum is (anti)foundational. Performativity relies neither on the determining essences nor on the intentional subject. Its foundation – mere doing – is a contingent one. Performativity is about bodies that are in incessant and manifold performing processes. These performances are imitations or bodily approximations of the norms, which also affirm and maintain the validity of the norm. Bodies perform their gender, thus participating in the production of the social reality that co-defines future acts of any other bodies. A Butlerian translation of Nietzsche, for the purposes of her nascent theory of performativity, would be: 'That the gendered body is performative suggests that it has no ontological status apart from the various acts which constitute its reality' (GT: 185). To this we can add, as Eve Kosofsky Sedgwick does, that the performative always carries the double meaning of the dramatic and non-referential, encompassing the polarities of non-verbal and verbal bodily action. Furthermore, the non-referentiality always includes aberrance, 'the torsion, the mutual perversion, as one might say, of reference and performativity' (Sedgwick 2003: 7).

Although the Butler of *Gender Trouble* is (and would remain) critical of the 'metaphysics of substance', in quite a Nietzschean fashion, she by no means refrained from shaping her understanding of performativity in terms of ontology. Bodily performances enact social reality in which they take place. The performative enactment is, so to say, bidirectional, it is simultaneously produced and productive. This can be also seen as the lasting trace of Foucault's understanding of power. What appears to be our deepest, most fundamental reality – our interiority, our being, regardless of our actions – is in fact 'an effect and function of a decidedly public and social discourse, the public regulation of fantasy through the surface politics of the body' (GT: 185). Certainly, one might wonder why a fantasy would be regulated and, even more so, why regulation would be linked to something interior. To this, Butler responds: 'If the "cause" of desire, gesture, and act can be localized within the "self" of the actor, then the political regulations and disciplinary practices which produce that ostensibly coherent gender are effectively displaced from view' (GT: 186). In that sense, what the theory of performativity seeks to show is that fantasy *is* regulated and that politics is somehow implicated in this regulation. Removing the self (in quotation marks) from the position of the necessary foundation enables the 'political and discursive origin of gender identity' (GT: 186) to come into full view.

Outlined thus, the theory of performativity offers a conceptual and a political corrective to the emancipationist aims of feminist theory. The theory of performativity aimed to emancipate lived bodies from (unliveable) essences, to emancipate agency from its phantasmatic foundations, to loosen the constraints of identities and open space for more collective struggles, an aim that remains as important for Butler to this day.

However, this 'outline' has instigated a host of complex questions which have occupied various interpreters of performativity. For the sake of clarity, they could be divided into three groups. The first group of questions deals with the 'performer': who performs if there is no doer behind the deed? What happens with the subject if the act cannot be localised within the self? Does the doer have a body, is it material, is it positioned within the material arrangements of reality, or is it somehow free-floating and unanchored? Does the actor have a soul – is there any room for psyche in the theory of performativity, or do the performative enactments take place exclusively on the surface of the body? The second set of questions is about the act itself and its invoked politicality: is a (political) act possible without a compact subject? What is the scope of an action and where does it take place? Is an act reducible to a speech act and is there performativity outside language? Is an act anything but a performance, understood as a the-atricalisation of an act? Lastly, the third group of questions revolves around the dispute on voluntarism/determinism: can there be any change within this rigid public regulation of our private practices and fantasies, or does it merely replicate what was formerly understood as biological determinism? Is there, quite the opposite, any restriction to the unrestrained will of the actor who derails gender norms seemingly on a whim? Is political agency reduced to a free play of signifiers, or genderfuck, or masquerading, or random slippages in the citational chain?

As already noted, possibly the key question that expanded the original outline of performativity is: why are we doing gender the way we are if there is nothing inside us that compels us to act thus? Put another way, is going against the grain of gender norms something now easy and playful, when we know that no interiority is there to bind us? This question, which was posed in *Gender Trouble* and has been framing feminist and queer theories and practices ever since, required that Judith Butler reflects further on the nature of the doer, or the acting subject. In that sense, the theory of performativity has evolved into a peculiar account of the performative constitution of subjectivity. On a different, related level, it demanded considerations of the nature of acts and action, with particular emphasis on the relationship between a performance (a bounded act, or a set of particular acts done by performing individuals) and performativity (reiteration of norms that precede, constrain and exceed the performer [Butler 1993b: 24]). The fundamentally political question – can possibilities be materialised differently? – belongs to yet a third plane, although still related to the problem of social transformation. A variant of this question, especially bearing in mind the somewhat offhand use of certain terms in *Gender Trouble*, would be: is the individual the one who breaks free from reiterative actions, or must the existing 'body politic' necessarily be called into question by collective struggle? 'Body politic' and politics of liveable life will later coincide and intersect when 'the performative emerges precisely as the specific power of the precarious [. . .] to demand the end to their precarity' (D: 121).

It was pointed out many times that *Gender Trouble* produced one gross misunderstanding of the performative, enabling the interpretations of gender as a choice, a role, a construction we build, 'as one puts on clothes in the morning, that there is a "one" who is prior to this gender, a one who goes to the wardrobe of gender and decides

81

with deliberation which gender it will be today' (Butler 1993b: 21). This misreading proved particularly important for Butler's later articulation of performativity as an account of agency, and the political articulation of the insurrection at the level of ontology. One of the more significant aspects of this shift in meaning has been the inclusion of Austin's understanding of performativity (Butler 1993b; BTM; ES), which had not been there from the start. It can be said that Butler's turn to language, through Derrida's reading of Kafka via Austin (Bell 1999), was supposed to complicate the initial idea of the performative act as a performance, which can always slide in the direction of the intentional subject. The turn to language, in which the bodily act became essentially supplemented by the speech act, could be understood as the key shift from individual acts towards the social constitution of action. In its subsequent iterations, the theory of performativity sought to explain how sociality both constitutes and constrains us, sometimes to the point of suffocation; how it generates inequality among lives at the fundamental level of our (gendered) existence; how it makes us vulnerable, exposed, precarious; how we live in a state of interdependence – so often socially, politically and psychically denied in favour of being considered discrete existences.

Notes

1. In one of her first texts, 'Sex and Gender in Simone de Beauvoir's *Second Sex*', Butler considered the question of the choice to become a woman. She rejects the interpretations which lead to an understanding that women choose their oppression, that is, being the second sex is their freely chosen project. To the contrary: 'the phenomenology of victimization that Simone de Beauvoir elaborates throughout *The Second Sex* reveals that oppression, despite the appearance and weight of inevitability, is essentially contingent. Moreover, it takes out of the sphere of reification the discourse of oppressor and oppressed, reminding us that oppressive gender norms persist only to the extent that human beings take them up and give them life again and again' (Butler 1986: 41). A woman indeed becomes in the mode of the Other, but there is no necessity to such becoming. Both becoming and women are imaginable as far more contingent domains of existence.
2. Butler rarely thematises feminist sources with which she contends. *Gender Trouble* is an exercise in 'French feminism' for which French feminist theorists had little sympathy (cf. Delphi 1995; Moi 1999; Berger 2014), rejecting it as Americanisation or genderisation of feminist theory

(Möser 2019). The related contention on gender and sexual difference (Braidotti 1994; Braidotti and Butler 1994) appears marginal for the development of Butler's feminist position (UG: 174–203; Pheng and Grosz 1998). Although she seldom named the feminists she opposed, in the early 1990s there were strands of US feminism that collided with Butler's anti-identitarian thought, such as certain forms of maternalist thinking (CT: 49), and Catherine MacKinnon's style of radical feminism. Her distancing from the current represented by MacKinnon was profound and far-reaching, and Butler expressed it openly and very early, declaring that it makes feminism 'into a position which asserts the systematic domination of women by men, distils both these categories into very fixed places of power, sees women as always in positions of relative powerlessness, as victims who then only get to claim power through recourse to the state – a very frightening prospect' (Kotz 1992: 86). Rather, Butler's affinity tended towards black and postcolonial feminism (PL: 47), which in its own way calls into question the (white, western) meaning of 'Woman'. Furthermore, there was a certain humility in her own role and participation in feminist debates (FCR: 132). Just as those she opposed, Butler was also cautious in naming her 'allies'. She expressed her debt to Denise Riley (GT: 4), and I believe that Butler's feminist positioning is very much in line with Riley's words: '"Women" is historically, discursively constructed, and always relatively to other categories which themselves change; "women" is a volatile collectivity in which female persons can be very differently positioned, so that the apparent continuity of the subject of "women" isn't to be relied on; "women" is both synchronically and diachronically erratic as a collectivity, while for the individual, "being a woman" is also inconstant, and can't provide an ontological foundation. Yet it must be emphasised that these instabilities of the category are the *sine qua non* of feminism, which would otherwise be lost for an object, despoiled of a fight, and, in short, without much life' (Riley 1988: 1–2). Indeed, when asked explicitly, Butler refused to offer a definition of feminism: 'I do not understand myself in a position to define feminism. It could be that I do not want feminism to have a fixed definition, but that is because I want it to remain alive, becoming more expansive, inclusive, and powerful' (Tohidi 2017: 462).

3. To this we should certainly also add Merleau-Ponty's understanding of the body as a historical idea rather than a natural species, and an active process of embodying certain cultural and historical possibilities (Merleau-Ponty 1962; Butler 1988: 520–1; Butler 1989). Although cautious towards the key phenomenological notion of intentionality (Phelps 2013), phenomenological thought is an important background for Butler's conception of the body (Stoller 2010; Foultier 2013; Käll 2015). Alongside the frames elaborated here, certain sociological and

83

anthropological ideas also had an impact on Butler's understanding of gender. In her text on performative acts (Butler 1988: 528), she explicitly references Kessler's and McKenna's (1978) thesis on gender as an 'accomplishment', and underscores her distance from Goffman's (1956) understanding of performance of gender roles and gender display. Kessler and McKenna are important for Butler because, drawing on Garfinkel, they argue that 'male' and 'female' are cultural events and the effects of gender attribution processes, rather than a collection of traits, behaviours or physical attributes (Kessler and McKenna 1978: 154). The idea of gender as some kind of action or 'deed' appeared in the sociological text 'Doing Gender', where gender is defined as 'a routine, methodical, and recurring accomplishment [. . .] Doing gender involves a complex of socially guided perceptual, interactional, and micropolitical activities that cast particular pursuits as expressions of masculine and feminine "natures"' (West and Zimmerman 1987: 126). The individuals 'do' gender, but that doing is socially situated, interactional and institutional, and always at the risk of gender assessment. To the question 'can we ever *not* do gender?', they answer in the negative: 'Insofar as a society is partitioned by "essential" differences between women and men and placement in a sex category is both relevant and enforced, doing gender is unavoidable' (ibid.: 137). Finally, Esther Newton's *Mother Camp* (1979) had inestimable significance for Butler's thesis that gender is drag, an imitation of the normative ideal. I discuss Newton's influence in Chapter 3.

4. *Gender Trouble* is organised around distinctions that play a fundamental role in the history of philosophical thought. On a closer look, it operates with quite a few of them, such as being/becoming; being/acting; essence/existence; thing in itself/phenomenon; essence/appearance; original/copy; inside/outside; contingent/necessary; natural/artificial; nature/construction; determinism/freedom.

5. In *Gender Trouble*, the notion of gender seems problematic; it makes trouble and gets into it, because of its reduction to two genders that, in fact, simply reinstates the binarity of sex (together with its fatefulness). *Gender Trouble* wishes to liberate gender from binarity, or from counting (Butler never cared about the possible number of genders, or to increase it), because identitarian formations of gender bring about new exclusions and, with them, also newer forms of violence. In its later iterations, especially in *Undoing Gender*, gender will function as a designation that is far more expansive and capacious, as it is by that time entirely untied from sex. 'To assume that gender always and exclusively means the matrix of the "masculine" and "feminine" is precisely to miss the critical point that the production of that coherent binary is contingent, that it comes at a cost, and that those permutations of gender which do not fit the binary are as much a part of gender as its most normative

instance' (UG: 42). Thus, gender functions as the mechanism by which feminine and masculine are produced, naturalised and normalised in their exclusionary binarity, but it can also serve for the denaturalisation and de-normalisation of that same binarity.

Chapter 3

Agency

Performativity as an Account of Agency

The theory of performativity has always been almost automatically linked to the performativity of gender. Gender is, as we have seen, one – albeit extremely powerful – norm that in multiple ways conditions the lives of the bodies in the world given to us long before we are capable of being autonomous. However, the idea that we *do* or *craft* our bodies into genders, that the reality of our bodies is the reality of our acts, unmoored from any givens, has from the very start demanded elaborate theorisation of what it means to act. On several occasions, Judith Butler has claimed that performativity is an account or a theory of agency (Butler 2009b: i; GT: xxv). Drawing on the notion that Butler's philosophy is an insurrection at the level of ontology, we can say that the account of agency she has attempted to offer refers to the crucial question of how reality might be remade (PL: 33).

The theory of agency can also be read as Butler's theory of the subject. This is why we must begin with the vexed debate on voluntarism and determinism – the unsolicited legacy of *Gender Trouble* – which further splintered into debates on subject constitution and the character of the agent. The debate revolves around two questions: does Butler's notion of agency enforce a subject who freely decides with which norm to comply with today and which to violate tomorrow? Or, contrarily, to what extent is the social character of reality permissive of a free action, if 'the social conditions of my existence are never fully willed by me, and there is no agency apart from such conditions and their unwilled effects' (FoW: 171)? The third issue, to which we will return in the latter part of this chapter, is how individualist this account of agency is, if it is bodies that act, but their acting is in some crucial sense a 'shared experience and "collective action"' (Butler 1988: 525)?

With her rejection of both biological and social determinism (GT: 10), yet without an unambiguous answer to the question of what urges us to act the way we do, Butler encountered accusations of radical voluntarism: if there are no internal restrictions preventing us acting as we please, we may act in whatever way we like. This is, for example, how Elspeth Probyn described the early celebration and appropriation of Butler's argument. We can have whatever type of gender we want, we wear it as drag and there are as many genders as there are people, 'in short, the sort of feel-good gender discourse at large' (Probyn 1995: 79).

Although such a conclusion certainly produced many liberating effects, the theory of performativity is more than a superficial reformulation of a Sartrean radically free actor. Doing is indeed crucial for it, and the possibility to do differently is crucial for its larger aims at social transformation. However, Butler was very cautious with the first principle of existentialism according to which 'man' is nothing but the sum of his actions, who, when choosing himself, consciously, intentionally and with total responsibility chooses mankind (Sartre 2007: 37, 25). Beauvoirian remodelling of the existentialist subject, who from then on became gendered, stood in the way of an unmoored, unconditioned act. If we are the sum of our actions, we are thus only in a conditioned way, where what conditions us also provides us with the notion of 'mankind' that comes to us from elsewhere and with significant limitations. No one is their own exclusive source: we only become in a social world that was already there when we were born into it. With advanced technologies, we begin to become even literally before we come into the world. With ultrasound, for example, we are gendered – socially defined – before we even have a body of our own (which in some parts of the world, where a male child is favoured, might even prevent someone coming into the world). Clearly, then, we are the actors of our existence – this is the very essence of performativity – but we are at the same time conditioned and constituted by the world in which we act. The notion of the social constitution of the act stands in the way of both radical voluntarism (I wake up and choose the body in which I will leave the bed), and radical determinism (something in me, anatomy which is my destiny, or something outside of me, an unbendable web of norms, precludes any kind of agency I might have).

In order to counter the argument from radical voluntarism, Butler develops a complex conception of performativity, expanding the initial Foucauldian frame of discursive norms to integrate Austin's theory of speech acts, Derrida's understanding of iterability,

Althusser's notion of interpellation and Lacan's conception of the symbolic. The performative subject of agency appears neither as radically free nor determined, but as constituted. The constitution of the subject is markedly social in kind. Thus, before we proceed to the concept of performativity, let us first briefly consider the notion of the social, especially since in Butler's early work it appeared in different guise (see Campbell 2002; Lloyd 2009).

Initially, Butler spoke of 'the political and cultural intersections' in which gender is 'invariably produced and maintained' (GT: 4–5). Gender appeared as the cultural interpretation of sex, as the cultural norm that provides cultural intelligibility and demands cultural transformation. Appropriating the language of feminist theory, in which nature was pitted against culture and which fitted well with the general academic jargon of the time, the language of *Gender Trouble* and, to lesser extent, *Bodies that Matter*, remained 'cultural'. 'Culture' encompasses various discourses though which norms speak to us, make us understand ourselves and the world around us, and reiterate what we understand. It encompasses daily rituals, some of which have institutional form. It manifests itself in the law's binding and prohibitive force, in scientific truths, religious beliefs and practices, and so forth. But, whatever form it takes, by being discursive the norm is always in language.

A certain movement from 'discourse' to 'language' would gradually put the notion of the social in place of the cultural. The life of bodies is marked by our linguistic existence: we require language in order to be (ES: 1–2). Language functions as the relay of sociality, of something markedly unchosen. Even before we begin to speak our mother tongue, we are addressed and named, and as such we become socially recognisable beings. To be addressed is a call to which we do not always respond, nor always entirely intentionally. Further, there is no intention in adopting a language, nor do we choose the names we adopt with it. Language positions and subjectivises us. The subject appears through language as a social being: I speak, but through me it is language that speaks (Olson and Worsham 2000: 738). Once we become self-conscious, as thinking and acting beings, our consciousness and volitions remain equally constituted by a plethora of normative discourses, which impacts how our understanding is formatted, how we think of and read reality. The social thus refers to that which belongs to us, although we never chose it. An unchosen array of apprehensions and affects is what constitutes us as *social* thinking and acting beings, together with various other forms of dependencies (on other people, relations, institutional support, infrastructure), which Butler later develops in her social ontology:

> The language we have for what is most intimately our own is already given to us from elsewhere. This means that in the most intimate encounters with ourselves, the most intimate moments of disclosure, we call upon a language that we never made in order to say who we are. In this sense, we are exposed to the social, impinged upon by the social, in ways that precede my doing, but any doing that might come to be called my own is dependent upon this very unchosen domain. (Reddy and Butler 2004: 116–17)

Our acts are bodily and linguistic. Moreover, they are linguistic as bodily, because *'speaking is itself a bodily act'* (ES: 10; UG: 172). Whatever agency we have, we have it as embodied beings that are socially constituted in and through language. It is in this vein that we should understand Butler's appropriation of Austin's theory of the speech act into linguistic agency, performativity as citationality, and the double movement of performativity that takes place always and only in the domain of the social.

Citationality: Agency under Constraint

The notion of performativity has a specific conceptual history, most commonly referring to John Austin's seminal work *How to Do Things with Words*. Austin differentiated between the descriptive statements and ones that do things. The first type of the statements would be, 'This is my wife' or 'I have put a bet that it will rain tomorrow'. But statements such as 'I take this woman to be my wife' or 'I bet £5 it will rain tomorrow' are not descriptive or constative, and cannot be said to be true or false. These sentences offer no description of what one is doing – their utterance is in itself a sort of doing (a wedding, or a bet). Since they perform an action and, through this action, produce certain immediate effects in reality, Austin calls such utterances performatives (Austin 1962: 5–7). Performatives can have force and referent value – they can be felicitous – only in appropriate circumstances that have a ceremonial or ritual character, as they fall under the domain of conventions (ibid.: 18–19). Let us briefly consider an utterance performative of a wedding. 'I take this woman to be my wife' produces concrete effects when uttered under certain conditions: during a wedding ceremony, in the presence of a priest or a registrar, if uttered by a man (a condition at the time when Austin gave his lectures, a universally valid rule until recently), if the man saying it is not already in a binding relation with another woman, if the woman he 'takes to be his wife' is not his mother, sister, daughter. Lastly, such an utterance does something only in a world of conventions in which it can actually bring about that some two persons, previously random individuals, become one person before God and in law, as had been the case for centuries. The utterance accumulates its authority (Butler 1993b: 19), and each of its repetitions functions as a layer which provides its newer iterations with performative power (Derrida 1988: 15; FoW: 168).

Austin's theory of the speech acts was, however, not among the sources for Butler when she first formulated her understanding of performative acts (Butler 1988), but rather came to her through Derrida's reading of Kafka's 'Vor dem Gesetz' (GT: xv; FCR: 134; Bell 1999). Taking a cue from Derrida, Butler shows no interest in a 'fantasy of sovereign power in speech' (Bell 1999: 164; ES: 48), or in the fact that I, the subject of the utterance, do something with the words when I utter them: for example, that I, a man, say the words 'I take this woman to be my wife', through which I become a husband. The dimension of 'my' intention – I want to get married, therefore, I have to say, and I do indeed say the proper words in appropriate circumstances – is less significant than the citational character of the speech act enacted by a supposedly free will. Discursive practices that enact what they name outlive the 'discursive event' of an act and surpass any intentions the speakers might have had. Although the intention does not disappear completely, it ceases to be conceived as capable of governing the entire scene or system of discursive practices (Derrida 1988: 18).

The performative dimension of the acts, in the Nietzschean sense, reveals not the doer but the doing. The instance of my speech act cites all previous performative instances of that act, becoming intermixed with its innumerable iterations. That iterability, the fact that what is said/done has been said/done innumerable times, is what gives authority to what I have said/done. In other words, the performative does something, enacts or produces what it names, because it is uttered again and again, and not because there is a subject who utters it. The theory of performativity, which thus foregrounds the doing, also implies a certain critique of the subject (Butler 2010: 150).

Unlike constatives that can be true or false, performatives behave like all conventional acts, which for Austin means that they can be done properly, or they may have infelicitous effects, failing to create some intended state of affairs. The notion of failure is important for Butler, but in a very Derridean sense, where it is not only a possible possibility, but a necessary one. Failure is, in fact, what enables felicitous or successful performatives (Derrida 1988: 15). Now, if failures have such a constitutive role for the production of the successful acts and thus for the upholding of the entire system of conventional signification, it becomes clear why their unravelling through parody of 'felicitous' performatives has had such allure (and to which the whole debate on agency in Butler has very often been reduced [Magnus 2006; Kim 2007: 97; Hood-Williams and Harrison 1998]).

However, the idea of failure had far more encompassing consequences for the theory of performativity – both in terms of subject constitution and the significance of agency. Namely, citationality is always an inherently incomplete process. 'Performativity never fully achieves its effect, and so in this sense "fails" all the time; its failure is precisely what necessitates its *re*iterative temporality' (Butler 2010: 153). As it takes place only in a mode of endless repetition, performativity is never successful in any definitive way. Thus, although repetitions produce sedimentation, congealment, ossification, from which they draw their performative authority, this authority is not incontestable. Its constitutive contestability is what requires ever more repetition, through which authority of citation gets renewed as recited. The 'necessary possibility' of failure within the performative structure is crucial for Butler's understanding of agency.

In addition, citationality expands the Nietzschean notion of doing into a countless series of acts, through which the subject gets reconstituted time and again. If performance could be taken as a singular act, performativity is never reducible to one act alone. Citationality shifts the emphasis from the volitional subject who does the citing, to the acts of citation. An act of uttering the sentence 'I take this woman to be my wife', which in correct circumstances for centuries established monogamous marriage between persons of opposite sexes, assumes reiteration of the norm, a series of its repetitions – countless utterances of the matching sentence through which countless marriages began. Who was the initiator, the first mover or creator of that history, when and why it began, is impossible to say with certainty (UG: 52). Iterability or citationality can indeed be seen as the operation of '*metalepsis by which the subject who "cites" the performative* is *temporarily produced as the belated and fictive origin of the performative itself*' (ES: 49).

The performative is then 'not a singular act by an already established subject, but one of the powerful and insidious ways in which subjects are called into being from diffuse social quarters, inaugurated into sociality by a variety of diffuse and powerful interpellations' (ES: 160). Applied to bodies becoming gendered, or to gender performativity, this linguistic conception means that there are certain bodily acts and norms that are cited by these very acts. What I take to be my sex, the very interior of my body, is a series of reiterations of hegemonic norm, 'conventions', into which I have been socially interpellated. The norm reiterates itself each time, from the ultrasound examination when the sex of the foetus is first determined, and in all subsequent invocations of that same sex, for example, for administrative purposes. These regulatory moments are not just boxes to be ticked. In addition to our name, date of birth and place of residence, they in fact index that we are something or, rather, someone capable of entering institutions, various kinds of relations or contracts. The instances in which we appear as somehow 'sexed' re-establish us as persons and provide us with a position in social reality. We may or may not be able to confirm this ascribed status: sometimes because we are incapable of doing so (as is the case with the newborn); sometimes because there is no good option to circle or tick; sometimes because it is done without our consent by others through whom the authority speaks.

The sexed I performs, but not intentionally. The one who performs the sex is not a rational and self-actualising subject who is the cause of its becoming, repeating sexedness knowingly and with purpose. There is no subject behind the repetitive acts, orchestrating or, as Derrida would say, governing the scene of its becoming. It is in fact the repetitions that enable the very constitution of the subject. Even more importantly, the time of this constitution is not external to the acts. The acts do not remain self-identical as they are repeated in time (BTM: 244): the subject is always constituted only temporarily – it *gets* constituted time and again through performative repetition. (The possibility of an 'infelicitous repetition' is, in this process, a necessary possibility and, as we will see later on, an occasion for subversion.) In that sense, the subject is neither given in advance, in some solid and unchanging way, as the one who first is and then does, nor is it constituted once and for all by some, so to say, great performative act that would bring its performance to an end. We repeat the norms of gender in order to live until we die.

The introduction of citationality provided an answer for something that seemed insufficiently clear in the early outline of the theory of performativity. There were both hegemonic norms and the possibility of resistance, but no explanation for what mediates between them. As Amy Allen claims, 'the upshot of this problem is that readers of *Gender Trouble* are left with the paradoxical feeling that resistance is either completely impossible or too easy' (Allen 1998: 461). With citationality, doing one's gender ceased to be thinkable as a singular willed act. The 'doer' of the norms is not a 'great performer' who performs their gender on the stage of the world, self-consciously choosing to liberate the world from the shackles of sex. The doer is performed by their doing through a ritualised recital of norms, which – to have any existence – require citation, reproduction, reiteration, that is, embodiment and incorporation. In Butler's version of performativity, it is not only that there is no doer behind the deed: there are neither doers nor norms without the repetitive doing under constraint.

Constraint is, as we have already seen, the crucial notion in which bodily, psychic and wider social limits converge to curb the wild freedom of action. Butler claims that constraint is what impels and sustains performativity (BTM: 60), what enables the subject constitution, but also keeps us opaque to ourselves (*Giving an Account of Oneself*, 2005 [hereafter GAO]: 20), incapable of giving a full and seamless account of how we began and continue to become. The unconscious losses, produced by the early interpellations through which we enter sociality, are an important site of storage of irrecoverable constraints. As Letitia Sabsay (2016: 54) claims, 'we could say that it is precisely the efficacy of the performativity of power in the unconscious that reifies gender and sexuality as identities at the imaginary level with such pertinence'.

Psychoanalysis thus seems to be a logical ally of any attempt to show that the subject is not self-identical and self-transparent, and does not act as a sovereign master of their intentions. It appeared in this form in *Bodies that Matter*, where Lacan's notion of the symbolic was deployed to counter the idea of the 'great performer'. Now, although a book entirely devoted to Butler's peculiar approach to psychoanalysis has yet to be written, the notion of constraint would certainly play a very prominent role in it. At present, I can only touch upon one aspect of Butler's use of Lacan's understanding of language, which has allowed her to expand the linguistic structure of performativity, and is crucial for her understanding of agency.

The symbolic in Lacan functions as the domain of the Law that regulates desire and the linguistic structure that establishes universal conditions for communication. For Lacan, the unconscious is structured like language, to which we all have access, but which none created. Once one enters into language, accepting its rules and, through them, the dictates of society, one is able to begin to communicate with others. Entry into the 'symbolic order' is made possible by the acceptance of the law, which for Lacan is the Law of the father. 'It is in the name of the father that we must recognize the support of the symbolic function which, from the dawn of the history, has identified his person with the figure of the law' (Lacan 1977: 67). Entry into the symbolic order is the moment of normative constitution of the sexed subject within language, as 'it consists in a series of demands, taboos, sanctions, injunctions, prohibitions, impossible idealizations, and threats' (BTM: 69–70). All these appear in the form of constraining performative speech acts ('you must not', 'you ought to', 'you have to', 'if ... then') endowed with the power to produce or materialise properly sexed subjects. In this sense, 'sex' is not something one is or has, but a symbolic position assumed under the threat of castration and punishment – that is, under constraint operative within the very structure of language.

The notion of constraint proved useful in explaining why agency cannot be, to quote Allen, 'too easy', but Lacan's binding understanding of the symbolic threatened to make it completely impossible. Thus, as good as this link with Lacan was for a defence against accusations of voluntarism, Butler had begun reading Lacan counter Lacan himself already in *Bodies That Matter*. Under the influence of Monique Wittig's understanding of language (GT: 157), Butler redefines the symbolic performatively in order to emancipate bodies from their positions determined by the markedly heterosexist structure of the symbolic. With this gesture, the Law of the Father becomes deprived of its fixed position, conceived as prior to and independent from any possible recitals of the Law. The assumption of a sex thus ceases to be understood as a singular act, a one-time entry-card into the social world. For Butler it is an interminable practice of citing the norm of 'sex'. What was supposedly there 'from the dawn of history' is recited anew with each repetitive reestablishment of sexed subjects, and is itself a product of citations that precede and outlive time-limited attempts of mortal subjects to approximate and embody the Law.

In Lacan, the symbolic is the universal, timeless and irreversible structure that governs the social domain of the temporary, ephemeral and volatile embodiments and incorporations. As such, it is of 'limited use for a theory that seeks to understand the conditions under which the social transformation of gender is possible' (UG: 44). In Butler, on the other hand, the symbolic too has a performative history, and is performed in time. Instead of being fixed in a timeless structure, the positions that produce the subject as sexed function as the citational practices that take place within constitutive constraints. Reinstating the subject-position reinstates both the position itself and the Law that positions it. Thus, not only do both sex and Law depend on their repetition and recital, but neither 'can be said to preexist their various embodyings and citings' (BTM: 71). Instead of being conceived as impervious to a reiterative replay and displacement, the performatively elaborated symbolic appears as the sedimentation of social practices (*Antigone's Claim*, 2002a [hereafter AC]: 19; UG: 44).

The theory of performativity dismisses the strict distinction between the symbolic and social law, introducing contingency and historicity in the Lacanian frame of structural necessity. If the symbolic/linguistic structure is temporally renewable, then the logic of performativity applies to it; and this produces the possibility of its amendment (Olson and Worsham 2000: 739). This certainly does not mean that the constraint disappears and limitations crumble. Instead, it means that there is space for something new and incalculable, performable *from the scene of constraint* itself. Not only does the possibility of agency appear within the less inflexible domain of the norm, 'which can never be fully extricated from its instantiation' (UG: 52), but an independent ontological status of the norm itself is negated, as the norm is only produced in its application. The norm is dependent on its being acted out in social practice and through the daily rituals of bodily life. It 'is (re)produced through its embodiment, through the acts that strive to approximate it, through the idealizations reproduced in and by those acts' (UG: 48).

The effective scope and importance of norms cannot be diminished – they have the power to define what is real and what remains in the shadowy regions of ontology. However, whenever a new citational chain is set in motion, each new citation of the norm opens itself to a necessary possibility of a failure, a slippage, a displacement, a wrong citation. Each thus reveals the social life of the norm, a life that is contingent, contextual, historically situated. It is precisely repetition that reveals the absence of destiny behind the norm, as either 'natural body' or calcified structure of the symbolic.

Contingent Foundations: Is There a Subject behind Agency?

Gender performativity was from the very start interpreted in two opposite ways: one interpretation allowed for the 'great performer', the other warned against the total abolishment of agency. If the first gave rise to a complex development of the theory of performativity, the latter idea, registered, for example, in *Feminist Contentions*, stimulated further elaborations of Butler's understanding of the subject formation and agency – importantly underscoring their contingent foundations.

The book *Feminist Contentions* presents an engaging form of role play among friends who shared an interest in philosophy and feminism, but seemed to differ on the question of postmodernism, one of the burning issues of the early 1990s. The contentions were many, but the central one, as Linda Nicholson noted introducing the debate, revolved around issues of subjectivity and agency. Seyla Benhabib took on the role of critic of postmodernism, understood as a quietist stance that undermines the 'theory which examines present conditions from the perspective of utopian visions' (Nicholson 1995: 4), a theory that claims to lay the foundations of agency. Despite her consistent dismissal of the caricatural moniker, Butler has observed that she appears as the symptom of 'postmodernism' (FCR: 133), and is therefore given the role of questioning the very possibility of agency. Although closer to Benhabib, Nancy Fraser seems to be positioned halfway, with a tentatively conciliatory role, while Drucilla Cornell, who was a latecomer to the discussion, was supposed to provide a certain balance to this 'gang of four' (Nicholson 1995: 1). The heart of these contentions, however, seems to be in an exchange between Benhabib and Butler. Benhabib begins the discussion with three deaths – of man, history and metaphysics – cautioning that feminist theory needs to be wary of their strong, postmodernist formulations. In her rendering, Butler appears to be the paradigmatic backer of the first death, that of man. What is the connection between the 'postmodernist' variant of Nietzschean–Foucauldian announcement of this death and agency, and how might performativity become emblematic of its abolishment?

A feminist, Benhabib is ineluctably critical of the western philosophical subject, yet is nonetheless concerned to keep some of its traditional attributes, primarily self-reflexivity, the capacity to act on principles, rational accountability of one's actions and ability to project into the future. The subject Benhabib wishes to preserve for feminism needs to be endowed with autonomy, rationality and, a fortiori, agency. The subject is, obviously, a (genderless) 'man', a 'better', upgraded version of the old humanist subject which, if extended enough, may also include women (and if need be, other minority realities as well). Again, as a feminist, Benhabib assumes that a subject is radically situated in 'various social, linguistic, and discursive practices' (Benhabib 1995a: 20), but that going beyond these conditions is precisely what attests to its possession of agency. In her view, the postmodernist subject stands on the opposite side, dissolved in yet 'another position in language'. Along with this dissolution, 'disappear *of course* concepts of intentionality, accountability, self-reflexivity, and autonomy' (ibid., italics mine). Having lost all human qualities, this postmodernist 'being' is just a grammatical construct entangled in the chains of significations and deprived of its role of initiator and author. In addition, a feminist appropriation of the trope 'no doer behind the deed' works against the fragile and tenuous women's sense of selfhood. It bids farewell to the self as the subject of a life-narrative, which can have detrimental consequences to female agency (ibid.: 21–2). The theory of performativity seems especially worrisome to Benhabib:

> If we are no more than the sum total of the gendered expressions we perform, is there ever any chance to stop the performance for a while, to pull the curtain down, and let it rise only if one can have a say in the production of the play itself? (Ibid.: 21)

Women would not fare much better, fears Benhabib, even if this (Goffmanesque, not Butler's) model of performativity is replaced by the speech act model, because the linguistic constitution of the subject (woman, gender identity) abolishes the human side of the subject:

> What does it mean 'to be constituted by language'? Are linguistic practices the *primary site* where we should be searching for an explication of gender constitution? What about other practices like family structures, child-rearing patterns, children's games, children's dress habits, schooling, cultural habitus etc.? Not to mention of course the significance of the words, deeds, gestures, phantasies, and the bodily language of parents, and particularly of the mother in the constitution of the gender identity of the child. (Benhabib 1995b: 109)

Furthermore, it is unclear what 'normative vision of agency follows from, or is implied by this theory of performativity' (ibid.: 111): the subject is entangled in power relations, as a subject-position in the web of discourses, but it remains uncertain how and to what purpose these power relations could or should be opposed.

The ontogenetic understanding of subject-constitution advanced by Benhabib is, of course, not in opposition to the idea of the stylised repetition of bodily acts, since the bodies repeat or cite the norms that come from elsewhere – including unchosen family structures and patterns, games, cultural habitus and cultural assumptions. The true point of collision refers to the 'place' of the subject who, for Benhabib, seems to be somehow able to step out of the conditions that constitute it, even transcend them. When the curtain is pulled down, Benhabib's version of the subject will have some other place to 'go', to spare time for reflection and decision-making, in order to potentially change what is restrictive about the conditions that constitute it. The power to leave them behind, if only for a moment, and to reappear when one has a certain say in the production of this play of subject-constitution, equals autonomy. There is, therefore, no possibility of emancipation without the pre-Nietzschean figure of the doer behind the deed, as it seems to be the necessary foundation of agency.

Contrary to this, the 'place' of the doer is, for Butler, in the doing itself. The subject *becomes*. It neither has a stable existence prior to or apart from the social field within which it operates (comprising all the practices Benhabib mentions, which also appear in linguistic form), nor is it endowed with agency by virtue of being the subject first, or by being rational, autonomous, and so on. It is false to presume that 'a) agency can only be established through recourse to a prediscursive "I", even if that "I" is found in the midst of a discursive convergence' (GT: 195), or, in Benhabib's register, an 'I' that precedes its ontogenesis, as some sort of irreducible remainder immune to the effects of practices that shape it. Yet, it is equally false to presume 'b) that to be *constituted* by discourse is to be *determined* by discourse, where determination forecloses the possibility of agency' (GT: 195). The subject becomes in and through the act. This places agency within concrete conditions, demanding no metaphysical foundations as its guarantee. Conditions – everything that enables and constrains the subject in its constitution or becoming – are themselves the contingent foundations of its agency.

Claiming that the subject becomes says nothing about its qualities. Who is the subject of agency? Is it a wo/man, flesh and blood, or a mere position in language? If the latter, as Benhabib seems to suggest, the subject is irrevocably deprived of its humanness, which was indeed recognised by some as Butler's 'antihumanism' (Lovibond 1996; cf. Ingala 2018a). Perhaps it will suffice to say that the subject is simply anyone who says 'I', when referring to themselves. The I-sign belongs to no one: until I say, referring to myself, 'I, Jane; I, Julia; I, Adriana', it remains anonymous, dissociable from anyone who may invoke it to refer to oneself as the subject. But each time the subject positions itself in the otherwise anonymous linguistic place of the 'I', it is constituted – the speaking body becomes a subject. And each time the 'I' is invoked, in using it, I cite all prior uses of this alluring word which, although most intimate, most 'mine', belongs to no one in particular. For Butler, this 'is *precisely* the condition of agency within discourse [. . .] That the subject is that which must be constituted again and again implies that it is open to formations that are not fully constrained in advance' (FCR: 135).

With this in mind, we can say that the subject is indeed an embodied someone whose body is a situation of possible interpretations of cited meanings, and flesh and blood to which this I repeatedly refers, each time reconstituting itself anew. The subject, the 'I', acts at times with certain intentions, which sometimes even prove to be quite autonomous; but these acts, of whatever kind, are never extricable from the conditions that constitute that very acting – be they linguistic or more broadly social. Acting is conditioned by powers that are not external to agency. The actor cannot stop the performance and demand the curtain be pulled down. There is no possibility of standing outside the discursive conventions or power relations by which the 'I' is constituted, no possibility to will away, however strong our will, all the norms that constitute embodiment. Our only possibility is to work through the very conventions by which we are enabled (FCR: 136), the ones that put us on the stage where family structures, patterns of upbringing, children's games, are played out, where we are dressed in certain ways and where the 'stage' represents our cultural habitus, with words, gestures and fantasies an integral part of the script.

Clearly, Butler departs from the dominant conceptions of agency relying on a self-referential, intentional subject, bearer of free will whose agency belongs to it as an internal – and potentially emancipatory – feature, untouched by the powers that remain fundamentally external to it. Surely, such an emancipatory model of agency served as an inspiration for many oppressed groups, women in particular. For Butler, however, this model fails to answer the question: why should agency, as well as the subject itself, be pre-supposed – secured in advance – rather than being accounted for by a complex interrelation of powers, discourses and practices that partake in its constitution? There is nothing in the subject that would be emancipatory per se, as its internal feature, that is prior to or apart from the fields of power in which any kind of emancipation may and does take place. The issue important for Butler regards the

> concrete conditions under which agency becomes possible, [which is] a very different question than the metaphysical one, what is the self such that its agency can be theoretically secured prior to any reference to power [. . .] What this means politically is that there is no opposition to power which is not itself part of the very workings of power, that agency is implicated in what it opposes, that 'emancipation' will never be the transcendence of power as such. (FCR: 137)

What is required for agency to have emancipatory or transformative dimensions is 'the difficult labor of deriving agency from the very power regimes which constitute us, and which we oppose' (FCR: 172) – to the extent that we oppose them. Whether we oppose them depends on the circumstances: the specific conflicts, institutional arrangements and historical conditions – the contingent foundations which galvanise transformative agency.

How Does the Subject Become?

The move from performance to performativity – with the introduc-tion of citationality and constraint – complicated the initial relation-ship between bodies and norms. The question of acts, or agency, of repetition under constraint and the possibilities of social transforma-tion, engendered a very specific understanding of the subject as well. Thus, before we go on to elaborate the transformative agency in Butler, we need to say more about the subject that emerges together with its contingent foundations.

The preoccupation with the subject precedes Butler's involve-ments with gender. The performative theory of the subject – which of necessity also appears as the critique of subject (Butler 1993a, 2010) – is a complex and composite theoretical enterprise. The notion of becoming is central to it, fusing Hegel's journeying subject with a circumscribed process of becoming a woman (or the Other of the subject), developed by Beauvoir. Phenomenology provided the notion of unbroken continuity of subject constitution, in which the subject does not appear as an actor who willingly decides on the process of its constitution, but is the activity of constitution itself (Käll 2015: 29). Acts of the constitution never happen in a vacuum, but only within the field of power relations: the subject becomes through the process of subjectivation (*assujettissement*). The limitations of Foucault's understanding of the subject's discursive constitution are mediated by Althusser's understanding of interpellation (Bell 1999: 164). The specific elaboration of Freud's understanding of melancholy provides Butler with a notion of subject constitution through pre-emptive losses (PLP: 132–3). From *Subjects of Desire* to *The Psychic Life of Power*, Butler's theory of the subject rests on an account of a desiring subject and presumes that the logic of identity is inherently exclusionary, which produces, as Jana Sawicki (2005: 392) notes, a 'queer subject of history, a permanent principle of destabilization at the heart of the subject'.

In Butler's first text on performative acts, she claims:

> As a public action and performative act, gender is not a radical choice or project that reflects a merely individual choice, but neither is it imposed or inscribed upon the individual, as some post-structuralist displacements of the subject would contend. The body is not passively scripted with cultural codes, as if it were a lifeless recipient of wholly pre-given cultural relations. But neither do embodied selves pre-exist the cultural conventions which essentially signify bodies. Actors are always already on the stage, within the terms of the performance. (Butler 1998: 526)

The subject of this passage is, obviously, the body, an embodied 'I' that acts, and gender is what this acting body performs. The body/ the subject does not pre-exist its acts, nor is it passively receiving the norms that have an existence of their own, separate from acts. The subject constitution takes place in social reality, which is the only reality in which subjects, embodied and situated in the social world and in relation to others, come into being (Käll 2015: 28). The subject may indeed sometimes choose to act in this or that way, stylising its embodiment within the limits of the possible or, at times, even breaking with them. No one, however, chooses the reality that enables its constitution. Whenever we act, we are already on stage, that is, in an unchosen social world. The performance is not the subject's 'project', in the existentialist sense of total self-constitution as a choice. Referring, quite interestingly, to the unnamed poststructuralist position, this early exposition of the double movement tells us that performance is also not entirely imposed either, such that it determines the subject. Acting takes place within the terms of the performance – the field of constitutive possibilities that depend on repetition, reappropriation and renewal for their existence. Norms too depend for their reproduction on bodies that act.

The mainstay of Butler's theory of the subject is, therefore, that there is no subject prior to or apart from acting. The subject is an effect of its bodily and linguistic acts, as much as it may be the cause of some new string of actions. Performativity goes against one-directionality of the subject, as it always involves a certain double movement: I acts and is acted upon by the norms that enable its very acting.

The subject-constitution is not limited to a certain portion of time. For example, gender constitution does not happen only under the influence of practices to which we are exposed in early childhood. The subject gets reconstituted in time, at no point taking a 'final' form, conclusively crafted once and for all (Butler 2007a: 182). This crucially temporal dimension – of becoming, rather than being – maintains an inherent instability at the heart of the subject.

That I act, that 'my' repetitions constitute me as a subject, through endless acts performed by 'my' body, also says something about the authorship and ownership over these acts that are 'mine'. I get constituted as a subject by turning the norm into that which belongs to who I am, and I am compelled to continue doing so in order to remain 'myself'. Materialising those possibilities that are there for me, I become those possibilities, and I realise myself through what is not exactly 'mine'. This can be also described as a form of instability – or dependency – at the heart of the subject, which never really comes to an end either.

Let us apply this to the constitution of the woman-subject. To begin with, one is not born a woman. In a social world in which gender binarity functions as the norm, what actually is born is a miniscule human who will, over the course of their becoming, affirm its humanness by becoming a woman. The physical act of emergence into the world has a social form: the umbilical cord is cut, and the so-called primary sexual characteristics of a newly born become observable. A person announces the first social fact about the newborn – 'It's a girl!' – calling a woman into being. Before the birth of this particular human, the 'primary sexual characteristics' have already existed in the social register as a discursive form of naming and norming. (The utterance 'It's a girl' automatically also means 'It's not a boy'. The trouble is, of course, when it is neither, when the primary sex characteristics are undefined or imprecise – when, in fact, there is no differentia specifica at all.) The announcement has performative and interpellative force, if by interpellation we mean a discursive production of the social subject (PLP: 5) through a discursive practice that produces what it names (BTM: xxi). In other words, long before this concrete human becomes able to refer to herself as a girl (to define herself as the subject of *her* gender, gender that 'belongs' to her), it will be subjected to the norm that provides social intelligibility, enabling others – parents, custodians, carers, relatives, childminders, doctors – to situate it within the frame of social reality.

Becoming a girl-subject is also a taxing and uncertain early achievement in the domain of the psyche effectuated by prohibitions of certain kinds of attachment that produce the incorporation of disavowed and unmourned losses. Through stylised repetition – imitation and appropriation – of possibilities, she finds it possible to respond to her social name, and the subject that addresses itself as 'I, the girl' becomes constituted as the girl-subject. Becoming this subject takes place within constraints: 'not to be a boy', not to be 'ambivalent', but to approximate an assumed status of the woman-subject. However, although the constraints are rigid, and although for a significant period of time they do not fall under the domain of the girl-subject's volition – a formative period of learning and adopting the codes of sociality and locating oneself within these frames – they are, for that reason, not the structurally static features of the self. Their dynamic nature is evident in the very necessity of their constant renewal. 'I perform (mainly unconsciously and implicitly) that renewal in the repeated acts of my person [which later provides and sustains the status of the girl-subject or woman-subject]. Even though my agency is conditioned by those limitations, my agency can also thematize and alter those limitations to some degree' (Olson and Worsham 2000: 739), but it can never abolish them entirely. The process of becoming the woman-subject does not end with the end of girlhood, or any other point in the life of a woman. She remains attached to the norms that constitute her into a 'she', continuously citing the norms of womanhood in order to live a legible, intelligible, liveable life, until she dies.

Agency, Power and Resistance

What are the implications for agency in this theory of the subject, if agency is only possible 'within the terms of performance' (Butler 1998: 526)? As has been shown, the subject gets constituted without a 'place' of shelter or freedom from power. This is indeed a Foucauldian framework, to which Nancy Fraser (1995: 68) also points during the philosophical exchange on the benefits of post-modernism for feminism. If we follow Foucault, the story of power is about the 'different modes by which, in our culture, human beings are made subjects' (Foucault 2002b: 326). Butler agrees: 'No individual becomes a subject without first becoming subjected or under-going "subjectivation"' (PLP: 11). Subjectivation (*assujettissement*) assumes that one becomes a subject only by subjection to power. Power says no: it halts, prohibits, constrains us; and precisely in this way also forms, delimits and animates within limits of the allowed. The human addressed as a girl is limited ('you are not a boy', 'don't act like a boy', 'girls don't do that'), and simultaneously produced into a girl-subject. Subjection to norms is the condition of possibility for becoming subject/ed. It is a regulatory principle of the production of the subject (PLP: 84; GAO: 17).

Agency is thus constituted by the very powers that enable the becoming of a subject. However, the powers that condition the subject do not deliver it 'ready-made', 'finished', in one go. The body is not a lifeless recipient of power, but a site of its continuous trans-fer – it acts and is acted upon. 'Power happens to the body, but this body is also the occasion where something unpredictable can happen to power itself' (Butler 2002b: 15), since the subject is always only 'partially constituted, or sometimes constituted in ways that can't quite be anticipated' (Bell 1999: 164). If power relations hold only to the extent that they are performed, renewed by the daily rituals of our bodily lives, it means that they are also open to the productive and non-mechanical aspect of performance itself. Ultimately, a radi-cally conditioned form of agency is possible due to this constitutive incompleteness of the subject (PLP: 14–15).

Anxious to show that agency is counter to any notion of a vol-untarist subject that exists apart from the regulatory norms it pro-claims to oppose, Butler introduced the paradox of subjectivation, claiming that the resisting subject is enabled by the norms it resists. This constitutive constraint does not preclude agency, but it does 'locate agency as a reiterative or rearticulatory practice, immanent to power, and not a relation of external opposition to power' (BTM: xxiii).

What is agency, then? If the subject becomes by and through acting, is it not, so to say, continuously agentic? Or, is agency some specific quality of a resisting actor, which would be, for example, Benhabib's understanding? Is agency, for Butler, always already there as a quality of iterable action, or is it reducible to resistance only? She claims that it is precisely the 'iterability of the subject that shows how agency may well consist in opposing and transforming the social terms by which it is spawned' (PLP: 29). Saba Mahmood once rightly noted that there are two simultaneous moves that Butler seems to be making: agency is indeed located within the structure of power itself, rather than in the rational, autonomous and therefore agentic subject, but it still seems that resistance is its paradigmatic instance. Thus, although the transcendental-humanist-liberal idea of the subject is disputed by Butler's understanding of subjection, 'what remains intact is the natural status accorded to the desire for resistance to social norms, and the incarceration of the notion of agency to the space of emancipatory politics' (Mahmood 2001: 211).

Mahmood wonders what remains of agency if it is not equated with a desire for resistance. This is an important question to which I will return later in this chapter. For the time being, let us remain with the designations Mahmood uses to describe Butler's understanding of agency. Can agency be identified with resistance, if not with the social transformation itself? Does agency equal freedom? What kind of politics is envisioned when we think of agency as political, and on what normative grounds can such a politics be said to be transformative or emancipatory?

In laying down the contingent foundations of her theory of the subject, through its various rearticulations and modifications, Butler never entirely abandoned its Foucauldian set-up. She did not heed Nancy Fraser's early warning that such an adherence necessarily stands in the way of normative thinking, that is, 'her poststructuralist Foucauldian framework [. . .] [is] structurally incapable of providing satisfactory answers to the normative questions it unfailingly solicits' (Fraser 1995: 68; similarly, Benhabib 1995b: 110; cf. Fraser 1996). Butler disagreed: her essay on Foucault's notion of critique (Butler 2001a), could be read as a longer affirmation of the importance of 'Foucault's contribution to normative theory, almost against the normativists themselves' (Zaharijević and Krstić 2018: 29–30). The Foucauldian coupling of power and resistance – together with its specific normativity – remained ingrained in how Butler understood agency.

In Foucault, power is irreducible to the figure of a mortal God, sovereign or any general system of domination – these are 'only the terminal forms power takes' (Foucault 1978: 92). 'Society is an archipelago of different powers' (Foucault 2012), prohibitive and enabling, productive and confrontational, intentional and non-subjective (Foucault 1978: 94). Resolved to de-economise power, to approach it not as a commodity that can be possessed, transferred or alienated, Foucault defines it 'as something that is exercised and that exists only in action' (Foucault 2003: 14). Power is everywhere: diffused, proliferating, cutting through social relations. It is exercised through and in relations; a search for the foundations of power – 'power as such', perfidiously concealed behind its own relations and manipulating them according to some plan – is futile. Power has no single source such as the state, the ruling class or patriarchy.

Yet, as much as it is an archipelago of powers, society is also an archipelago of resistances. As they are myriad and interrelated in myriad ways, there is no single locus of Power, there is no single 'locus of great Refusal, the soul of revolt [. . .] source of all rebellions, or pure law of the revolutionary' (Foucault 1978: 96). For Foucault, no one thing is solely of the order of oppression or solely of the order of liberation (Foucault 1996b: 339). Equally, there is no pre-given, privileged or single subject of resistance (Foucault 1980b: 208). Resistances happen within concrete, given, limiting and enabling conditions. If successful, resistances can cause the operation of existing power relations to change, on a small or a large level. They might lead to their redirection, restructuring or reversal. Still, they never lead to an ultimate overthrow of power. No resistance has the capacity to engender total freedom from power as such. Even when particularly forceful and with far-ranging effects, resistances do not do away with power, but create new power relations.

Resistances do not make us ultimately free or autonomous, but do – to a point – desubjectivise. Resisting or opposing makes us, in other words, critical towards being governed (Foucault 2007a). Certainly, desubjectivisation is in itself neither 'good' nor 'bad': what is transformative about it is that it opens up possibilities not previously disclosed, accessible or available to us.

Desubjectivisation is an ambivalent concept. It entails the possibility to become freer, but not free in any absolute sense. In Foucault, freedom never arrives as a permanent and incontrovertible state upon the resolution of some 'ultimate resistance'. No liberation project can have entirely transparent, one-directional and calculable effects, and no liberating process produces freedom as a final consequence. Discussing gay communities and what would later emerge as identity politics, Foucault once insisted that the victories won in the 1970s, however important, do not amount to freedom as such: what was needed next was the creation of new forms of life, relationships, through ethical, sexual and political choices (Foucault 1996b: 383). Freedom is not vouched for by any liberationist project, nor is it guaranteed by laws and institutions, because '"liberty" is what must be exercised' (Foucault 1996b: 339; cf. Birulés 2009; McWhorter 2013). Only such exercises can control the new power relations introduced by liberations themselves (Foucault 1997b: 283–4).

Butler's understanding of power and power relations is largely compatible with Foucault's, as she has insisted on various occasions. Agency is, however, not a Foucauldian term, and its equation with resistance complicates matters. In addition, freedom – a concept far from univocal in Foucault himself – remains undefined in Butler. She once referred to what freedom is not. Her refusal of 'the classical liberal and existentialist model of freedom' (GT: 169) was in a sense Foucauldian, as it entailed the rejection of an assumed barrier between the volitional subject untouched by power, and its 'outside', infested with power. However, rejecting these models did not lead her to embrace and further develop some other recognisable model of freedom. Moya Lloyd noted that although politically committed to freedom, Butler remained silent on what it means to be free, 'viewing judgements of this kind as the (provisional) outcome of democratic contestation rather than the purpose of political theory. Instead her aim, indeed the aim throughout her work is to uncover how restrictive norms might be challenged' (Lloyd 2007: 133). The act of challenge, or the act of resistance, seems to be freeing, but it does not amount to freedom as such. Freedom needs to be exercised as a continual resistance to the restrictive norms.

Subversion has been frequently framed as the specifically Butlerian form of challenge to norms. There were some who understood 'more subversive' models of gender performance as prominent instances of resistance, while others saw them as Butler's recommendations of patterns for simulation (Hennessy 2000). Butler certainly contributed to shaping such views: several sentences after the stated rejection of the models of freedom that are based on an impossible fantasy of full-scale transcendence of power, she goes on to say: 'In my view, the normative focus for gay and lesbian practice ought to be on the subversive and parodic redeployment of power' (GT: 169). 'Normative focus' and 'ought to' are strong formulations, and the exactness with which she defines the subject of the said practices leaves little room for ambivalence. However, even if we accept that the queer subject – which did not yet 'exist' at the time of *Gender Trouble*'s writing (partly because it would only be invented by this book) – had a privileged position at the time of emergence of queer theory, I wish to offer a somewhat different reading, one to which Butler's more recent work gives support.

Resistance is not a possibility restricted to any chosen subject. It is, in contrast, available to all, opening up through the repetitive stylisation of the body. Challenging the norms through which this stylisation takes place, resisting our very becoming in a certain way, means to question the terms by which one is constituted. If one is constituted as abject, unreal, one certainly may have the urge to resist such a constitutive social reality more than those who get a social confirmation of their reality. This, ultimately, is what the insurrection at the level of the real is about, to which Butler is, to paraphrase Lloyd, politically committed.

To redeploy and displace – Foucault's spatial and strategic formulas which Butler often used to describe agency – is to work within the very terms of performance (Butler 1998: 526). Redeploying and displacing power relations means that resistance is exercised from within the power relations themselves. Thus, to redeploy and displace is what one can do *in medias res*. After all, *Gender Trouble* urges us to focus on what can be done or enacted now, rejecting both narratives proposing emancipation from within the past or a utopian future out of reach. The search for an imagined past in which there was no power, or a future where there will be only good power, hinders us, albeit in different ways, from focusing on what is at hand: to act politically and exercise political agency.

Repeating Differently: Rearticulation, Resignification

Philosophy should help us engage in 'the displacement and transformation of frameworks of thinking, the changing of received values and all the work that has been done to think otherwise, to do something else, to become other than what one is' (Foucault 1997c: 327). Butler is agreeing strongly with Foucault that the purpose of philosophy is not to supply us with the vision 'that will redeem life, that will make life worth living', seducing us away from the lived difficulty of the political. Holding on to this 'urge is the very sign that the sphere of the political has *already* been abandoned' (FCR: 131). Such 'normative commitments' entail certain similarities of critical reading of Butler's and Foucault's respective conceptions of why resistance, freedom or agency is exercised, and who conducts it. Namely, if power is ubiquitous, and if there is no clear criterion for separating 'good' from 'bad' powers (or resistances, which, even if initially emancipatory, can and have taken various unemancipatory turns, the Iranian revolution being one prominent example [Foucault 2018], or the current classificatory and identitarian normalisation of queer positions [Sabsay 2016]), on what grounds are we to formulate our political aspirations and normative visions? Second, can agency in Butler ever liberate itself from Foucault's individualist exercise of freedom? Or, in other words, is there any space in this conception for a 'we', that is, a collective struggle?

We have touched upon the first dilemma in the debate with Benhabib. To philosophically assume a subject with agency – prior to its formation within the political field – means that 'the terms of a significant social and political task of transformation, resistance, radical democratization' (CF: 46) have not been taken into account. Political agency is contingent and contextual, not bound to the prescriptions of a politico-theoretical programme.[1] The absence of prescriptions on what is to be done, does not, however, mean that political agency is uncritical. As interrogation of the established domain of ontology, critique is crucial for Butler's notion of political agency. Asking 'What, given the contemporary order of being, can I be?' (Butler 2001a), is where both the practice of critique and exercise of freedom begin. In the register of performativity, the question of transformative agency is how, from within the field of power relations and repetition itself, to produce a transformation beyond the limits of our endless iterative practices?

Early on, Butler claims that considering the possibility of social transformation is one of her central tasks. However, the way she termed the processes leading to transformation is, admittedly, quite peculiar: displacement, redefinition, resignification, redeployment, rearticulation do not belong to terms with obvious revolutionary potential. In the most provocative part of *Gender Trouble*, 'From Parody to Politics', Butler defined agency in the frame of resignification: agency is to be located in the possibility of a variation of a regulated process of repetition (GT: 198). Such a definition leaves

one with an uncertain feeling that all politics is exhausted in variation. In addition, she also defines a 'critical task for feminism', which
becomes to locate strategies of subversive repetition and affirm the
resignifications of the regulated processes that provide the immanent
possibility of their contestation (GT: 201). Since it is not a question
whether to repeat or not – we cannot decide to pull the curtain down
for a time to reflect on further production of the performance – the
task of feminism becomes *how* to repeat and, through a radical proliferation of gender, '*to displace* the very gender norms that enable
repetition itself' (GT: 203). Even if citationality enters the picture,
mollifying, to paraphrase Amy Allen (1998: 461), the paradoxical
feeling that agency is either completely impossible or too easy, two
significant questions remain. First, how does one repeat with displacing effects (and how is one to know that these effects are displacing)?
Or, framed in the jargon of critical normativists, even if we accept
that agency is articulable as resignification, we remain in the dark
regarding the kinds of resignification that lead to advantageous,
acceptable or desirable changes. Claiming that we need to repeat
differently says nothing specific about how this 'difference' ought to
look. The second question seems even more troublesome: is subversion the only aim of this (political) action, or would it be more accurate to say that its aim is 'parody', even parody of the political itself?

Responses to Butler's understanding of agency varied. Martha
Nussbaum (1999), for example, reads Butler's theory as no more
than the parody of the political itself. However, Nussbaum's vitu-
perative piece can serve as a true model of dismissive, outright
hostile, vitriolic writing. Different in tone and aim, other feminist
critiques have pointed to certain problems with Butler's notion
of agency, which seems to take place outside social and historical
circumstances, and 'remains abstract and lacking in social specificity' (McNay 1999: 176; cf. Nelson 1999). Butler's insistence on
the significance of context and historicity, which was exceptionally
rarely followed by examples from either history or present contexts,
justified such claims. Cincia Arruzza speaks of 'historicity without
history', stating that Butler 'neither historicises her own categories
nor addresses the historical conditions that make her own description of gender possible in the first instance' (Arruzza 2015: 36, 42).
Similarly, Lloyd contends that Butler deploys the term 'social' pro-
fusely, without examining 'the historical practices that themselves
generate the social' (Lloyd 2008: 104). Butler is indeed quite cautious
with examples, because her famous example of performativity, the

drag queen, turned into a paradigm, which led her 'to be wary of one's [own] examples' (Butler 1993a: 111). This is, of course, only part of the explanation. The absence of historicisations where they were expected as 'promised' generally fits well with Butler's understanding of the type of genealogy she proposes to offer – a 'specifically philosophical exercise in exposing and tracing the installation and operation of false universals' (Butler 1993b: 30) – which is, so to say, an odd, ungenealogical genealogy. Butler's exposition of false universals is also open to objections of neglecting various 'ontogenetic' explanations, as Benhabib would have it, and to speaking in an antihumanist tongue (Fraser 1995: 67). From here, it is only a small step to the charge for obliteration of the corporeal dimensions of performativity and agency (Clare 2009). Some critics wonder about the normative orientation of Butler's 'specifically philosophical exercise', because it does not pretend to be emptied of value statements, some of which, moreover, aim at political application. Is this a 'ludic' form of politics that promises to transform patriarchy 'through an indefinite series of individual acts ("performance") of parodic repetition' (Ebert 1993: 39), or a postmodernist politics fetishising sexual identity and promoting 'bourgeois humanist individuality as a more fluid and indeterminate series of subversive bodily acts' (Hennessy 2000: 120–1; cf. Glick 2000)?

Figured as repetition variation, agency seems too diffuse, too disorienting, politically unfathomable. Quandaries remain: to repeat differently, but to what purpose? What parameters do we use to measure difference? How do we know that different is different enough? How do we know that we have achieved our politically relevant goal, if this is what political agency is about? Ultimately, even if it is not summarily dismissed as ludic or postmodernist, a different repetition might have trouble escaping the individualist trap of the 'great performer', leading some to claim that Butler's 'theory remains confined to the perspective of the isolated individual either resisting their subjectification or confronting their oppressor' (Boucher 2006: 114), and that 'it fails to explore fully how the active appropriation and reshaping of values and resources by actors may result in changes at a collective level' (McNay 1999: 190).

The Individual, the Collective, the Social

In the text on the politics of performativity, Geoff Boucher argues (2006: 129) that Butler, like Foucault, dethroned the omnipotent subject in order to save the political individual. For Boucher, a subjectless conception of agency provides Butler with the opportunity to develop her understanding of an individual resisting their subjection through oppositional cultural practices. Among the many issues regarding agency, the question of the character of the performative subject – is it exclusively individual, or can it have a collective expression? – seems to have true pertinence. The question itself received greater attention from Butler in more recent years, especially in *Notes Toward a Performative Theory of Assembly* (2015b). My claim is, however, that she engages with this topic throughout her work: from early endeavours to link subversion with the queer, through dispersed, but insistent, critiques of the autonomous subject, to her commitment to radical democracy and equality of precarious lives. In this matter, Butler's social ontology of the body is equally important as the performative theory of assembly. Now, although these directions may seem scattered, what links them is Butler's multivalent notion of the political. Comprising many layers, without neat coherence between them, her notion of the political includes the feminist credo that the personal is political; 'queer structure', to which she holds steadfastly in her texts, even when the term 'queer' itself became less frequent; persistent commitment to collective struggle;[2] advocacy for a politics that goes beyond mere inclusion, extension of rights and reform of laws; faith in action not mediated by state mechanisms, and equivalent distrust of the state;[3] Gramscian trust in the power of civil society, in 'our' power to change things, through the laborious, unending task of cultural translation, through exercising non-violent expansion of the universal and joint defence against it shrinking (Butler and Connolly 2000; Olson and Worsham 2000; Heckert 2011; McCann 2011; Willig 2012).

Butler never offers a synthetic overview of these issues, which is why the notion of the political, central to all her endeavours, remains relatively elusive. Yet, we can claim that two impulses – anti-identitarianism and politics *in medias res*, which function as the political engine in *Gender Trouble* – remain implicated in all later developments of her understanding of the political. These two impulses do not follow causally from her critical approach to established ontology or the metaphysical foundations of the normativist theories of the subject, which functioned as an implicit (insidious, installed [GT: 203]) assumption of feminist theory. If we understand *Gender Trouble* as a philosophical toolbox for unravelling gender (and sex), then its possible political application needs to include engagement against identity's necessary exclusions, which are at work if the subject of feminism remains an unproblematised notion of 'woman'. Second, the political implication of contingent foundations of agency assumes that we need to be able to act politically *in medias res*, acting from a plurality and in coalitions which would not be based on identities – an idea at the very heart of the early notion of queer.

The claim that politics based on identity is of necessity exclusionary, and that it inevitably only reproduces inequality, remains a permanent feature of Butler's political thought. For example, in *Frames of War*, arguing for urgency and a radical democratic response to matters at hand, she underlines that the focus of left politics should not be on identities, but on precarity and its differential distribution. Precarity cuts across identity categories, 'thus forming the basis for an alliance focused on opposition to state violence and its capacity to produce, exploit, and distribute precarity for the purposes of profit and territorial defence' (FoW: 32). The second idea that politically animates *Gender Trouble* refers to the demand to act here and now, using the resources presently at one's disposal, in an unauthorised, even insurrectionary way. Thus, in *Dispossession* we read that 'performativity names that unauthorized exercise of a right to existence that propels the precarious into political life' (D: 101; cf. ES: 147). Such an entry takes place when the uncounted start to count themselves, to appear and, thus, to matter.

The appearance of the precarious produced a radical shift in Butler's thought. This shift, however, did not mean a radical break with the theory of performativity. Rather, it built on it, productively engaging its inconsistencies and tensions. I would claim that, in the sphere of the political, the crucial tension regards the question of individual and collective agency, that is, the question of 'we'. This 'we' needs to be based neither in identity, nor collective consciousness (or experience), nor function as an aggregate of discrete individuals. The question – whether political agency is about 'a way of politicising personal life' (Butler 1986: 45) or about liveable life – seems to be the crux of this tension. The exercise of freedom is, for Butler, not reducible to the Foucauldian care of the self and the aesthetics of existence, but requires the production, multiplication and diversification of possibilities for a liveable life. 'Freedom is more often than not exercised with others', and presumes 'a set of enabling and dynamic relations that include support, dispute, breakage, joy, and solidarity' (NT: 27). The following sections of this chapter delve into the political forms of this exercise, beginning with subversion and ending with assembly.

THE INDIVIDUAL: SUBVERSION, PARODY, DRAG

In one of her first texts, 'Sex and Gender in Simone de Beauvoir's *Second Sex*', at the moment when Butler defines body as situation and a field of interpretative possibilities, she goes on to say that 'the body becomes a peculiar nexus of culture and choice, and "existing" one's body becomes a personal way of taking up and reinterpreting received gender norms' (Butler 1986: 45). Although she immediately follows up this claim by saying that there are limitations to how we personally choose to do ourselves, and although the existentialist 'project' gives way to the Foucauldian proliferation of corporeal styles, the individualist dimension of this very early claim still remains: 'To the extent that gender norms function under the aegis of social constraints, the reinterpretation of those norms through the proliferation and variation of corporeal styles becomes a very concrete and accessible way of politicizing personal life' (ibid.). Even though it does not appear as bluntly in *Gender Trouble*, this 'concrete and accessible politicisation' reverberates through the notion of subversion, which was, for some, Butler's central contribution to political theory (Chambers and Carver 2008: 137) or political philosophy (Solana 2017: 16).

The prominence of the notion of subversion cannot be overestimated – after all, it is in the subtitle of *Gender Trouble*. But this is also where the trouble with subversion begins. First, the notion itself is almost entirely undefined. Second, through it, politics often becomes one with parody. And, as it was strongly identified with the practices of drag, political agency seems to be something theatrical, belonging to the genre of comedy. Bearing in mind Moya Lloyd's important suggestion (2007: 51) that subversion is a third type of politics, in addition to reform and revolution (which can be exemplified by Rubin's and Wittig's ideas of destruction of the sex/gender system or heterosexuality), the question that presents itself is: what exactly characterises this political column? Is it, perhaps, its playfulness? Further trouble with Butler's supposedly central contribution to the political is that it simply disappears from later texts, without a clear explanation why.

When it comes to its definition, the most one can hope for is the statement from an early interview: 'subversiveness is not something that can be gauged or calculated. In fact, what I mean by subversion are those effects that are incalculable' (Kotz 1992: 84). Surely, subversion in *Gender Trouble* is presented as a desirable and political practice. We are led to this conclusion indirectly, from Butler's criticisms of strategies that can never become sustained political practices and are based on an unacknowledged emancipatory ideal, or remain grounded in a subject with godlike dimensions (GT: 110, 127, 158). Thus, if something is to produce certain political effects, it cannot come from a point external to the practices themselves, that is, it cannot be guided by ideals impossible to maintain, nor done by subjects who presumably have access to a 'truer reality' than the one they inhabit. If subversion is possible, it will happen 'within the terms of the performance' (Butler 1998: 526), with our bodies here and now, on the horizon of 'an open future of cultural possibilities' (GT: 127).

Subversion is, therefore, a possible action against the norm or a system of norms. What makes it possible is not the heroic will of an actor who has the power to refuse and destroy them, but the instability of the norms themselves (Deutscher 1997: 26). The actions take place within a normative matrix with an immanent potential for self-subversion, as it is neither founded on structural necessity of the symbolic law, nor dictated by the laws of anatomy. The performative double movement assumes both inherent erosiveness and instability of the enacted norms, and the possibility to further erode them through subversive bodily enactments, in which they may become a site of parodic contest.

But why would this contest be parodic, and not, as we have become accustomed with the teleologies of emancipation – as Saba Mahmood called them (Mahmood 2001: 210) – hard fought in blood, sweat and tears? Why are these practices fundamentally disordering and why does the subversive actor appear in drag? We should recall that in the subtitle of *Gender Trouble*, subversion subverts identities. Subversion redirects or rearticulates repetition of acts that take place within a highly rigid regulatory frame. This frame congeals over time to produce the appearance of the substance of identities of man and woman, that is, as an external expression of a hidden inside, mediated through the heterosexualisation of desire. In such a normative frame, only men and women exist as intelligible, legible, recognisable, while all other embodied variations of sex, gender and desire occupy positions of 'developmental failures or logical impossibilities from within that domain':

Their persistence and proliferation, however, provide critical oppor-
tunities to expose the limits and regulatory aims of that domain of
intelligibility and, hence, to open up within the very terms of that
matrix of intelligibility rival and subversive matrices of gender disorder.
(GT: 24)

The way the term 'critical' is used in this quote could be understood
as both referring to critique, a process of desubjectivisation of those
deemed to be 'logical impossibilities' within the matrix of intelligibility, and as a kind of critical strike against the domain that produces
ostensible coherence of gender through political regulations and
disciplinary practices. Subversion would, in that sense, be a certain
'strike back' at power, positioned beyond the master/bondsman
logic, perhaps in the sense borrowed from Butler's own reading of
Foucault's 'tactic of nondialetical subversion', in which the 'constant
inversion of opposites leads not to a reconciliation in unity, but to a
proliferation of oppositions which come to undermine the hegemony
of binary opposition itself' (SD: 222, 225).

Subversion introduces a disorder into the syllogistic coherence of
the norm – I was born female, therefore I become a woman, therefore I desire persons of the opposite sex – exposing this coherence as
possible only in a 'hetero-reality' (Lloyd 1999: 197), a heterosexist
matrix that regulates bodily acts. 'The target of Butler's politics of
subversion must be that assemblage, the matrix itself, heteronor-
mativity' (Chambers and Carver 2008: 148). What is subverted is
the ostensible naturalness of heterosexuality (Lloyd 2007: 50), and
the cultural logic of straightness based on binary disjunction (Disch
1999: 548). Subversion does not assume that one 'leaves' the matrix
in order to strike back at it. It is only from within the repetition of
regulatory practices that maintain the matrix that subversion, in
repeating differently, possibly alters those terms. What is subversive
about subversion is that it *reveals* the norm as contingent, cultural,
historical sedimentation that designates us as either real or suspended
as unreal, untrue, abject creatures.

Almost in passing, Butler ascribed this revelatory role to a specific
stage actor: drag. This actor then turned, as Jay Prosser commented
(1998: 24), not only into a queer icon, but something of an icon
for the new queer theory itself. '*In imitating gender, drag implicitly
reveals the imitative structure of gender itself – as well as its contingency*' (GT: 187). Drag appeared in *Mother Camp*, an anthropological study published in 1979, which examined the phenomenon of

professional impersonators, 'persons who most visibly and flagrantly embody the stigma' (Newton 1979: 3). Their 'work is defined as "queer" in itself', since 'no one but a "queer" would want to perform as a woman. It is the nature of the performances rather than homosexuality per se that accounts for the *extreme* stigmatization of drag queens' (ibid.: 7). In their performance, the impersonators play with two powerful oppositions: masculine/feminine and outside/inside. Feminine belongs to 'woman', which Esther Newton anthropologically locates to be a *social* category peculiar to American culture, which otherwise has relatively few ascribed roles (ibid.: 102). This category is based on strong bonds between biology, nature and sex-role symbols. The performance of drag queens 'wrenches the sex roles loose from that which supposedly determines them, that is, genital sex', demonstrating by their very acting that 'if sex-role behavior can be achieved by the "wrong" sex, it logically follows that it is in reality also achieved, not inherited, by the "right" sex', which is why it can be classified as 'an appearance', an 'outside' (ibid.: 103). The passing of persons in drag reveals the imitative structure of the real itself: 'it seems self-evident that persons classified as "men" would have to create artificially the image of a "woman", but of course "women" create the image "artificially" too' (ibid.: 5). Thus, the queer transgender has a double function in the unveiling of the norm: they parallel the process by which heterosexuality reproduces binarised gender identities and therefore itself, and, at the same time, they contrast with heterosexuality's naturalisation of this process. 'For whereas the constructedness of straight gender is obscured by the veil of naturalization, queer transgender reveals, indeed, explicitly performs its own constructedness' (Prosser 1998: 31). These acts of revelations have a parodic quality, because they expose gender norms as altogether mimetic, unoriginal and untrue in any metaphysical sense. The parody mocks not women themselves, the 'original', so to speak – Butler explicitly states that the parodic performance is a part of 'hegemonic, misogynist culture' (GT: 187) – but the notion of originality, the notion that there is an internal schema, essence, cause, original to be copied (Butler 1991). Drag reveals all gender as parody.

However, drag was too powerful an example: it rapidly turned into a paradigmatic 'gender troubler' whose acting became entirely equated with the desirable subversive politics. This ushered in a host of misconceptions of agency in Butler as a voluntarist, unbound, theatrical collection of parodying acts done by a special kind of

performer. It also gave rise, as Eva von Redecker (2017: 89) beauti-
fully points out in her examination of parody in Butler, three axes of
critique in terms of laughter – the first worrying that Butler makes
parodic laughter hollow, the second that it cannot be more than a
helpless giggle, the third insisting on defining the difference between
mean laughter and clever parodies.

Butler would return to her example again and again (BTM: 85ff.,
175ff.; PLP: 144ff.; UG: 213ff.), claiming that 'there is no necessary relation between drag and subversion' (BTM: 85), shifting the
emphasis from specific actors who undo gender to the norms that
both constitute and undo gender:

> When one performance of gender is considered real and another false,
> or when one presentation of gender is considered authentic, and another
> fake, then we can conclude that a certain ontology of gender is condi-
> tioning these judgments, an ontology (an account of what gender *is*) that
> is also put into crisis by the performance of gender in such a way that
> these judgments are undermined or become impossible to make. The
> point to emphasize here is not that drag is subversive of gender norms,
> but that we live, more or less implicitly, with received notions of reality,
> implicit accounts of ontology, which determine what kinds of bodies
> and sexualities will be considered real and true, and which kind will not.
> (UG: 214)

If the early account of subversion offered an opportunity to focus
on individual actors who, on or off stage, reinterpret and resignify
norms through the proliferation and variation of corporeal styles,
the rejection of 'the great performer' entailed a shift in focus to the
reality of norms. Even though the notion of subversion would be
lost in that move,[4] I wish to claim that it added a crucial dimension
to further forms of politicisation of performativity. Namely, subversion is not only a revelatory but also an insurrectionary action. To
repeat differently is a form of unauthorised exercise of a desire to be,
to persist within a reality of social fantasies that organise material
lives of embodied individuals. Drag showed that certain ontological
presuppositions are at work, and that they may be open to rearticulation. Since rearticulation depends on the logic of iterability, subversive acts also function without prior legitimacy, challenging 'existing
forms of legitimacy, breaking open the possibility of future forms'
(ES: 147).

This 'breakthrough' of the 'constitutive outside' – necessary to
provide naturalness, originality and unity to the 'coherent inside'

– can undo, and in the last thirty years has undone, the sedimented coherences in laws, public policy, culturally accepted behaviour and private lives of innumerable individuals. Although this breaking open takes place in and through various individual bodily acts, these acts are still not modelled on sovereign agency (Chambers and Carver 2008: 147). They are local, contextually enabled performances, whose effects could not have been gauged or calculated in advance, because they were unauthorised.

Alison Stone claimed (2005: 15), almost prefiguring performative theory of assembly, that Butler's understanding of coalition establishes a possibility of a collectively subversive action. In my understanding, although it never appears as a collective act, subversion is also not narrowly individualistic either. Still, a certain hesitation is in order here, because the alternative social ontology Butler later proposes, in which clearly no one remakes reality alone, was still in the making.

THE SOCIAL: AGENCY AND DEPENDENCE

The rejection of the 'classical liberal and existentialist model of freedom' (GT: 169) did not, as previously mentioned, provide an alternative working definition of freedom. Although Butler did develop a particular understanding of agency, it was clearly not modelled on autonomy, while her emerging performative theory of subject constitution stood in the way of the liberal-humanist understanding of sovereign mastery. On the other hand, a widespread tendency to interpret her notion of agency as reducible either to subversive (drag) performances, or to linguistic formation given in a distinctly antihumanist language, led her to a more intense focus on the reality in which agency takes place. This turn will have important consequences for subsequent elaborations of the ideas of interdependence, dispossession and vulnerability, that is, the major building blocks of the social ontology of the body.

The reality in which we craft ourselves into genders is a reality of norms. Our acting, or whatever agency we may have, takes place in the social world. Taking place is, however, too vague an expression for what happens to us while we act in a world that enables and constrains our acting. The social world is what we depend on. This dependence is precisely what orchestrates the materialisation of our possibilities, and also our consent and reproduction of power relations.

119

In the books written after *Bodies That Matter*, especially in *Undoing Gender*, the social world and our dependence on it have a prominent place. Certain reworkings of discursive constitution of the subject also shifted in that direction. Butler adopted Althusser's understanding of interpellation to show that a 'certain social existence of the body' is only enabled through appearing in and by virtue of language, through interpellation and naming. Our very existence is fundamentally dependent on the address of the Other. We are crafted into addressable, recognisable beings by a world that provides us with social definitions (ES: 5). Reworking Foucault's theory of subjectivation within a psychoanalytic frame enabled Butler to further develop the notion of dependency on the powers that subject us. Now, a child's primary dependency, before it can make decisions on who cares, does not amount to political subordination in the usual sense, but it does indicate that our formation is impossible without dependency. Primary dependences, recalled and exploited through our longing for recognisable and enduring social existence, and guaranteed by social categories, work in the service of subjection – 'which is often preferred to no social existence at all' (PLP: 20). With the concept of subversion fading into the background of the theory of performativity, Gramsci's understanding of hegemony proved useful to allow for the possibility of social transformation of everyday relations. Thus, Butler claims that her understanding of performativity is 'not far from' the theory of hegemony, as they both emphasise 'the way in which the social world is made – and new social possibilities emerge – at various levels of social action through collaborative relation with power' (CHU: 14).

In order to be who we become, we are dependent on the social world into which we arrive. The act of arrival, of course, says something about the one who has arrived. However, it also says something about arrival 'in the world, in discourse' (BTM: 173), in the sphere of social names, and the relations of power one finds to be limiting only much later, if ever. Even when one chooses to oppose these 'resources', one neither becomes independent of them, nor can this opposition provide a position of sovereign mastery over them. To constitute oneself as a subject, to be able to say 'I' in the first place, one depends on language, which is never quite one's own and is indeed complicit with power. But, in order to have agency, one need not restore the (fantasy of) sovereign autonomy in speech or lift oneself up beyond language. Thus, instead of demanding more control, more mastery, we may concede the idea that 'speech is always in some ways out of our control':

> Untethering the speech act from the sovereign subject founds an alterna- tive notion of agency [. . .] Whereas some critics mistake the critique of sovereignty for the demolition of agency, I propose that agency begins where sovereignty wanes. The one who acts (who is not the same as the sovereign subject) acts precisely to the extent that he or she is constituted as an actor and, hence, operating within a linguistic field of enabling con- straints from the outset. (ES: 15–16)

It is, however, not only speech that remains beyond our control. All the resources that prompt us into our social being are only somewhat controlled by us; we hold them only to an extent in our possession. If we cannot be without doing, then what conditions our doing is what conditions our very existence. If we are so conditioned, we cannot decide at some point to remake the world in a way to become its masters, makers of the world itself. If we do have any agency, it is not to be found in the denial of the conditions of our constitution. 'If I have any agency, it is opened up by the fact that I am constituted by a social world I never chose' (UG: 3).

However, our mastery proves most elusive in what seems to be our most obvious, most immediate possession – our bodies. It is as embodied subjects of agency that we can neither abstract nor tran- scend sociality. Our bodies bind us to the here and now, tether us to the place they occupy. Even if our mind is elsewhere, the body places us *in medias res*, at the heart of social reality. It seeks support, leans on, has various undesired and unchosen groundings – it invariably needs infrastructure. This physical need demonstrates that the reality of the body is not identical with social reality. In its physicality, the body is indeed material and extended, heavy and massive, but the reality which recognises its mass, which defines the space it occupies, in which the basic processes of feeding and sleeping transpire and have a name (also requiring a roof, a bed, a spoon), is a social reality. Bodies *live* in discursive reality, which constitutes them in time that is not a present simple of the body itself. Norms 'continue to act according to an iterative logic that ends for any of us only when life ends, though the life of norms, of discourse more generally, continues on with a tenacity that is quite indifferent to our own finitude' (SS: 5). But if discourse is understood to be 'also social action, even violent social action' (GT: 225), where violence turns into a 'discourse in action', violence itself happens to the body. The body is our outside, it is in the public sphere, exposed to different forms of touch. 'In its surface and its depth, the body is a social phenomenon' (FoW: 33), which is why 'my body is and is not mine':

> Given over from the start to the world of others, it bears their imprint, is formed within the crucible of social life; only later, and with some uncertainty, do I lay claim to my body as my own, if, in fact, I ever do. Indeed, if I deny that prior to the formation of my 'will', my body related me to others whom I did not choose to have in proximity to myself, if I build a notion of 'autonomy' on the basis of the denial of this sphere of a primary and unwilled physical proximity with others, then am I denying the social conditions of my embodiment in the name of autonomy? (PL: 26)

If *my* agency is, by my very embodiment, only somewhat mine, then I am the locus of my own acts and intentions and I am, at the same time, a locus over which I can never have sovereign mastery. The body is in the world and it is always, regardless of our will, open and exposed to its relations. This openness is not reducible to primary bodily dependency in the earliest forms of support and care – throughout its becoming, the body depends on the materials that the world makes available for it. 'The ideal of radical self-sufficiency is jeopardized by the body's permeability and dependency [. . .] the body constitutes a site of contested ownership, one which through domination or the threat of death can always be owned by another' (PLP: 54).

The last quote looks as though it could have been taken out of some of Butler's latest texts. In fact, it appears in 'Stubborn Attachment, Bodily Subjection', a rereading of Butler's first exposition of the master/bondsman scene. In *Subjects of Desire*, bodies were smuggled in 'where they are almost never to be found as object of philosophical reflection, much less as sites of experience' (PLP: 34). Smuggled in, the bondsman now appears as *the* body, and the condition for the master *not* to be the body (SD: 53). An act of emancipation on the part of the bondsman would seem to require a full split from the body he essentially was while he was in a state of bondage. In other words, a full-scale autonomy would not only assume emancipation from the master but also an emancipation from the body, which remains constitutively open to becoming the possession of another. Freedom, in Butler's reading of Hegel, entails an escape from bodily permeability to a sphere in which no bodies exist at all. 'There', where there are no more bondsmen and where, by implication, all should be sovereign masters, there must also be no bodies.

Subjects of Desire implies that the body is a necessary ground for freedom and the point of its mediation. This has implications for our understanding of autonomy. Namely, the body that performs its becoming fits neither into the figure of a bondsman nor of that of a master – it is neither entirely subjected, nor is it somehow wondrously free of all subjection. Performative embodied agency never overlaps with autonomy as radical self-sufficiency, sovereign mastery or independence from what makes us social beings.

The Social: Repetition and Risk

If, therefore, there are bodies and there are norms, if they are in an almost closed circuit of repetition, and if autonomy is inherently constricted by its social conditioning, what remains of political agency? Benhabib's curtain never falls. The body as the site of agency dispossesses rather than making us into possessors of ourselves. Our embodiment forever forecloses the possibility to push ourselves into a sphere where there are only fully volitional, bodiless masters, or to settle ourselves somewhere apart or beyond the social reality which turns our becoming into endless repetitions. Indeed, this is the ambivalent scene of agency in Butler. The power that the subject of agency has is not the power to triumphantly deny or transcend its social conditions or its own embodiment. Yet, agency is nonetheless a power derivable from the conditions that enacted the subject into being, and wielded by the same subject throughout its compelled and incomplete process of becoming. 'The subject is itself a site of this ambivalence in which the subject emerges both as the *effect* of a prior power and as the *condition of possibility* for a radically conditioned form of agency' (PLP: 14–15). Although radically conditioned by it, agency is not completely constrained by the prior workings of power. In that sense, it may exceed the power by which it is enabled (PLP: 15). In addition, the subject wielding agency, already sullied by the 'taint' of the powers that have subjected it, is not primarily self-reflexive, capable of acting on principles, rationally accountable for their actions and able to project into the future. The subject wields this power that is agency, not on account of its rationality and autonomy, but by virtue of its acting. Agency is a possibility intrinsic to the acting of the subject constituted by that very acting. There is no 'special subject' of agency, just as there are no 'special conditions' for agency.

Recall that the theory of performativity is in itself an account of agency. The incessant and continuous acting, not predetermined by any essence, is the condition of possibility of agency. But, as we are clearly aware, not all acting produces social transformation. Examined in the light of citationality, acting – citing of norms through bodily acts – is part of an unstable and incomplete process of repetition that fundamentally depends on new reiterations. Norms are sustained through their continuous reproduction, which depends on our acting under the constraint of a rigid, regulatory frame. However, the fact that norms require reiteration in order to be, opens up a space for 'anomalous or subversive practices' (CHU: 14), that is, for repetitions that have made it possible to subvert the norms they are supposed to reinforce. It is crucial to note that reiteration is an occasion – a possibility – for a norm to be subverted: 'resignification isn't necessarily subversive; the fact that norms must be cited in order for them to remain in force does not mean that citationality is a sufficient condition for subversion, only that it is a necessary one' (Allen 1998: 462; CHU: 41). With Saba Mahmood, we could claim that agency is the 'capacity for action that historically specific relations of subordination enable and create' (Mahmood 2001: 210). Thus, action itself may provide just another layer in an already sedimented norm. On the other hand, it could also go in a different direction, either unintentionally, anomalously, in a form of a slippage – exposing the norm for what it is – or else it may have subversive, insurrectionary potential to induce transformative effects.

The theory of performativity is an account of agency because it rests on the assumption that to act is to potentially produce new possibilities. Defining action as the most important human activity, Hannah Arendt related it to the possible production of something new, to the 'fact that man is capable of action, that the unexpected can be expected from him, that he is able to perform what is infinitely improbable' (Arendt 1998: 178). Leaving aside, for now, how Arendt understood the relation between action and the political, as well as the Arendtian 'man' – a peculiar political figure to whom the body belongs only ambivalently – we can say that the power of acting is interchangeable with the power to create beginnings. Before it becomes realised in this or that way, the 'beginning' can be seen as a possibility, as potential for something new. If such potential is inherent to every action, then agency appears not only when one expects the unexpected, but equally in entirely expected outcomes of actions, that is, in the domain of the most probable.

Given that we act in order to be, that our actions transpire in the domain of everyday social relations, the political impetus of these actions needs to be understood within the domain of the probable – although from a horizon of an improbable, incalculable future. 'Social transformation occurs not merely by rallying mass numbers in favour of a cause, but precisely through the ways in which daily social relations are rearticulated' (CHU: 14) – by anyone. There is neither a special subject of agency, nor does agency entail special circumstances that must include rallies or partisanship. Quite 'unpolitical' actions have a profound political potential. If our actions are shaped by and, at the same time, shape social reality, acting differently has the potential to question established reality.

If the political takes place *in medias res*, within acting itself, in this body and in this social world, then political agency is acting that reveals established reality precisely as established. It opens up possibilities within the real itself and seeks to preserve them as viable options. Since it takes place within the terms of performance, here and now, political agency is a moment in the process of desubjectivisation and does not assume a set of rules to be followed to reach a prefigured aim. Besides, political agency that the theory of performativity delineates is truly egalitarian: anyone can perform differently. There are no actors privileged based on a particular feature – just as 'there is no necessary relation between drag and subversion' (BTM: 85). Political agency is not consigned to a specific group or heroic individuals of the teleologies of emancipation or, for that matter, to Arendt's 'men' who act together, gathered in the agora.

Significantly, it now seems that the transformative potential that agency has does not realise itself only in a parodic play (see Zaharijević 2021a). Since different repetitions may question our reality, repeating differently necessarily assumes a risk of an unintelligible, unliveable, impossible life, especially for isolated individuals:

> The subject is compelled to repeat the norms by which it is produced, but that repetition establishes a domain of risk, for if one fails to reinstate the norm 'in the right way', one becomes subject to further sanction, one feels the prevailing conditions of existence threatened. And yet, without a repetition that risks life – in its current organization – how might we begin to imagine the contingency of that organization, and performatively reconfigure the contours of the conditions of life? (PLP: 28–9)

Put this way, performance ceases to be easy-going or mirthful. It also seems that there is nothing really theatrical about it, even in the Brechtian, serious sense. Risk – putting one's life at risk in order to risk the very reality in which some lives are socially dead or expandable – is an integral part of political agency. As it happens in and through the body acting, political agency inevitably entails risks. 'The body imposes a principle of humility and a sense of the necessary limit of all human action' (NT: 47). The body's mortality, vulnerability, permeability and dependency on various types of support always turns the stage on which the body performs its agency into a potential scene of violence. For this reason, political agency may indeed expand the space of what matters, but the body always remains at its centre. Agency can produce an organisational reconfiguration of life, but the price may be violent death.

The Collective: How Not to End up Like Antigone

Let us return to individual and collective agency. Early on, Butler claims that the 'act that gender is [. . .] is clearly not one's act alone', but a 'shared experience and "collective action"' (Butler 1988: 525). At first glance, it may seem that the notion of a shared experience could have been derived from feminist standpoint theory. Developing the idea that women have access to particular knowledge based on their universally shared experience, standpoint theory drew on the Marxist argument that the oppressed class has special access to knowledge not at the ruling class's disposal. Shaping this knowledge would culminate in the articulation of class consciousness and, in the Marxist version, the realisation of the historical mission of the proletariat. 'Like the lives of proletarians in Marxist theory, women's lives in Western capitalist societies also contained possibilities for developing a critique of domination' (Hartsock 1997: 368). However, Butler's antiessentialist and antifoundational theoretical assumptions make this link untenable. The presumed unity of women's experience can be established only at the expense of varieties of experiences of different women, often accommodating and hierarchising interlocking systems of oppressions. (This is, significantly, something that Hartsock acknowledges, claiming that Marx made no theoretical space for any oppression other than class, which she then repeated with women.) Further, it is fair to assume that Butler agrees with Joan Scott that experience is neither the origin of explanation, nor authoritative evidence that grounds what is known. Rather, experience itself seeks historicisation for which one needs to 'attend to the historical processes that, through

AGENCY

discourse, position subjects and produce their experiences' (Scott 1992: 25).

The shared character of experience needs to be located in the way we participate, through our individual acts, in a shared, almost collective action of sustaining the social reality of norms. Marx claimed that men make their own history, but not as they please. 'They do not make it under circumstances chosen by themselves, but under circumstances directly encountered, given and transmitted from the past. The tradition of all the dead generations weighs like a nightmare on the brain of the living' (Marx 1972: 10). In Butler's register, this nightmarish unchosenness is part of the social conditioning that both enables and constrains any 'making of history'. Our individual acts of embodying our assumed genders are conditioned by 'the tradition of all dead generations' that still live, and are reproduced, recited, renewed through the acts of those living (also making us into ancestors who will weigh on future generations). Perhaps this is also how we should understand the phrase in quotation marks: 'shared experience and "collective action"'. Because one's act is never one's act alone, the action is always already 'collective'. The act is also collective because, in making one's history, one does not do it as one pleases. This applies both to the stylisations of the body and to the stylisations of the will, which Butler discusses in her 'ethical' texts: 'There is no "I" that can fully stand apart from the social conditions of its emergence, no "I" that is not implicated in a set of conditioning moral norms, which being norms, have a social character that exceeds a purely personal or idiosyncratic meaning' (GAO: 7).

Let me end this chapter with a short reading of *Antigone*, a defiant maker of her own history and a very special character in the history of dramatic expositions of womanhood. Butler reads *Antigone* searching for a different symbolic framework of kinship, and Antigone's improper appropriation of mourning shows that 'there is no commandment that can outlaw grief, even as it seeks to outlaw its public form' (Stauffer 2003), what proved exceptionally important only a year after the publication of *Antigone's Claim* in 2000. However, I will focus on Butler's reading of *Antigone* from the perspective of agency. I would like to show why, although the titular character appears a heroic subject whose actions perform a series of transgressions, she cannot truly function as the paradigmatic figure of political agency.

The plot of Sophocles' play is well known. Against the will of the new king, Antigone wants to bury her brother and wants to do so

127

publicly. She knows that Creon's law condemns Polynices as a traitor to lie unburied outside the walls of Thebes. She nevertheless claims her right to mourn – and mourn properly, observing the proper ritual – invoking the pre-eminence of divine over human laws. Creon personifies the state and wants to confirm his sovereignty which Antigone knowingly challenges and, when questioned over her actions, repeatedly denounces. The king, enraged by her defiance, condemns her to be immured in a cave, which she bewails without truly regretting her actions. These actions are in opposition to the royal edict, but they also go against the admonitions of her sister Ismene, and lead her to reject the love of the crown prince, Hemon, through which Antigone rejects a future as queen and mother. Antigone hangs herself, in response to which her betrothed and his mother, the king's wife, also commit suicide. Ignoring the warnings of the blind prophet Tiresias, Creon allows for this tragic chain of events to take place in order to protect order and the rule of law.

What can we learn about political agency from this heroic figure? Antigone is a complex figure who, as Oedipus' daughter, does not choose her complexity – she is thrown, fatefully, into a very tangled kinship skein: her father is her brother, her mother is her grandmother, her brothers are her nephews, her maternal uncle was about to become her father-in-law, her cousin was intended to be her husband. For this reason, Butler insists she cannot signify kinship, but kinship's fatal aberration (AC: 15). She is a woman only ambivalently, too. Being a woman – at a time when women, even when daughters of kings, were not recognised as citizens – Antigone acts 'against' her womanhood. Instead of enacting 'her feminine role as guardian of the realm of the home [. . .] she displaces the political boundaries and the proper limits of the polis' (Athanasiou and Tzelepis 2010: 108). She is punished, perhaps additionally, for disrupting the gender order: not only does she defy sovereignty, she also calls into question the masculinity of the sovereign (who cries: 'I must be no man at all, in fact, and she must be the man, if power like this can rest in her and go unpunished' [Sophocles 2003: 74]). By flouting the law, Antigone thus renounces her femaleness, rejecting an existence of 'only and exclusively [. . .] the fleshy prerequisite of biological life' (Athanasiou and Tzelepis 2010: 108). 'Through a powerful set of physical and linguistic acts' (AC: 2), Antigone defies the state, and by refusing to stay alive and become a wife and a mother (her name means 'one who will have no progeny'), 'deinstitutes heterosexuality' (AC: 76). 'O tomb! O bridal bedchamber! O deep cave of a dwelling place [. . .] now by force he's leading me away, without a nuptial bed, without a wedding ceremony, and receiving no share of marriage nor of rearing children' (Sophocles 2003: 94–5). At a time when women were considered to be essentially unpolitical, she demands to be at the centre of the *polis*, to be political 'like a man'. But for her to be political is, of course, impossible: the chorus both reprimands her ('your self-willed temper has destroyed you' [ibid.: 93]) and praises her, calling her glorious and αὐτόνομος, 'answering only to the laws of yourself' (ibid.: 90). Her autonomy is reflected in her being the only mortal who, guided only by her own laws, will go into Hades alive. Her words very much resemble those of the sovereign:

> She is exploiting the language of sovereignty in order to produce a new public sphere for a woman's voice – a sphere that doesn't actually exist at the time. The citation of power that she performs is a citation that, yes, is mired in established power [. . .] but it also uses the citation in order to produce the possibility of a political speech act for a woman in the name of her desire that is radically delegitimated by the State itself. (Olson and Worsham 2000: 741)

By her doing and undoing – rites, speech, sex, laws – Antigone produces a radical crisis in established power, without being an outsider to it. She is herself engendered by those social (and kinship) relations that enabled sovereign power to be established. The tragic moment of her impossible autonomy is not only that death must be the chosen outcome, but also in the exposure of bareness of sovereign norm, which leaves the king without kin or heir.

It may seem that Antigone presents us with a perfect example of agency in the political individual who resists subjection through oppositional practices. She is the paradigmatically autonomous figure (and the first to be labelled as such, since *Antigone* is 'the oldest extant Greek text in which the word αὐτόνομος appears' [Safatle 2016: 257]), determined to remain her own legislator, even if this means legislating death to herself. Because she is denied her right to mourn, although it is an inherent part of femininity, Antigone's insistence on grieving for her brother paradoxically ends up undoing her femininity: by mourning, she forecloses the possibility of fulfilling her role as mother and queen. She speaks 'like' a king and her speech is in opposition to his; but in speaking 'like' the king, she calls the sovereign speech act into question. Antigone appears almost as the Arendtian 'man' in the agora who speaks and acts, performing the most political of all human activities. But Antigone is not a man; and for continuing to speak and act 'as if' a man, she is to be entombed, while the site of the political, the Theban *polis*, crumbles upon her physical and linguistic acts. Being neither proper woman nor man, Antigone confuses the space of the human. 'If she is human, then the human has entered into catachresis: we no longer know its proper usage' (AC: 82).

Despite all this, Antigone cannot serve as a model of political agency for us to emulate. Antigone dies. She pays for her defiance with her life. The risk she was prepared to take led to her bodily disintegration. Thus, the main question for political agency is: what would it mean for Antigone to have stood up to Creon *and lived*? Butler's answer to this question turns from the heroic individual to the social world in which political agency can only take place:

> We should be able to live in a world in which our demands for justice do not cost us our lives. We want to survive; we want to make such claims and survive. So the question that Antigone raises for me is, *what kind of world would it have been or could it be in which Antigone could survive?* (Reddy and Butler 2004: 122)

In an interview given at the time of Occupy Wall Street, Butler reshapes her answer in a more collective direction: 'The only way she could have lived is if she had had a serious social movement with her [. . .] It's really important to be able to re-situate one's rage and destitution in the context of a social movement' (Bella 2011).

Political agency, then, revolves around two interrelated issues: how to preserve the undetermined character of subversion, 'a politics of the incalculable, a non-programmatic and ungrounded politics of possibility' (Chambers and Carver 2008: 142), *and* not have Antigone die? The political moral of her story is that the individual, however autonomous – which in Antigone's case goes along with deep entanglements of many unchosen layers that fatefully condition her autonomy – cannot stand up to social reality *alone*. We want a politics that challenges social intelligibility and political represent-ability, but without tragedy, without staking life. The question of survival is, in a sense, a prerequisite for a successful or, rather, live-able political agency. 'It seems to me that you survive in community or in solidarity, with others who are taking the risk with you. So there might be a kind of collective effort that allows for those risks to be taken, pose a certain danger but not a suicidal one' (Butler 2007c).

What does it mean that there are others who are taking the risk 'with me'? One way of approaching this would entail assemblies or social movements: Antigone leads or participates in an insurrection against the tyrant, or in a massive public mourning, a kind of collective act of defiance of a sovereign edict. Not only does she then perhaps not die, but her body is shielded and sheltered by other bodies, gathered together and acting in concert. But there is also another approach to this question, which combines our bodily singularities, the social world in which these bodily existences walk and talk, and a (perhaps unseen, unheard) collectivity of others who take the risk together with me. Even individual actions thus have a certain collective quality, since 'the "I" is invariably implicated in the "we"', as the 'I' is always already social (D: 107). And since 'my' actions bear a constitutive social imprint, reproducing this imprint anew, my actions are performative of some *we*. This is not necessarily a *we* of a social movement or a rally. This *we* may as well belong to the most quotidian practices, those we ordinarily do alone; on occasion, however, in some places on Earth and in some historical circumstances – perhaps even now – they cannot be done without putting our lives at risk.

One such action is walking. Today, a woman cannot walk in Maidan Shahr without a niqab, while in Toulouse a woman cannot walk in a niqab. Refugees from the Middle East cannot walk in Podlaskie Voivodship, held as they are at the Polish border, even as they are also egged on by Belarusian security officials. Transgender women cannot walk in broad daylight in Belgrade, in Ankara, in Springfield, in Ceará:

> If and when it does become possible to walk unprotected and still be safe, for daily life itself to become possible without fear of violence, then it is surely because there are many who support that right even when it is exercised by one person alone. If the right is exercised and honored, it is because there are many there, exercising it as well, whether or not anyone else is on the scene. Each 'I' brings the 'we' along. (NT: 51)

The social stakes of my agency are never individual, but are always a matter of shared, collective performance. Thus, even if it is a singular body that does the walking, and experiences it without the threat of violence, 'to walk' means that there is a public, a common and shared space in which walking is possible, because there is 'group, if not an alliance, walking there' (NT: 51).

Lastly, something needs to be said about those others, with whom we take the risk in solidarity. Early queer anarchism rebelled against identity politics, gathering together those who were ready to join a

131

collective struggle: 'It didn't matter what you did, or how you did it, or how you felt about what you did; if you were willing to affiliate, that was politically viable' (Kotz 1992: 83). Queer politics was understood as politics of democratisation (Butler 1993b: 19), both with regard to its undetermined subject and to its demands. It should come as no surprise that Butler advocated for radical democracy, which appears as the double task of cultural translation and sustaining competing universalities. There is a trace of the old parodic critique in the newer form of contentious politics, striving as it does to proliferate antagonisms, rather than institute a new order or hegemony (Redecker 2017: 288). In the second phase of her work, centred around precarious life, 'the others' would finally appear as unified, but the category of their unification is carefully chosen never to allow its transmutation into identity. It is important for the differences within these 'others' and their competing demands for universality to never be irreducibly blended together, while allowing everyone in the collective struggle to still demand the end of precarity. Precarity is a 'rubric that brings together women, queers, transgender people, the poor, the differently abled, and the stateless, but also religious and racial minorities: it is a social and economic condition, but not an identity' (NT: 58).

The manner of the political articulation of demands is also performative. If we seek what we do not have and are barred from having, then we can, like Antigone, reach out for power that does not belong to us, acting as if we were entitled to it: 'sometimes it is not a question of first having power and then being able to act; sometimes it is a question of acting, and in the acting, laying claim to the power one requires' (NT: 58). However, if such politics *in medias res* initiates the struggle against social death, seeking to support life – then this politics cannot be strictly individual (making it always potentially suicidal, like Antigone's). At this point, it becomes clear why a theory of assembly finally manages to offer a frame for a collective struggle: at its core it holds the collective power of the assembled bodies who perform plural forms of agency in concert (NT: 9).

Notes

1. In a 1999 interview with Vikki Bell, Butler gives a telling answer about her understanding of the relation between theory and politics. 'I think what's really funny – and this probably seems really odd considering the level of abstraction at which I work – is that I actually believe that

politics has a character of contingency and context to it that cannot be predicted at the level of theory. And that when theory starts becoming programmatic, such as 'here are my five prescriptions', and I set up my typology, and my final chapter is called 'What is to be Done?, it pre-empts the whole problem of context and contingency, and I do think that political decisions are made in that lived moment and they can't be predicted from the level of theory [. . .] I suppose I'm with Foucault on this. I'm willing to withstand the same criticisms he withstood. It seems like a noble tradition' (Bell 1999: 166–7). Without fail, Butler returns to this in 2015: 'Of course, the theory of gender performativity that I formulated never prescribed which gender performances were right, or more subversive, and which were wrong, and reactionary, even when it was clear that I valued the breakthrough of certain kinds of gender performances into public space, free of police brutality, harassment, criminalization, and pathologization. The point was precisely to relax the coercive hold of norms on gendered life – which is not the same as transcending or abolishing all norms – for the purposes of living a more livable life. This last is a normative view not in the sense that it is a form of normality, but only in the sense that it represents a view of the world as it should be. Indeed, the world as it should be would have to safeguard breaks with normality, and offer support and affirmation for those who make those breaks' (NT: 33).

2. This commitment can be observed in various places and guises. For example, we find it in 'Against Proper Objects', where she discusses the, in her opinion, wrongheaded tendency of disciplinary factionalisations between queer and feminist (women's or gender) studies in the interest of provisional institutional legitimation: 'methodological distinctions perform the academic version of breaking coalition' (Butler 1994: 21; cf. UG: 181–5). Further, in addition to her opposition to institutional separatism that works to keep thought narrow, sectarian and self-serving, in 'Merely Cultural' she responds to the charge that newer forms of left politics reduce activism to mere assertion and affirmation of cultural identity, by demanding a rethinking of the splintering of material and cultural. Instead, Butler contends that political formations overlap, that they are mutually determining and take place in convergent fields of politicisation. 'In fact, most promising are those moments in which one social movement comes to find its condition of possibility in another' (MC: 37). Finally, the same motif of collective struggle can be observed in the more recent context of anti-gender mobilisation. Butler ends her 2021 *Guardian* article with a call to 'gender critical' feminists to turn away from reactionary powers that target trans, non-binary and gender-queer people. 'Let's all get truly critical now, for this is no time for any of the targets of [anti-gender] movement to be turning against one another. The time for anti-fascist solidarity is now' (Butler 2021).

3. Butler has shown some sympathy towards anarchism, echoing the positions of, for example, Gustav Landauer or Howard Zinn (cf. Zinn 2009: 653; Lynteris 2013; Redecker 2016). She links critique to deliberative democracy, an open and uncensored consideration of political values and actions, 'and to anarchism – an operation of thought and action that is not regulated in advance by state or corporate power'. Critique cannot be reduced to either, but both are historically and philosophically tied to it (Willig 2012: 142). Certainly, this is part of the Foucauldian critical tradition, which never opts for radical anarchy, for radical ungovernability, but still includes significant resistance to governability (Butler 2001a). This is why Butler always remained sceptical about full institutionalisation of critical and political agency. In Butler's performative theory of assembly there are also 'anarchist moments or anarchist passages', that mark the new time and space for popular will, in which the assembled bodies exercise the 'performative power to lay claim to the public in a way that is not yet codified into law and that can never be fully codified into law' (NT: 75).

4. The absence of subversion is quite conspicuous in texts after *Bodies That Matter*. Indeed, even there, faced with the criticism of privileging not only certain actors, but also certain spheres of reality (centred exclusively around gender and sexuality), Butler goes on to say that the goal of a more complex mapping of power 'cannot be pure subversion, as if an undermining were enough to establish and direct political struggle. Rather than denaturalization or proliferation, it seems that the question for thinking discourse and power in terms of the future has several paths to follow: how to think power as resignification together with power as the convergence or interarticulation of relations of regulation, domination, constitution' (BTM: 184). In her introduction to the second edition of *Gender Trouble*, subversion fared quite badly, as a notion brimming with normative expectations, which ends up being undefendable: 'The effort to name the criterion for subversiveness will always fail, and ought to. So what is at stake in using the term at all?' (GT: xxiii). The question really at stake is what will qualify as 'human' and 'liveable'.

Part II

Liveable World

Chapter 4

Liveable Life

What Counts as a Life?

In a conversation with Fina Birulés (2009) published under the title 'Gender Is Extramoral', Judith Butler asserts: 'one could say that all my work revolves around this question: what is it that counts as a life?'. Such a statement must be startling. The notion of life did not appear so often in the preceding elaboration of the theory of performativity. Yet, the statement clearly refers to the whole of Butler's work. In addition, given that she refuses to define life, as it 'tends to exceed the definitions we may offer [. . .] so the approach to life cannot be altogether successful if we start with definitions' (Schneider and Butler 2010), it seems that we are here faced with a certain conundrum. What is this 'life' that all of her work revolves around, and has it been with us all along?

Importantly, Butler's question is not about what a life is, but what counts as a life. The inconspicuous term 'counting', possibly one of the most Butlerian terms, should thus serve as a link. Not only does it connect the phases of Butler's work, but it also points in the direction we should think about life. What counts as a life; who counts as living; what living counts as possible; and who counts as a life for which living is in some sense foreclosed? Can we, in fact, ever really say that such life is counted? 'To live in the shadowy regions of ontology' is to live a life that does not count (Meijer and Prins 1998: 277). Talking with Birulés, Butler argues that gender is extramoral. Genders are, in themselves, neither good nor bad and, therefore, there are no genders that are 'better' than others. If there are, however, restrictions regulating what counts as the body supported in its desire to persist, we find ourselves in the midst of a different discussion, which is primarily political in kind. This discussion revolves around the life of the body, as well as conditions for life's flourishing, and, ultimately, around inequality. In other words, the main question of the discussion is: what makes for a liveable life?

Life has had a long trajectory in the history of philosophy, but 'live-able life' emerged out of the theory of performativity. The phrase has become a cornerstone of Butler's philosophy written after *Precarious Life*, galvanised by the questions 'what counts as a livable life and a grievable death?' (PL: xvi), and what counts as normatively human? At first, it might appear that these questions are entirely beyond the scope of the theory of performativity. *Precarious Life* responded to circumstances produced by the monstrosities of war that made Butler turn to 'philosophy and peace' rather than continue working on gender (see Stauffer 2003). However, the tools used to address these novel issues were engendered by the theory of performativity, even if they were now less applied to questions posed previously. This is important not only because it helps connect various directions of a work organised around 'registering events and movements in the world and transposing them into theoretical idioms' (O'Hana 2017), but also because it provides links between variously precarious lives and contingent foundation of equality among them. 'Livable life' made its appearance later, but it was there *in nuce* all along (cf. Lloyd 2007: 134; Loizidou 2008: 145; McNeilly 2015: 149–50).

In 1999, when revisiting the ideas and aspirations behind *Gender Trouble*, Butler wrote:

> I also came to understand something of the violence of the foreclosed life, the one that does not get named as 'living', the one whose incarceration implies a suspension of life, or a sustained death sentence. The dogged effort to 'denaturalize' gender in this text, emerges, I think, from a strong desire [. . .] to live, to make life possible, and to rethink the possible as such. (GT: xxi)

If we take this claim seriously, there is every reason to say that live-able life has been both central and present all along. Yet, the term 'liveable' remained undefined in her texts, even when it began to appear with a certain regularity, accompanying an equally undefined notion of 'life'.

To what does 'liveable' in liveable life refer? If we consult diction-aries (noting, of course, differences across languages), this attribute can be understood as referring to something 'cosy', 'homey', 'com-fortable', 'habitable', but also something akin to 'bearable', 'endur-able', 'sufferable'. A liveable life would then, by inference, be some kind of life in which we have enough space, where this capacious-ness feels warm and familiar and where we can count on permanent shelter and support of some kind. A liveable life is a life that one can inhabit, living with innumerable inconveniences that inevitably arise. The English dictionaries suggest yet another meaning: a life worth living. However, I would propose we read liveable life as one that can be lived, that we are able to live. In that case, two questions present themselves. Is 'liveable life' a pleonastic expression, where liveability is not more than an inner capacity of the body to keep on living, some simple feature of life that does not stop on its own? Or, conversely, if we are the inhabitants of our own lives, would that mean that it is upon us to make them more capacious and homelike, indulging in some sort of DIY or life-related feng shui? The answer to both questions is negative. Although life is centrally related to the desire to persist (even in unliveable conditions, even under threat to survival), and although we certainly can and should do things to have a more meaningful existence on Earth, liveable life in fact refers to the conditions provided to us by the world we inhabit, through the bodies we inhabit.

Although it made its grand appearance in the title of *Precarious Life*, life had to wait for *Frames of War* for a more careful elaboration (Power 2009). Rejecting thinking of life as such, like she rejected thinking of the body as such, Butler rather urges us to consider what qualifies as a life: how is it that we apprehend this qualification and through which frames? The frames are epistemological, related to the question 'how do we know?', but they are not to be dissociated from the operations of power that shape how we see, apprehend and acknowledge that some lives indeed qualify as having a full life, while others seem expendable. For that reason, the question of life is not only epistemological, but also ontological: we cannot say what life is without accounting for the operations of power through which a life is produced (FoW: 1). This production involves bodies and norms, because 'to live is always to live a life that is at risk from the outset and can be put at risk or expunged quite suddenly from the outside and for reasons that are not always under one's control' (FoW: 30). Being lodged in the body, which is invariably 'exposed to socially and politically articulated forces as well as to claims of sociality – including language, work, and desire' (FoW: 3), life cannot be extricated also from ethical and political dimensions of the fundamentally unequal production of lives and their unequal exposure to violence.

So, responding to the question from the beginning of this chapter – what is 'life' and was it with us all along? – we can say that, despite its centrality, life in Butler remains undetermined, but the conditions that each life requires in order to be liveable have to be both thinkable and politically fought for. This struggle is for a plurality based in equality and against violence.

Survival, Life and the Good Life

If we seek to understand what liveable life is – and not what it is not – we encounter a problem. Only once does Butler provide a positive reference to it, hinting that liveable life can be seen as the good life. The reference to 'a good life, a livable life' (NT: 208) requires certain caution, not only because it reiterates and reclaims Adorno's suspicions that one could live a good life in a bad one, but also because it appears in the form of repetition. However, since we know that reiterations do things, let us try to use it to consider what it means to say that a liveable life is a good life. Let us, for the sake of argument, pit it against mere survival. This opposition does not belong to Adorno's register, but it is operative in theorists with whom Butler is often in discussion: Arendt, Foucault and Benjamin. It is also important to remember that we perform norms not only to be intelligible, but literally to survive.

Adorno claimed that there can be no right life in the wrong ('Es gibt kein richtiges Leben im falschen', a sentence that apodictically concludes his ruminations on 'asylum for the homeless' [Adorno 1951: 55–9, 59ff.]). The possibility of leading a good life while the world is falling apart is an old one, known at least since the Stoics. How can one will to do good and live as good, when the world is replete with corruption, inequality, exploitation and various forms of alienation? The social conditions that inform our individual understanding of what is or should be good themselves create obstacles to a moral life. Adorno believed that the existing norms and moral principles only amplify social domination, and that in the false totality of advanced capitalist society, the good life becomes impossible (Schweppenhäuser 2004: 328). This, of course, does not mean that we should lead a 'bad life'. Adorno, in fact, insists on the necessary task of appropriating morality, at the same time opposing forms of ethical violence, a recourse to ethics in an attempt to suppress the difficulties of the contemporary ethos of life. Adorno's lesson, important also in Butler's ethical considerations expounded in *Giving an Account of Oneself*, is that no individual, no 'I', can be understood outside the sociality it belongs to; it cannot be 'espoused as a pure immediacy, arbitrary, or accidental, detached from its social and historical conditions' (GAO: 7).

In contrast to the single positive reference of 'a good life, a livable life', there are many terms in Butler's work associated with unliveability (see Zaharijević and Bojanić 2017). Unintelligible and abject, ungrievable and precarious, jettisoned and dispossessed: these seem to be the many names of lives that are real and lived, but somehow lived as unreal, almost spectrally, in a certain suspension. These lives are illegible, expungable, eradicable. We can say that, as such, these are bad lives, lives lived badly. This statement is emphatically not ethical, but political, because deprivation – unreality, spectrality, suspension – is not a consequence of someone's choice, of someone's wanting to do bad. Such lives are marked by a constitutive lack of reality; they can be said to be produced as spectral, suspended, deprived of reality. The badness of these lives is produced as bad by the norms through which the world confers value and meaning. Let us thus reverse the basic ethical question and ask, 'how can I live a life that is not bad?' The presupposition of this question is obviously another, a political one, 'how can I live?', in which life almost appears in survival mode. The emphasis moves from the 'I' to the conditions of a life which is mine. In order not to allow for ontologically deprived lives, we need to first ask, 'what makes for a livable world' (UG: 17)?

The question of the 'world' refers to the arrangement of the social and historical conditions of life. These will surely include items under the rubric of infrastructure and institutions, necessary for any body to survive and flourish, to be sustained in a material and symbolic sense. But the question of the world also refers to what has thus far been termed 'social reality', the reality of norms, of discourses that turn us into intelligible and, in a certain way, valuable beings, creatures worthy of being taken into account, protected and, in the final instance, grieved. For something to be apprehended as a life, it first must have a 'right to ontology', to a rightful place in the social reality that enables others to perceive and count it as real, to apprehend it as qualified for life. The right to an ontological status cannot be taken as self-evident, so long as there are gradations of humanness that allow for some lives to be less real than others. 'The domain of ontology is a regulated domain: what gets produced inside of it, what gets excluded from it in order for the domain to be constituted is itself an effect of power' (Meijer and Prins 1998: 280). This is why the question of power and norms precedes the question of what a life is, or what will be recognised as life.

Perhaps the distinction between lives that matter and those that do not can be seen as fertile ground for biopolitical operationalisation of a distinction between qualified and bare life, that is, a life worth living and a life reducible to mere survival? The circumstances of war in which some lives are deemed worthy of all kinds of protection, while others appear radically dispensable, seem only to augment such an operationalisation. Thus, it may seem that the venerable distinction between *bios* and *zoe*, restored of late in biopolitical discussions, is also at work here. Indeed, Butler herself referred once to Agamben's *Homo Sacer*, arguing that there are certain normative conditions that must be fulfilled for life to become life. Once again, life appears in two senses, as the 'minimum biological form of living' and the one which 'establishes minimum conditions for a livable life with regard to human life' (UG: 39, 226).

Defining the pair *vita nuda*/political existence as the fundamental categorical pair of western politics, Agamben strongly emphasised the difference between two essentially distinct forms of life, conserved in Greek: *zoe* is an expression of a mere fact of living; *bios*, on the other hand, refers to a 'qualified life' (Agamben 1998: 12, 11). The first is excluded from the *polis*, the latter is impossible without it, since *bios* is essentially *bios politicos*. The *polis* itself 'comes into existence, originating in the bare needs of life, and continuing in existence for the sake of a good life' (Aristotle 1991c, 4 [1252b29–30]). Thus, a qualified life is a good life is a political life.

It is, however, not only on Greeks that Agamben relies in amplifying this dyad. In a different formulation, bare life and good life also appear in Walter Benjamin's 'Critique of Violence'. Benjamin emphasises the falseness, even ignominy of the proposition that existence (*Dasein*) stands higher than mere existence (*gerechtes Dasein*), 'if existence is to mean nothing other than mere life'. If life is, in contrast, the irreducible total condition that is 'man', then this can never coincide with the 'mere life in him' (Benjamin 2004: 251). Countering the stance of Kurt Hiller, a radical pacifist and a prominent gay rights activist, for whom the simple sanctity of life entails a prohibition on violence (Bojanić 2019), Benjamin insists that 'however sacred man is [. . .] there is no sacredness in his condition, in his bodily life vulnerable to injury by his fellow men' (Benjamin 2004: 251). 'Man' is neither exhausted in the mere life (*bloßes Leben*), nor is 'he' reducible to the uniqueness of his bodily person (*leibliche Person* [ibid.]).

This distinction has found yet another afterlife: in Arendt's *The Human Condition*, the living body, *zoe*, finds itself outside the public zone, where specifically 'human life' takes place. For Arendt, there are two dimensions of life, one cyclical, repetitive and bodily,

142

pertaining to all living creatures, the other linear and narrative, pertaining to humans. A life with a story, able to constitute a biography, is a life whose beginning and end are, so to say, partially removed from the cyclical, endlessly repetitive movement of nature. The 'biological process in man' is surely the motor of our stories, but unlike the 'story-telling', it forever retains the character of unceasing natural movement. *Bios*, a life that constitutes bio-graphy, belongs to unique, irreplaceable, unrepeatable beings who live in the world 'which existed before any one individual appeared into it and will survive his eventual departure' (Arendt 1998: 97). To be in the world with a story requires, for Arendt, speech and action, two central features of the political. Arendt also draws on Aristotle and his definition of life being 'action and not production', *praxis*, not *poiesis* (Aristotle 1991c, 6 [1254a7]). It is interesting to note that at this point in the *Politics*, where property and slavery are defined, we are still outside the proper sphere of the *polis*; rather, we are in the household, the domain where *zoe* reigns. In the very section where life is defined as action, we learn that action is administered not by the owner of the property, but by the owner's human possession, the slave, defined as the instrument or tool for action (Phillips Simpson 1998: 30).

Mere, natural, naked, bodily life and good, human, qualified, political life are merged in Foucault's exposition of modern biopolitics (or what is perhaps more adequately termed 'zoe-politics'). 'For millennia, man remained what he was for Aristotle: a living animal with the additional capacity for a political existence; modern man is an animal whose politics places his existence as a living being in question' (Foucault 1978: 143). For modern man, the 'biological life' becomes an object of political struggle. With power transforming into biopower, power over life, the political has become organised around arrangements and distributions of physiological features of life according to their value and social utility. Such power 'effects distributions around the norm' (ibid.: 144) – the very same that gives rise to the questions of 'man' and 'sex'.

Now, Butler is hardly a typical biopolitical thinker (cf. Deutscher 2017: 144–51). However, in her reading of Adorno's understanding of the impossibility of a good life in a bad life, she suggests that a very old question, 'how am I to lead a good life?', is bound up with biopolitics. By this she means those 'powers that organize life, even powers that differentially dispose lives to precarity as part of a broader management of populations through governmental and nongovernmental means, and that establish a set of measures for the differential valuation of life itself' (NT: 196). The question of my life is inextricable from the response of the world that values my life more or less than other lives. My life unfolds in a world in which the right to ontological status and an undamaged future is differentially distributed.

Bearing all this in mind, it seems that the question 'whose lives matter' is a paradigmatically biopolitical question. However, despite a singular, unhappy reference to Agamben, Butler does not employ the *zoe/bios* distinction. She is indeed interested in a human life, a life that can (potentially) constitute a biography. At the same time, she refuses the distinction between the political and non- or pre-political life, as well as the parallel distinction of private and public, which keeps certain lives forever in the shadowy domains of reality. The lives that are 'bad' or 'damaged', deprived of a right to ontology or a sense of a tenable future and remaining on the side of mere survival, are very much politicised and political, as they too are distributed around the norm defining the human. Human life is, ultimately, impossible to separate from the body, always potentially exposed as it is to harm and vulnerable to injury by fellow men. It is therefore neither reducible to a biological minimum, nor a passive piece of flesh. The body is rather 'a living set of relations' (NT: 65) that furnishes the demands for a liveable life with meaning.

The point where the liveable and good life coincide reads thus:

> We cannot struggle for a good life, a livable life, without meeting the requirements that allow a body to persist. It is necessary to demand that bodies have what they need to survive, for survival is surely a precondition for all other claims we make. And yet, that demand proves insufficient since we survive precisely in order to live, and life, as much as it requires survival, must be *more* than survival in order to be livable. (NT: 208)

Obviously, Butler does not elaborate on the symbolic homelessness of modern man. However, she takes from Adorno the idea of an unchosen badness which not only configures our personal responses to it, but also situates ethics at the heart of politics – a politics that emphatically takes bodies into account. My life is reflected back to me from a world in which I try to constitute a certain biography and become in certain ways, and in which my becoming is recognised as valuable, as mattering. *My* life depends on norms, infrastructure, institutions, other lives and discourses provided by the world which, as Arendt said, existed before any one individual appeared in it and

will survive their eventual departure. In that world, I may be produced in an invisible or valueless biography, even barred entirely
from biography, a being whose speech about their life is unfathomable and untranslatable into any idiom. My humanness can be apprehended only doubtfully or ambivalently. 'Whether or not I can live
a life that has value is not something that I can decide on my own,
since it turns out that this life is and is not my own, and that this is
what makes me a social creature, and a living one' (NT: 200). So
long as the norm of the human allows for some humans to live bad
or shadowy lives, the differential distribution of survival and (the
good) life will keep certain portions of humanity barred from 'more
than a survival'.

Butler refrains from saying how good a liveable life should be. She
refrains from offering prescriptive models of liveability, which would
inform us how to lead a good or at least a better life. The only thing
we learn is that there is something 'more' to liveability than survival
– and this 'more' shifts us from ethics to politics. Liveability reveals
a fundamental inequality in the midst of life, an inequality that
demands insurrection at the level of ontology. The aim of this insurrection is to abolish the shadowy regions of the real that produce
lives that always potentially fall back on survival.[1]

The Desire to Persist

There is, however, more to survival than 'mere survival'. For Butler,
survival does not fit into a dyad comprising bare life/political existence, the most fundamental categorical pair of western politics, as
Agamben would have it. Survival is important – and it is important
to socially and politically safeguard it – because the desire to live well
presupposes the desire to live (SS: 65).

'Can the "Other" of Philosophy Speak?', the final chapter of
Undoing Gender, itself a peculiar trajectory of reading practices,
gives Spinoza a seemingly strangely prominent position in Butler's
personal history of philosophy. She describes the *Ethics* as her first,
autodidactic and 'premature' encounter with philosophical thought,
and the idea that a primary human passion is to persist (UG: 235). In
Spinoza, everything endeavours to persist in its own being, and this
endeavour (*conatus*) or power is the actual essence of the thing in
question, infinite in time. In the human, *conatus* appears in the form
of will, appetite or desire (Spinoza 1901: 136–7). Desire is the actual
essence of man, insofar as it is 'determined to act in a way tending

to promote its own persistence' (ibid.: 173), thus prefiguring Hegel's notion of desire as desire for recognition (SD: 7). For Spinoza, bodily existence is what constitutes the essence of the mind, so the mind will endeavour to affirm the existence of the body (Spinoza 1901: 138). This self-preservation principle is further confirmed by the claim that no virtue can be conceived as prior to the endeavour to preserve one's own being: we cannot desire to act and live right, 'without at the same time wishing to be, to act, and to live – in other words, to actually exist' (ibid.: 203).

Yet, instead of an egoistic individual at the base of Spinoza's thought, Butler extends the desire to persist to involve a desire to live in a world that reflects the possibility of that persistence, which also reflects and furthers the value of others' lives (UG: 235; SS: 65). We will return to the second part of this claim in the next chapter. For now, let us remain for a moment on the first part. Being fundamentally ecstatic, desire depends on its externalisation. The desire to persist, to not encounter our own destruction, depends on something which is external to us, on a world which is outside but is constitutive of what we are. Up to this point, the question of survival has appeared several times in relation to embodiment of norms. Materialising the norm means embodying available possibilities, which are to an extent unchosen by us. In our long processes of becoming, we can persist on condition that possibilities remain available, that is, that they not become negated. For bodies that struggle to comply with norms, norms appear as both what guarantees life, and what, if lived, threaten with effacing this very life (UG: 217). 'If there are no norms of recognition by which we are recognizable, then it is not possible to persist in one's own being, and we are not possible beings: we have been foreclosed from possibility' (UG: 31).

The Psychic Life of Power offered a theory of subjection that tried to show why we remain stubbornly attached to what subjects us, and how our original dependency coupled with a desire to persist renders us vulnerable to subordination. Becoming a subject is becoming subjected to norms that provide us with recognition, protecting us from becoming (socially) dead or perishable. If becoming within the available set of norms for some of us includes wretchedness and pain, then 'a subject will attach to pain rather than not attach at all' (PLP: 61). In other words, when norms are in opposition to our desire to persist, we reach for options that are available, regardless of the fact that they produce a contradictory and 'bad' life. A desire to persist is a desire for possibility – a possibility to be and remain real.

'How is survival to be maintained if the terms by which existence is guaranteed are precisely those that demand and institute subordination' (PLP: 27), asks Butler? Is subjection to norms, produced by a desire to persist, equal to 'love of the shackles' (PLP: 27), and autonomy is nothing but illusion? As discussed in the previous chapter, our fundamental dependence on the world in which we come to be turns autonomy into something 'always conditioned and, to that extent, subverted by the conditions of its own possibility' (PLP: 204). What Butler reads from Spinoza is that we persist in our own being only within 'the risky terms of social life':

> To persist in one's being means to be given over from the start to social terms that are never fully one's own [. . .] Only by persisting in alterity does one persist in one's 'own' being. Vulnerable to terms that one never made, one persists always, to some degree, through categories, names, terms, and classifications that mark a primary and inaugurative alienation in sociality. (PLP: 28)

Instead of 'love of shackles', subjection to norms functions almost as a struggle for life, a striving to affirm ourselves as real and persist as possible beings. An endeavour to persist in one's own being implies that we will submit to a world that enables us to persist. And if possibilities the world makes available also come to threaten us, then our life is no more than mere survival.

Yet, the desire to persist is not exclusively related to our psychic life. Taken by itself, the life drive is not sufficient; it needs to be supported by something outside itself (FoW: 21). 'Life is sustained not by a self-preserving drive, conceived as an internal impulse of the organism, but by a condition of dependency without which survival proves impossible', which is of the kind that 'can also imperil survival depending on the form that dependency takes' (FoW: 46). Thus, survival, that is, the perseverance in one's own being, is possible only on condition of dependency – on norms, infrastructure, institutions, other social beings – and on condition of interdependence, in which the unchosen structures of the world become implicated in my own survival. Survival is 'dependent on what we might call a social network of hands' (FoW: 14), which seeks to minimise the unliveability of lives (NT: 67).

The Possible Life

A life that cannot be lived is an impossible life. The absence of possibilities restricts the sphere of life sometimes quite literally, through restricted movement, breathing, speech, assembly, expression of intimacy, dignified death. We have become accustomed to understanding these possibilities as rights that are politically there for us, regulated either on account of our humanity or citizenship. Moving, breathing, speaking, loving and dying, however, are 'activities' that also exist in a pre- or non-legal sense, which take place regardless of their being legally sanctioned. Thus, the fact that they are instituted as certain prerogatives (I move in part because the right to free movement belongs to me, both in accordance with Article 13 of the Universal Declaration of Human Rights and with Article 39 of the Constitution of the Republic of Serbia) does not mean that their regulation is the precondition of their possibility. That they are regulated shows that, as activities, they can be allowed or prevented, sometimes forcibly and arbitrarily, despite their very basic character. In certain circumstances, such as a pandemic, they can be limited or denied: in a state of emergency certain rights are suspended, allowing the state to restrict the most elementary activities such as walking, gathering and speaking. Further, in a world of countries and citizenship – that is, nationally restricted possibilities – what is possible on a given territory will not necessarily be possible on another (for example, the basic right to work stops being a right if we find ourselves on a territory that is not 'ours'). In war, many rights become suspended, perhaps even indefinitely.

Rights can be conceived as regulated possibilities integral to our humanness. They, however, possess rich histories. With this in mind, it can be said that our basic activities have been recognised as human in phases, and that these phases were quite uneven. Indeed, the very regulation of possibilities needs to be seen as an outcome of many and various attempts and struggles to push through the limits of the human. Transforming basic possibilities into rights and acknowledging that they may and should belong to everyone has required a multitude of historical rearticulations of the norm of the human. Each of these rearticulations we now read in terms of rights – among many others, the right to strike, the right to be included in the universal claim of suffrage, the right to child custody, the right to social property, the right to gender definition, the right to religious freedom – demanded an insurrection at the level of ontology, which preceded or went along with politically organised forms of rebellion.

If the possibilities – to move, speak, express my intimacy and grieve over the loss of a relation, to work, to die in a dignified way – are there, but are still not possible for me, then I live a life that cannot be lived. The demand for access to possibilities is the demand for one's reality to be recognised. I demand that in the extant registers of what is real, my existence stops being unreal and impossible. If I am not the only one to demand this, if we are rising up together, it may lead to the expansion of the space of the real. Importantly, any such expansion testifies to the mutability of the limits of the real, to their expandability, transforming also the zone of possibility. We can say that all existing rights are recognised possibilities that, once recognised, transform the register through which the real gets established as the only possible one.

The three subsections that follow, on recognition, appearance and the jettisoned life, will examine the (im)possibility of life from different angles, relying on Butler's reading of Hegel, as well as on her overt disagreements with Arendt and those less overt with Agamben. The question of the impossible life assumes a world in which formal equality is taken to be achieved in the greatest part of the globe. Despite formal equality, however, there are lives that remain unequal or less equal. The reason for this is that the possibilities, even when they are regulated as rights and thus formally granted, still depend on social norms.

To Recognise

> To ask for recognition, or to offer it, is precisely not to ask for recognition for what one already is. It is to solicit a becoming, to instigate a transformation, to petition the future always in relation to the Other. It is also to stake one's own being, and one's own persistence in one's own being, in the struggle for recognition. This is perhaps a version of Hegel that I am offering. (PL: 44)

Recognition is the central motive of the encounter of the two self-consciousnesses in Hegel's *The Phenomenology of Spirit*. Some 'you' has to appear on the scene in order for an 'I' to become conscious of itself. But this 'you' is a challenger: invoking and validating the self in the self-consciousness is at the same time a possible revocation and invalidation of it, which in its fierceness resembles the Hobbesian war to death. The struggle between the two 'I's in Hegel, however, is not motivated as in Hobbes by distrust of others or self-subsistence, but by their equal desire for recognition: 'Self-consciousness exists in and for itself when, and by the fact that, it so exists for another; that is, it exists only in being acknowledged' (Hegel 1977: 111). The struggle of the two 'I's is necessary and radical. Since the only way for a self-consciousness to reach its own certainty is through the existence of another self-consciousness in which it loses itself, and from which it wants to return to itself, and since this action is doubled, it can resolve only in struggle, in the death of the other, that is, in the staking of life. The encounter that transforms a consuming desire into a desire for recognition takes place when the *Phenomenology*'s solitary traveller 'leaves' the world of sense-certainty and 'enters' the world of those desiring the same thing. The first 'social' situation in Hegel, that of domination, ultimately arises out of the conflict between two 'I's that equally desire recognition of the other, but where one submits because its mere life, survival, is dearer to it. In effect, it becomes a bondsman.

Crucially, what makes Hegel's scene of recognition so different to the Hobbesian vision of the state of nature is the emphasis on relationality. Self-oriented individuals in Hobbes are also situated within the frame of encounters, albeit exorbitantly unwanted and completely irresolvable without the establishment of a mortal God, the sovereign instituted through the compact on peace and protection. Such is the nature of their encounters that they forever remain atomised loners, whose (subsequent) sociality is equally artificial as the 'artificial eternity' of the 'artificial man' (Hobbes 1965: 149). In contrast, the demand for recognition, constitutive for the Hegelian self-consciousness, is an expression of a desire for recognition of the other and by the other. This desire is at the same time self-determining and ecstatic (SD: 50): estranging – as it finds its expression in another; and assertive – as it affirms the desiring one. Recognition makes us ecstatic, out-of-ourselves, as we need to be among others in order to be something at all. The *self*-consciousness is never *self*-sufficient and in itself. 'One could say that Hegelian self-consciousness is the locus for a fundamental experience of non-identity that is manifested through the material relations between the subject and the other, such relations being understood through the figures of labor, desire and language' (Safatle 2016: 29).

Hegelian staging of recognition leads to destruction or subjection, and many important readers of Hegel have put particular stress on the struggle and emancipation that follows. For Butler, however, it seems that it is the relational character of the subject, constituted prior to struggle proper, that matters most. In her latest readings of Hegel (Butler 2019b; but cf. SD: 50), this paradigmatically combative scene enables non-combative conclusions: the self-consciousnesses are mutually related, and would be deprived of knowledge of themselves without being recognised by another, which implies their interdependence (Hegel teaches us that knowing ourselves does not imply an inward turn, for we gain knowledge of the self only in the social world). However much we have striven towards a monological ideal of self-sufficiency, the demand for recognition makes us into creatures that exist exclusively in the mode of dialogue (Taylor 1992: 33–4).

Therefore, to seek recognition assumes the existence of others who will acknowledge and accept the legitimacy of our demand. The subject's becoming is possible only by virtue of others. A self-consciousness is a self-consciousness only in demanding recognition for itself in an encounter with another self-consciousness. However, Hegel is insufficient to explain how it is possible to seek recognition and still be unrecognisable. The story of the two self-consciousnesses has nothing to say on the unequal distribution of recognition (Zimmer, Heidingsfelder and Adler 2010). Although one becomes a socially viable being through the experience of recognition – and this experience is constitutive for any social being – Hegel is of no use in explaining the conditions under which recognition itself becomes possible. For that we need to introduce sociality or norms, in a Foucauldian register, through which recognition becomes a site of differential production of the human. 'To the extent that desire is implicated in social norms, it is bound up with the question of power and with the problem of who qualifies as the recognizably human and who does not' (UG: 2).

The journeying experience of the Hegelian subject is in many respects unique. The world opens – starts to appear – to the subject through its various trials and tribulations of becoming intelligible to itself. The subject appears, so to speak, together with the world; they are co-constitutive. In our becoming subjects, we are not so demiurgic. On the contrary, one is 'fundamentally dependent upon terms that one never chose in order to emerge as intelligible being' (D: 79). The terms which ought to determine and affirm who we claim we are, are already out there in the social field, ready-made for us before we begin to articulate any demands of our own. Now, if we assume, following Spinoza and Hegel, that everyone desires to persist in their own being, then the striving for recognition appears as an extended form of the desire to persist in the world, among others.

Birgit Schippers (2014: 26) rightly insists on the importance of the difference between recognition and recognisability in Butler's thought. The first, in Hegelian fashion, refers to reciprocal acts where two 'I's demand recognition from one another. 'One comes to "exist" by virtue of this fundamental dependency on the address of the Other' (ES: 5). The 'Other', of course, appears in many guises: as the self-consciousness seeking reciprocal recognition from me, as the Althusserian figure of the one who interpellates me, as the Levinasian Other who obligates me. But, Butler is critical of the demiurgic and essentially dyadic structure of these encounters. Each of these 'Others' is not just some 'you' and recognition is not an autochthonous act. It might be such in Hegel, where it appears as the 'first encounter', constituting the very idea of encountering, of relationality, and thus sociality. However, the context in which 'you' and 'I', as actual persons in the quotidian meaning of the referent (that is, not as Hegelian self-consciousness), encounter one another complicates the dyadic relation between us: there is always a boundless field of 'others' who shape 'our' encounter. 'The participation of all or of many within a society is necessary; it is what guarantees that the performance is continually repeated' (Ferrarese 2011: 763) and recognised as successful according to social norms. Thus, recognisability refers to the conditions under which any acknowledgement of the demand for recognition is made possible. Others appear as other 'you's, but also as norms sedimented into terms we use to demand recognition: they are 'themselves conventional, the effects and instruments of a social ritual that decide, often through exclusion and violence, the linguistic conditions of survivable subjects' (ES: 5; cf. GAO: 29). And if there is a 'you' who confers recognition on me, I will probably be able to survive. But the 'two of us' are also in various ways part of relations that are not dyadic in kind, and 'always refer to a historical legacy and futural horizon' (UG: 151). Thus, to be survivable, the norms that decide upon the possibilities of survival need to enable me to demand recognition from anyone, without risk from exclusion and violence.

In that sense, recognisability refers to the normative or regulatory schemes of recognition that define who will be at all able to appear as a recognisable being. Let us perform a small thought experiment and try to put Antigone and Creon in place of two Hegelian genderless, even human-less 'I's who appear to one another as self-consciousness seeking recognition. The suggestion is unusual, especially given that Antigone does later appear in *The Phenomenology of Spirit*. She is figured as the pre-political opposition to politics, in contrast to Creon who is representative of the ethical order and the state. Representing kinship and femininity, in Hegel's rendering Antigone turns into 'womankind in general', and into an internal enemy of the community which 'only gets an existence through its interference with the happiness of the Family' (Hegel 1977: 288). However, since we are engaging in the thought experiment, let us ask a perhaps paradoxical question. Can we somehow imagine that Antigone is not a defender of the hearth and spirit of family piety (ibid.: 447), but a self-consciousness striving for recognition? Could we, against the grain of authoritative interpretations, claim that Antigone is in fact the very embodiment of the desire for recognition, although hers is the body of a woman? If such a claim does not seem to work, perhaps the reason is that Antigone is a woman. She can hardly be figured as a self-consciousness striving for recognition – despite her willingness to put her life at stake, despite the fact that her acts call kinship into question, leading not only to the fulfilment of the promise of her name, but also causing deaths that preclude her various forms of subjection. In the schemes of recognisability available both in Theban tyranny and in Prussian enlightened monarchy, Antigone is not recognisable in the frame of struggle for recognition. This turns her into an impossible insurgent who dethrones the tyrant, and into an impossible journeying subject in the most famous story on the subject's appearance in the history of philosophy. If she can be recognised at all, it is only as womankind in general, as 'the irony of community' (ibid.: 288).

The invocation of Antigone with emphasis on the troubling fact of her gender could misleadingly suggest that Butler considers recognition in the context of identities. Recognition is, however, never reducible to an acknowledgement of identities (FoW: 163), not only due to their inherently exclusionary logic.[2] For Butler, recognition should reach beyond what possibilities are already available. It is fundamentally about opening up possibilities for something new to appear.

In 2008, Butler was featured in Astra Taylor's eight-part film, *Examined Life: Philosophy Is in the Streets*. Appearing alongside Sunny Taylor, a painter, writer and disability activist who is in a wheelchair, they are shown walking down a San Francisco street. Butler is the first to speak: 'I thought we should take this walk together and one of the things I wanted to talk about is what it means for us to take a walk together.' They agree that nobody goes walking – or can go walking – without there being something that supports that walk. Recognising differently-abled people obviously requires more than acknowledging that certain difference is there. It considers our built environment as an unequally distributed resource. Furthermore, the demand for recognition requires from all of us to understand both movement and space differently, to understand what possibilities there are for movement in space that make some of us less present, and thus less real. Our desire to be depends very much on the conditions that make the realisation of that desire possible. In that sense, meeting such a demand for recognition involves a social and political readiness to recreate the space that allows for different forms of movement. This means the redistribution of funds from, for example, the production of arms to an ambitious reconstruction of the general infrastructure of cities and towns. But it also, importantly, involves our becoming aware of what bodies can do, what they are permitted to do, how that is not ours to choose, and how dependent we are as social beings on one another, but also on norms that decide on our liveability (Butler and Taylor 2008; Abrams 2011). If this is taken into account, social reality cannot simply remain as it was prior to the 'transformation' effected by such a recognition: something in the order of intelligibility, and in this case, something in our understanding and practice of moving, also has to profoundly change.

To Appear

The demand for recognition is made by those not yet recognised. The place that 'belongs' to them in the existing distribution of the real is too narrow and incapacious, exposing them to a lack of relation or to a dangerous relation. One seeks recognition because in the existing categorial apparatus, normative discourses, infrastructural arrangements, their place is a non-place. Within the existing possibilities in the order of the real, this subject remains less possible, without a foothold. How can we exist without a place that in some ways enables us, allowing us to move at all or to move without a threat to life? This question introduces another aspect of possibility, which primarily refers to the spatial character of embodied life.

In an interview with George Yancy (2015), Butler discusses the chant 'Black Lives Matter' against the rejoinder that all lives matter. No doubt, Butler's idea of liveable life is equalising, meaning that all lives do matter. But, so long as there is only one kind of life – white life – that is given recognition, emphasis on the obvious, that black life is a life too, claims something that has historically not been realised. If whiteness is understood as a background to (universal, human) experience, as an ongoing history which 'orientates bodies in specific directions, affecting how they "take up" space' (Ahmed 2007: 150), then non-white bodies appear as insufficiently universal, insufficiently human, as 'spaced-out'. If (universal, human) experience is epidermalised as implicitly white, then non-white bodies appear in it with a difference that denies them universality. Insisting on that difference is the demand for recognition that all lives never really included *all* lives. It is a demand that now, in this moment, lives that have historically not mattered, have been unworthy, were considered 'only a fraction of life' (Yancy and Butler 2015), emancipate from their historical abjectness, reconfiguring in the process the very notions of the human and universal.

Writing recently on the sudden and senseless murder of black people, Kimberlé Crenshaw succinctly states that their deaths were a direct consequence of their being Black. For them 'the violence of the past is the violence of the present' (Crenshaw 2020). The offence of Ahmaud Arbery, a 25-year-old Black man, was 'jogging while Black' (ibid.). In our social organisation of the visible, his mere skin colour signalled depravity and danger, his embodied presence justifying the violence mobilised to subdue the implicit threat he posed (see Butler 1993c). Arbery, it has been suggested, would have avoided getting killed had he not gone jogging in broad daylight. Had Arbery not appeared, had he not gone jogging in public, he might be alive.

What does it mean 'to appear'? Can we appear at all if we make only spectral, damaged or attenuated claims to the human (Feola 2014: 135)? What if we try to pose as human, but 'no recognition is forthcoming, because the norms by which recognition takes place are not in your favor' (UG: 30)? If we are abject, do we ever *appear*?

The figure of the 'abject' holds a prominent place in *Bodies That Matter*, referring to those beings who live in unliveable and uninhabitable (yet densely populated) zones of the social (BTM: xiii). Julia Kristeva gave this strange notion conceptual life. According to her, in its opposition to the subject, the abject is more and less than an object: it is 'the jettisoned object', radically excluded, radically separate, loathsome, 'not me. Not that. But not nothing either. A "something" that I do not recognize as a thing [. . .] On the edge of non-existence and hallucination, of reality that, if I acknowledge it, annihilates me' (Kristeva 1982: 2). The proximity and indistinctness of the abject is disturbing, as it rips an ostensibly seamless texture of social life. The abject is there, but illegible, ambiguous (ibid.: 9). This ambiguous zone – neither this nor that – is an abjected outside, uninhabitable but inhabited, invisible or framed to be unseen, yet densely populated. Jettisoned from the 'symbolic system', 'it is what escapes that social rationality, that logical order on which a social aggregate is based' (ibid.: 65).

Butler uses the idea of abject to explain how the domain of 'unthinkable, abject, unlivable bodies' (BTM: x) is produced as the constitutive outside to intelligible bodies. The zone of uninhabitability is the limit to the subject's domain, its autonomy and life, and also a limit to what qualifies as 'human' (BTM: xiii, xvii). The production of the '*un*symbolizable, the unspeakable, the illegible is also always a strategy of social abjection' (BTM: 142), which depends on the space in which the symbolisable, sayable, legible appears. The space of appearance is where we are made to be seen, heard, 'read' by others, symbolising something unambiguous, included, within. In that sense, for Butler, 'appearing turns into an issue of social and political recognition' (Pulkkinen 2018: 136).

The intrinsic relation between appearance and reality found one of its most powerful articulations in the work of Hannah Arendt. Action, the central notion of her political thought, is tied to the idea of appearance. The political emerges from acting together, that is, 'the sharing of words and deeds' (Arendt 1998: 198). Contrary to labour and work, action and speech do not leave material, tangible traces, and they do not outlive the moment of their actualisation. However, what they produce in a fleeting moment of their actualisation has no correlate in poietic human activities. The 'product' of speaking and acting together is the *polis* itself. Far more than a physical city-state, the *polis* is what holds people together and provides them with 'the space of appearance in the widest sense of the word, namely, the space where I appear to others as others appear to me, where men exist not merely like other living or inanimate things but make their appearance explicitly' (ibid.: 198–9).

The space constituted in common, through action and speech, is public space. (The word 'public' is itself full of cues. The Greek κοινή refers to what is common and shared. *Populus* [people] and *pubes* [grown-up, person of age] merge in the Latin *publicum*. German *Öffentlichkeit* points to the openness, where the public – those who listen to the one speaking – is in the open [*das Offene*], and not in the invisible, inaccessible spaces normally considered to be walled in, that is, private. Russian общественность and гласност combine 'society' with 'voice', that which can be and – in public – will be heard. The curious Slavic word *javnost* combines an uttered response/report [*javiti*] with the state of being awake [*java*]. Etymologically, it relates to a specific form of sociality, when shepherds returned their herds from pasture and gathered together after a while – when one finally, after a long time, hears the voice of another. This, the word seems to suggest, is something that cannot take place in dreams; it demands acting together at one place common to all.)

The public is the space where human beings appear explicitly through speech and action. 'To be deprived of it means to be deprived of reality, which humanly and politically speaking, is the same as appearance. To men the reality of the world is guaranteed by the presence of others, by its appearing to all; "for what appears to all, this we call Being"', as Aristotle says in *Nicomachean Ethics*, 'and whatever lacks this appearance comes and passes like a dream, intimately and exclusively our own but without reality' (Arendt 1998: 199). Humanly and politically speaking, what does not appear remains unreal and in a certain sense un-human, since it is only human beings who 'have the privilege of appearing to one another, distinguishing *themselves* in their in-born uniqueness, such that, in this reciprocal exhibition, a *who* is shown to appear, entirely as it is' (Cavarero 2000: 20). The 'who' that appears is a life that constitutes a biography.

Posited as such, the public realm – the space in which the political takes place – seems egalitarian: the presence of others to and with whom one appears safeguards the reality of the world. The trouble is, however, that, for Arendt, the space of appearance strictly depends on the existence of the opposite, non-appearing realm that ought to be out of reach. The private is the limited reality of family life, warmth of the hearth (Arendt 1998: 59), natural in its cyclicality, coming and passing like a dream. Now, if all humans moved unhindered through these spheres according to their possibilities and needs, alternately appearing and disappearing, perhaps this co-dependence of the private and the public would not be a problem. One appears, so to say, for a time, and then disappears to nourish themselves under the cover of the dreamlike private. Configured thus, the private and the public are complementary spaces, in which the one who moves through and between them is the one who sometimes speaks and acts, and sometimes sleeps and loves.

This is, however, not how Arendt imagined this distinction. Figuring it upon the image of Athenian democracy, she accepted that there must be those who are never part of the public, although they will be found in the nooks of the private. The private – the household interior – is shadowy (ibid.: 38), related to an uncertain kind of existence, an existence unseen and unheard (ibid.: 50). The private, for Arendt, is always in the dark, referring to the darkness of *physis*, of bodily functions, toil, love, something deprivative, intimate, protected, concealed, invisible (see Loidolt 2018: 135–8). But, if this is so, the reality of the world does not open to everyone. Those who remain in the shadow, who do not speak or act in public, are not entirely endowed with reality. They lead what Arendt defines as 'an entirely private life', deprived of the essentially human. They are deprived of a reality that comes from being seen and heard, as well as the possibility to achieve something more permanent than life itself (Arendt 1998: 58):

> The political realm [. . .] is the public sphere in which everybody can appear and show who he himself is. To assert one's own opinion belonged to being able to show oneself, to be seen and heard by others. To the Greeks this was the one great privilege attached to public life and lacking in the privacy of the household, where one is neither seen nor heard by others. (The family, wife and children, and slaves and servants, were *of course* not recognized as *fully human*.) In private life one is hidden and can neither appear nor shine. (Arendt 2005: 14, italics mine)

Arendt offers a social ontology in which appearance is intrinsically related to being, where to be is to be in public. To be (a human) is to act, that is, to create and perform the reality in which one appears. However, this powerful conception directly depends on the dark side of the same social ontology, assuming the existence of spaces that not only temporarily hide from appearance (as shelters, fortresses), but are entirely deprived of appearance (within ontological walls). The unyielding 'of course' from the passage quoted above, affirms not only the division between public and private, but also the givenness of the differential distribution of humanness across this divide. Certain spaces are spaces of appearance, such that anyone can appear in them, as long as they are fully human, that is. Those fully human can show themselves, be visible and audible, since these are spaces that affirm their humanness. But this historically obdurate 'of course' belongs to a social reality in which some are constituted *as* politically meaningless beings (indistinct, illegible, unintelligible – as

Barbarians speaking in a *bar-bar* tongue never to become κοινή, the language of the 'politēs'). As such, they are constituted precisely as invisibly human, as unreal humans, sometimes monstrous and liminally dreamlike (Zaharijević 2020a: 152).

Butler's understanding of the political can hardly be understood without Arendt, from whom Butler draws, among other things, acting in concert, performative aspects of the political, plurality, and the unchosenness of cohabitation (D: 122). As shown by Emma Ingala (2018b: 35–40), what strongly binds these two thinkers is the relational nature of the political subjects, the emphatically compromised sovereignty of political actors and their agency, and the common space of appearance always created performatively with others. Nor can the significance of appearance in Butler's understanding of the real be overestimated: our bodies are indeed in the world, with an invariably public dimension, making us into social beings.

However, the aspect of non-appearance – a conspicuous admission of a limit to reality (and humanness) in Arendt's 'of course' – is the basis of Butler's continuous contestation of Arendt. The fact that for Arendt there is '*only one basic world-opening activity that indeed is in need of visibility: acting/speaking*, which amounts to *the actualization of plurality*' (Loidolt 2018: 140) is especially problematic for Butler. As early as *Antigone's Claim*, she criticises Arendt's lack of acknowledgement that the internal boundaries of the public were secured through the perpetual production of its constitutive outside. Women and children, slaves and servants, all non-property-holding males, but rather themselves property, 'were not permitted into the public sphere in which the human was constituted through its linguistic deeds. Kinship and slavery thus condition the public sphere of the human and remain outside its terms' (AC: 82). The 'fully human' was applicable to certain human beings, consigning others not only to the outside of the public, but also to the outside of 'full humanity'.

What forms the 'constitutive outside' changed over time. The norms defining the boundaries of private and public, non-appearance and appearance, less-than-human and human have histories of their own. And although these histories can be told as social histories, pertaining to something on the other side of the political, cut off from the space where the true political takes place, the political itself would remain untransformable if its constitutive exclusions remained unrecognised. Women as paradigmatic bodies, slaves as tools for action, metics as the first named form of immigrants were variously excluded from access to the space where *humans* show themselves and shine. The fact that these were 'entirely private lives', deprived of the possibility to achieve something more permanent than life itself, cannot be considered the choice made by women, slaves or metics. As Athena Athanasiou and Elena Tzelepis powerfully state,

> the Athenian polis is the biopolitical site in which women, along with slaves and foreigners, constitute the irreducible limit of humanity: the marked and dreaded Other who is banished from the political domain as mere body, and, at the same time, represents the abjected ground on which the body politics claims to be constituted [. . .] In the discursive regime of the ancient polis, where the political is emphatically defined as the sexually neutral domain of disembodied reason and essential logos, the female body – or, perhaps more accurately, the female as mere body – is considered to be essentially unpolitical. (Athanasiou and Tzelepis 2010: 110)

The fact that these lives, neither seen nor heard by others, existed as unpolitical – and not of their own will – points to what a political life, a good life, was and ought to be, as well as what it ought no longer be.

In this neat division of spheres, mere survival belongs to bodily life. At first glance obscured, the distinction between body and mind resurfaces as the difference between *zoe* and *bios*. The bodies that appear in public seem somehow to be 'bodiless', as their bodily needs are catered for elsewhere, in the darkness of the private. (In a different place, Arendt also considered what the non-bodiless bodies looked like in public. Referring to 'rebellions of the belly', meaning in particular the women who marched on Versailles while their children were starving in squalor, Arendt claims that their force appears irresistible as it 'lives from and is nourished by the necessity of biological life itself' [Arendt 1990: 112]. It seems that biological lives in political, public space never appear as plural, but only as 'a multitude united in one body' [Cavarero 2021: 146].)

On the other hand, bodies that are 'fully embodied', and therefore precluded from the space of the political, remain behind the ontological walls of the private. The private is private (deprived) because it is short of the political. Those who never cross its threshold remain consigned to *zoe*. For centuries, the self-evidence of this precept produced ontological deprivations in the organisation of the space of the political.

Butler makes a distinctly feminist argument when she claims that

> the foreign, unskilled, feminized body that belongs to the private sphere is the condition of possibility for the speaking male citizen (who is presumably fed by someone and sheltered somewhere, and whose nourishment and shelter are tended to in some regular ways by some disenfranchised population or another). (NT: 45–6)[3]

But Butler also goes beyond this essentially feminist formulation, demanding a different social ontology, one in which there are no differential conditions that determine what is worthy of appearance and what remains excluded, jettisoned and abject.

Appearance is generally inseparable from the corporeality that is seen, felt and understood in certain ways. The presumably bodiless beings that speak and act cannot be separated from bodies, even for a moment. A speech act is a bodily act: an audible utterance necessitating a larynx and lungs (among other things). If, on the other hand, we do not appear, it is because we are not assigned a place of appearance in the world. That is to say, there is either a lack of norms that situate one's body in the space of productive meaning, or the presence of norms that exclude and render abject. The universal is either simply foreclosed to some bodies, or they turn into particularities, given a side-place to the universal. Thus, we have the political in which there are humans and, on the side, there are women, slaves and foreigners.

A social ontology that insists on bodies would have to demand the destabilisation of the distinction between *zoe* and *bios*. There is no sphere in which we are not embodied. It is bodies that have an unalterably public dimension; they appear, becoming visible and audible to others. The meaning of the public/private distinction is not derived from the capacity of bodies to appear, but from a differential historical framing of various appearances and the unequal valuing of different bodies. Appearance is always bodily and always imbued with norms that order the social positioning of the bodies (whether they appear, becoming either a 'political existence' or mere life). The destabilisation of these age-old distinctions has been in play whenever the demands for recognition were made by those 'of course not fully human'. Feminists have fought for the politicisation of the private under the banner 'the personal is political' long before this slogan was even invented. But Butler goes one step further by claiming, in contradistinction to Arendt, that the private is always already

JUDITH BUTLER AND POLITICS

political, indeed that it is the constitutive outside to the political itself and its condition of possibility.

To Be Jettisoned

The private, however, need not be considered only in terms of privacy. It seems that the argument about the outside that shapes the 'inside' has held up over time, even when the private sphere was considered much more porous and less fixed. The private can be understood as the space produced by closing off – or walling in – the open, where humans shine. Not shining are all those who, leaving the obscurity of the private, do not appear, although as bodies they have to appear: be they Athenian women, the emerging labouring classes in the industrial revolution, slaves on cotton plantations, Jews in ghettos, gay men cruising during the AIDS epidemic, documented and undocumented immigrants who, driven by war or destitution seek shelter in wealthier countries – in a word, people who were or could be 'stripped of genealogy, cultural memory, social distinction, name, and native language, that is, of all the elements of Aristotle's *bios*' (Ziarek 2008: 95). The 'private' is thus rather a broad and indistinct domain in which inequality is allowed – even desirable – despite the fact that not only the aim of the political, but also the mode of its constitution, on which point Butler agrees with Arendt, should be equality.

Butler's first comprehensive critique of Arendt is to be found in a little book, *Who Sings the Nation-State?*, whose ultimate goal is the rejection of the deep divide between *zoe* and *bios*. The book title refers to a group of undocumented residents, who in the spring of 2006, at the time of intense debates in Congress on changes to US immigration policy, demonstrated in several cities in California. These protests, which surely influenced Butler's later elaboration of the performative theory of assembly, had a singular trait: the undocumented Mexican residents who gathered in the streets of Los Angeles sang the *Star-Spangled Banner* in Spanish. The US President specifically condemned the act of singing in a language other than English: 'I think people who want to be a citizen of this country ought to learn English. And they ought to learn to sing the anthem in English' (qtd in Holusha 2006) – the only language that is 'ours', defining our national identity and the boundaries of the *polis*. Had the protesters sung the anthem in the official language of the *polis*, their gesture could have been understood as a peculiarly formulated plea for integration ('we sing your anthem, we are learning your language, please recognise our request to legally reside in your country'). But a rendition in Spanish (by a plurality) makes the singing itself into an articulation of plurality (Butler and Spivak 2007: 59). It displaces the anthem from its monolingualism, turning it into an object of a translation and a demand for the redefinition of the language through which the *polis* speaks. (The demanded redefinition is, in a sense, only catching up with reality, as the *polis already* speaks in various languages, Spanish being the second most represented.) The Spanish rendition of the anthem becomes a speech act of sorts, and the established space of the public gets unsettled when the street – the space of appearance par excellence – becomes a place from where bodies and voices announce their desire to end disenfranchisement. In 'normal' circumstances, the undocumented immigrants, singing the American anthem in Spanish, are there, but are consigned to the dark space of non-appearance. In 'normal' circumstances, they are inaudible, since the 'politēs' do not speak this (barbaric) language. When the invisible and the inaudible take to the streets and speak by singing the very symbol of the *polis* – to which they do not belong and which relegates them to a non-place – they performatively enact their right to assembly, to plurality, to a place (ibid.: 63), although no such right exists for them as of that moment.

The figure of the stateless reveals starkly the paradox of human rights. Insofar as they are human the stateless possess inalienable rights; yet, being 'without a state', they lack the frame in which any rights can be recognised. The poetic French term 'apatride', referring to one without a fatherland, a patria and patrimony, has a rather bureaucratic echo in another French term, 'sans-papiers'. We see in this pair a profound tension between rights that belong to us on account of our humanity, and rights that we have on account of citizenship, but can also lose or not have. In a world organised into discrete nation-states, one can lose a state. The nation, however, remains inscribed in one's first paper, the first administrative recognition of someone's existence, alongside one's name, sex and place of birth. This paper often also includes information on the 'blood' of the newborn, which, together with place, defines the boundaries of citizenship on the basis of *ius soli* and *ius sanguinis*. Who we are remains cached in our birth certificate, the paper confirming that we were born somewhere, engendered at a given moment, in some nation(-state). The paper is a state acknowledgement of the status of being born, of coming to be. That paper – as well as our mother tongue, the language of 'our' anthem – ceases to have power and ability to guarantee rights when we find ourselves on foreign ground which defines itself by its own monolingualism, if not 'monosanguinism'. For this reason, persons 'without papers' (or those whose papers are void) are those who, moving across borders, become undocumented, and thus 'illegal' humans. They are 'living proof' that the world recognises only humans with papers. Herself 'stateless', Hannah Arendt's consideration of this issue led her to introduce the famous concept of the right to have rights. 'The same essential rights were at once claimed as the inalienable heritage of all human beings *and* as the specific heritage of specific nations [. . .] the practical outcome of this contradiction was that from now on human rights were protected and enforced only as national rights' (Arendt 1962: 230).

Could we then say that in the world of nation-states, 'humans' whose inalienable rights become meaningless by their status of illegal aliens, are in a sense banished from humanity? Perhaps we could claim that they are stripped of all qualities and relations, reduced to a bare life (*zoe*)? Without papers, without language and legally provided possibilities to act, these humans 'appear' – to invert Arendt – not as 'men', but precisely as 'physical objects' (Arendt 1998: 176). Perhaps they are then nothing more than *bloßes Leben* (Benjamin 2004: 251)?

Giorgio Agamben reintroduced bare life to contemporary philosophical discussions, referring to a conception in which the biological fact of life is given political priority over the way it is lived. Unlike the Greeks, for whom the simple, natural life (a merely reproductive life) remained confined to the sphere of *oikos*, and was strictly excluded from the *polis*, for modern man the realm of bare life, originally situated at the margins of political order, gradually begins to coincide with the political realm (Agamben 1998: 12). The 'biopolitical body of the West (the last incarnation of *homo sacer*)' (ibid.: 105) appears as a threshold of absolute indistinction between the outside and the inside, the included and the excluded, *zoe* and *bios*. 'When life and politics – originally divided, and linked together by means of the no-man's-land of the state of exception that is inhabited by bare life – begin to become one, all life becomes sacred and all politics becomes the exception' (ibid.: 86). With power becoming biopower, the distinctions between the excluded bare life, formerly consigned to a particular place or category, and the included rights-bearers, begins to collapse. Instead of being somewhere outside of the city, bare life 'now dwells in the biological body of every human being' (ibid.: 81). In today's biopolitics, we all become a *homo sacer*, potentially reducible to living but without rights. Biological life is in this case the object of management techniques in various spaces where law can easily be set aside, which becomes painfully obvious in cases of 'deprivation of citizenship, the interning of refugees, border detentions, those interned without due process, those interned as lesser forms of life, or those possessing lesser (or no) rights' (Deutscher 2017: 132).

Claiming that Arendt and Agamben share an understanding of *zoe* and *bios*, Butler says that the two can be distinguished, although exclusively for analytical purposes: the Socratic good life, so dear to Arendt (Arendt 2005; Canovan 1990), must be at least implied in life itself, in our sheer capacity to live (Birulés 2009). More life is already assumed in mere life, as Bonnie Honig suggests. 'If democratic politics is about risk and heroism', orienting us towards the gifts of life and making us strive to produce a biography, 'it is also just as surely about generating, fairly distributing, demanding, or taking the sources of life – food, medicine, shelter, community, intimacy, and so on' (Honig 2009: 10–11). The Arendtian premise that the sphere of a merely reproductive life – the dark nooks in which bodies are fed, nourished, kept clean and healthy – is unpolitical needs to be rejected. In the same vein, practices that enable the survival of *bios* are not reducible to the physiological fact of living. We might say that hunger, the need for sleep, illnesses, gravidity, exposure of the body in its materiality (to a potential violence which is always more likely to happen if hunger, illness and gravidity are at an advanced stage) belong to a merely physiological arrangement of our bodily life. But even so, what enables the body to assuage hunger, to obtain care and attendance, to maintain a healthy pregnancy and give birth, to remain protected from arbitrary violence – in other words, to remain alive – belongs to the sphere of the political for which speech and action will be employed.

Life does not have a basis and superstructure: each sphere in which life takes place is saturated with power. Thus, the notion of bare life feeds on an exclusionary logic whose ultimate aim is to depoliticise life (Butler and Spivak 2007: 38). Indeed, it relies on a tacit assumption that there were times when certain lives were understood as exclusively *zoe* and 'non-political', and that this must have been good for the political, for the *polis*, because the 'political lives' (*bios*) were such precisely because the two were separable and separated.

Lives that (have to appear but) do not appear in a humanly qualified way – in the Athenian *polis* or in contemporary nation-states – inhabit excluded zones that are also politically produced. Due to their exclusion, those 'non-appearing' are indeed barred from recognition as qualified lives, but they are as such neither mere physical objects (even if they often 'appear' as abject), nor bare physiological (biological or 'natural') processes simply declining to terminate. The naturalness of human life, as well as its reified and abject status, is always an effect of various political processes of naturalisation, objectification and abjectification – all diverse forms of derealisation.

One of the oldest forms of allocation of recognition is the predetermination for a pre- or non-political life on the one hand, and for the qualified political life, on the other. This 'predetermination', which has for centuries been understood as something entirely natural – in the case of women, in the most direct, 'anatomical' way – is itself politically produced. To claim that we are now living at a time when the distinction between bare life and political existence is becoming blurred is to accept that for women, slaves and metics, politics has always been a form of biopolitics.

Agamben ominously claimed that 'if there is no longer any one clear figure of the sacred man, it is perhaps because we are all virtually *homines sacri*' (Agamben 1998: 68). However, the functioning of all previous political communities that had a clear understanding of their insides and outsides was made possible by multitudes of those politically preordained to live a merely reproductive, politically unrecognised life. Their reducibility to a mere biological reproduction codetermined and co-defined political from within. In that sense, politically qualified life, itself a result of concerted action, has always been regulated by norms of recognisability that distributed appearances, denying or granting the right to appear, distributing positions of mere life and bearing rights differently. In Butler's understanding, all lives are steeped in power, and none is ever outside of the workings of the political. It is the way in which lives are politically conditioned that reflects on their possibility to be something more than mere life.

Agamben's understanding of qualified and unpolitical lives, however, also has an important aspect regarding agency. If we are all becoming sacrificeable at the altar of our biopolitical communities, political agency is taking place in an indistinctly shrunken space, that is, slowly evaporating. In Agamben's view, no one is exempt from this thinning of political agency, but those possessing lesser or no rights seem to appear as the very embodiment of bare life, as harbingers of our bleak collective future. Now, there is a wide array of candidates who fit the elastic criteria of such partially (or entirely) unrecognised lives, excluded from the position of rights-bearers. If we follow Butler, it is of great importance what language we use to describe those unrecognised lives. If we understand them as bare life, as the 'deanimated givens' of political life (NT: 79), we implicitly ratify a perspective that consents to the existence of the politically living dead beings – even though our nominal aim is to call this into question. This perspective disregards and devalues forms of political agency emerging 'in those domains deemed prepolitical or extrapolitical and that break into the sphere of appearance as from the outside, as its outside, confounding the distinction between inside and outside' (NT: 78). If we wish to take into account exclusion itself – enabled by and maintained through the distinctions of *zoe*/*bios*, private/public – not only as a political problem, but as part of the workings of the political, we need to reject the notion of bare life.

This is precisely what Butler does when, discussing statelessness, she claims that no life stands outside the political. When a state unbinds, releases, expels, banishes, dispossesses us, 'we are not outside of politics [. . .] This is not bare life, but a particular formation of power and coercion that is designed to produce and maintain the condition, the state of the dispossessed' (Butler and Spivak 2007: 5). Deprived of legal protection from a state they have lost, these paradigmatically expendable lives do not reside in zones outside of the political. Their life is steeped in power (ibid.: 9), defined through manifold modes of deprivation, destitution and dispossession. It is politically produced as the very state of the stateless:

> The stateless are not just stripped of status but accorded a status and prepared for their dispossession and displacement; they become stateless precisely through complying with certain normative categories. As such, they are *produced* as the stateless at the same time that they are jettisoned from juridical modes of belonging [. . .] they are, significantly, contained within the polis as its interiorized outside. (Ibid.: 15–16)

Lives that are lived from the interiorised outside, that inhabit the uninhabitable zone of unrecognition, are, Butler maintains in *Who Sings the Nation-State?*, jettisoned lives. Their exclusion, unrecognition and non-appearance is operated from within the political that assigns them their particular, legally unrecognised place. Jettisoned life does not return to a state outside the polity (ibid.: 36). It is not cast out from the *polis* in a state of radical exposure, as Agamben would have it, where it could be sacrificed, but is 'bound and constrained by power relations in a situation of forcible exposure' (FoW: 29). Radically disenfranchised, these lives are situated at the nexus of the political, saturated with the very power relations that determine which life is qualified and which is jettisoned. Although they live as 'spectral humans, deprived of ontological weight and failing the tests of social intelligibility required for minimal recognition' (Butler and Spivak 2007: 16), never qualifying for a life that shines, they are not, for that reason, on the outside of the political. The state of being jettisoned, cast away from the space in which rights are fulfilled, is indeed a situation of extreme precarity. However, a jettisoned life is never bare, barren, naked and stripped of agency. It can transform its destitution into a politically performative tool; it can rebel from within its precarious state (cf. Ziarek 2008: 103; Cabrera 2018: 9).

Revisiting Arendt in a more conciliatory tone than in *Who Sings the Nation-State?*, as if wrenching her from Agamben's reading and onto her own side, Butler writes:

> Those who have been dispossessed of rights are actively dispossessed: they are not jettisoned from the polis into an apolitical realm [. . .] The rightless and stateless are maintained in conditions of political destitution [. . .] Indeed, Arendt writes quite clearly in *The Origins of Totalitarianism* that the ostensible 'state of nature' to which displaced and stateless people are reduced is not natural or metaphysical at all, but the name for a specifically political form of destitution. (PW: 150)

Let us, once again, return to the undocumented workers who sing the US national anthem in Spanish. They may, for our present purposes, represent today's rightless and stateless, framed by a normative regime that classifies some 'bodies as "genuine" and others (be it emaciated bodies of refugees squashed in lorries in which they have been smuggled to the "West", or confined to the leaky Tampa ship hopelessly hovering off the shores of Australia) as "bogus"' (Zylinska 2004: 526). As bogus, they can be deported, or jettisoned to an 'indeterminate place'. The place is, nonetheless, entirely determinable, appearing on the maps of immigration routes, regardless of the fact that it often remains out of sight, unseen and unheard of by those who are, as yet, not *homines sacri*. Mexican immigrants are surely not entitled to the same prerogatives as US citizens. Their spectrality – an effect of displacement and dispossession – in the space of appearance speaks of their profound political destitution. But a life steeped in political deprivations is not *ipso facto* deprived of agency. When they gather to sing together, they obviously do not sing 'from a state of Nature. They're singing from the streets in San Francisco and Los Angeles' (Butler and Spivak 2007: 67). By singing the national anthem in Spanish on the streets, they are altering the space of the political from the very heart of public space. Their bodies appearing in public becomes 'a turbulent performative occasion' (D: 178). On the street 'we act, and act politically in order to secure the conditions of existence' (NT: 58), the basic possibilities without which lives – both in the sense of mere and more life – remain impossible.

While Agamben dejectedly predicts that we are all becoming *homines sacri* – including those of us who have thus far been privileged members of the *polis* – and that little can be done about it, Butler responds that 'the performative emerges precisely as the specific power of the precarious' (D: 121). Precisely because there is no space beyond or outside the political, agency is always possible, and the conditions of precarity make it urgent – sometimes literally a question of life and death.

Precarious and Dispossessed Life

Now, it can be said that the immigrants are not 'private' persons in the same way that women, slaves and metics of the Athenian *polis* were. A similar argument can be made for various (alien) others, like 'racialized strangers', precarious workers, or trans and queer people (although the latter are in many parts of the world seen as the very paradigm of private lives, as those who must remain in 'their four walls'). What these different groups of people share is their unequal access to the space of appearance and fragile or non-existing recognition, due to which they live jettisoned lives, being assigned to a nonplace. In that sense, they are exposed to greater precarity and various forms of dispossession.

Precarious life is one of the central notions of Butler's entire work, so much so that from *Precarious Life* onwards, precarity gradually became a concept on par with performativity. Although at the beginning of this chapter it appeared conjoined to other names for 'unliveable' life, precarious life differs from the concepts we have examined thus far. I suggest we read precarity together with dispossession because both terms crucially relate to the bivalent traits of our being/ becoming *in the world* as humans, and both involve a certain criticism of ownership. Both are bivalent, and in Butler's philosophy this

169

important bivalence has to do with equality (see Zaharijević 2022). Namely, precariousness and dispossessability are what makes all humans equal, while precarity and dispossession are modes of social and political production and institutionalisation of our inequality.

The term 'precarious' refers to something uncertain, dependent on the will of another or circumstances beyond one's control, being exposed to or involving danger and insecurity. In Roman law, where the ancient institute of *precarium* first appears, that 'something' always related to possession, to something we can claim as our own. In this tradition, then, *precarium* stands at the opposite end of the scale from *dominium*. 'Ownership is the largest interest that one can have in things; *precarium*, or tenancy-at-will, is the smallest. Yet, a person holding *precario* had the benefit of possessory interdicts, and was called a possessor' (Hunter 1803: 379), despite the fact that they were deprived of *animo domini*. They are thus an owner even in the absence of *animo domini*, or the 'intention of the sovereign', that is, without the power to assert sovereignty or ownership over a thing. According to the Victorian jurist, in terms of law and reason, *precarium* is a 'startling inconsistency' and an 'extraordinary anomaly' (ibid.: 380). The inconsistency is that the tenancy-at-will could be converted into a tenure in perpetuity, on the basis of which a tenant could hold the tenancy in defiance of his patron (ibid.: 381), to whom the 'intention of the sovereign' (*animo domini*) belongs. Insubordinate tenancy was later regulated by turning *precarium* into a convention according to which one is allowed to use or exercise a right freely until revocation, which, however, can take place at any time and at the whim of the holder of *animo domini*.

In Butler's use of 'precarious life' we can recognise certain echoes of the original usage of the term. There is the possessor without sovereignty, and a 'tenant' with defiant possessory interdicts, whose tenancy-in-life nevertheless does not depend exclusively on the sovereign. Thus, a precarious life could be translated into a life owned, but only tenuously; acquired by supplication, but always open to arbitrary denial or seizure. A precarious life is a life of a 'tenant' who, from the very outset, acquires their tenancy with a great level of uncertainty, in the knowledge that, although obtained for now, the 'rights to tenancy' can be withdrawn at any time. In such a life, one 'begs', even while at the same time expressing defiance against the concatenation of powers on which one depends and over which one cannot be sovereign. In a world characterised by precarisation, the implacable production of adjustments to insecurity (D: 43), precarious life can extend to include insignificance, disposability, a sense of damaged present and an unliveable future.

Put another way, a precarious life is simply the life of the body in the world. Our being in and of the world is what at the same time constitutes and dispossesses us as embodied lives (PL: 24). If dispossession is the removal of that which makes something possible to remain in place (Devenney 2020: 74), we are simultaneously put and removed from our place, which makes both the idea of place and its being ours quite ambivalent.

As the long exchange between Judith Butler and Athena Athanasiou clearly shows, there are two valences to dispossession. One directly refers to loss, denial, deprivation: that is, taking something away, whether land, property, citizenship, basic means of livelihood. In this sense, it is an intended production of loss and deprivation. However, for one to become dispossessed of what belongs to them, one first must be 'dispossessible', that is, not in control of the world on which one still depends with one's belongings. The second valence of dispossession seems to be no less negative, as it points to the limits of one's self-sufficiency and reveals that one is always only partially and incompletely in possession of oneself. Dispossession indicates that dependency and independence are not entirely detached from one another, that relationality is implicated in autonomy, that the world does indeed penetrate through what was thought to be the impenetrable boundary of the skin. In the liberal political imaginary, the second valence has to be understood as deprivative, because 'the "I" is always to some extent dispossessed by the social conditions of its emergence' (GAO: 8), and it is only in and from dispossession that the I can give any account of itself. For Butler and Athanasiou, however, this is what positions the self as a fundamentally social, ecstatic being, moved by forces that precede and exceed it, 'driven by passions it cannot fully consciously ground or know [. . .] dependent on environments and others who sustain and even motivate the life of the self itself' (D: 4). Our being 'out there' contests the idea of an individual as an absolute owner over their primary possession, defined from Locke onwards as life and limb, our living body. Since, as an embodied life, I am inherently dispossessible, I am only ever an incomplete, partial owner of whatever is 'mine'.

When we say that lives are dispossessed, we are in fact underscoring that lives 'take place': we are born into an unchosen world – somewhere, at some moment – in which we continue to lead a complex process of living, an action only partially undertaken autonomously. We are not in control of the various factors on which we depend for our persistence and thriving. Sometimes these factors are epidermalised, as Fanon (1986) described the fundamental other-ing of people of colour; sometimes one is unlucky to be born or live in a war zone; or else one comes from an indebted country, the debt having been taken on against the people's will. We are then not only deprived of a viable status or position, but also assigned a status of deprivation, lack, of a spectral existence, without place, power or possessions.

Butler claims that 'one's life is always in some sense in the hands of the other' (FoW: 14). The 'other' is at times someone we know: perhaps we were the ones to entrust them with our life. At other times, however, the 'other' merely belongs to the world we inhabit, someone I do not know and might never even meet. Lives are thus by definition precarious – because they do not persist in and of them-selves, but are always and from the start given over to the world. Each and every one of us is dependent on a relation between the world and the body that makes our life precarious. No one is in total possession or in complete mastery of an entire social field – of (all) others, of norms, of language, discourses, institutions, infrastruc-tures. In that sense, all life is heavily dependent on sociality. One can, of course, debate its degree, but the fact of dependency is beyond dispute. Precariousness is not the internal feature of a monadic indi-vidual, of this or that life, but a state integral to life itself as a condi-tioned process (FoW: 23).

Since no life has been, as yet, capable of transcending injurability and mortality, precariousness and precarity appear synchronously. Precariousness can be understood as an existential category applica-ble to all lives equally: each life 'begs' for norms that allow for more possibilities, for relations and an infrastructure that enable its thriv-ing. Precarity, on the other hand, is not a generalisable condition of the human, but a politically and socially produced state in which some lives have to 'beg' more not to be exposed to violence and dis-possession. While precariousness refers to the primary vulnerability to injury and loss, precarity is 'a condition of induced inequality and destitution' (D: 20; FoW: 25; NT: 33). The synchronicity of precariousness and precarity is important, because the first does not refer to some pre-political state of the body, to a purely existential condition (Ingala 2018b: 44). Bodies live through materialising possibilities that are available to them, and precariousness is thus always materialised as a particular degree of precarity, which makes it 'indissociable from that dimension of politics that addresses the organization and protection of bodily needs. Precarity exposes our sociality, the fragile and necessary dimension of our interdependency' (NT: 119).

Precariousness of bodily life is a ground for equality among lives (FoW: 22), but it is, at the same time, also the ground for their inequality. Precariousness and dispossessability could be understood as ineradicable human openness to destitution. We all depend on sociality, which is politically organised and managed: the first is what makes us equal, the latter introduces differences in how we are positioned, seen and heard, in the world. This is, upon the whole, why Butler declines to define life. Life is a given, and it is given as precarious, bound to the world, in need of a relation, and in need of a relation that is not violent.

Life That Matters, Grievable Life

At the beginning of this chapter I suggested that liveable life should be understood as a life that can be lived. 'Life worth living' in Judith Butler's philosophy has a different name: grievable life. The notion of grievability appeared in Butler's thought together with precarious life. However, while the latter describes the existential state of human bodies living in the world, grievable life has a regulative function: it says something about the worth ascribed to lives in and by the world. While all lives are precarious, not all are grievable. 'Grievability is a presupposition for the life that matters' (FoW: 14). Such a life is a life that mattered while it was lived, which appeared as worthy of value, and not already lost before it departed (Schneider and Butler 2010).

Recall that 'mattering' is a significant word that previously used to accompany bodies. *Bodies That Matter* showed that not all bodies materialise in a 'proper' way, as they do not all have a stable position in the hegemonic system of signification; in short, not all qualify as fully human. Minority realities that Butler describes as the 'domain of abjected bodies' are deprived of an appropriate place in the established ontology of the human. However, what seems to have interested her most at the time, in 1993, is the potential challenge bodies 'produce to a symbolic hegemony that might force a radical rearticulation of what qualifies as bodies that matter, ways of living that count as "life", lives worth protecting, lives worth saving, lives worth grieving' (BTM: xxiv). Obviously, grieving is already there in

1993, attached to the worth of a fully human life; but its understanding would be greatly expanded after the war-related events of the first decade of the twenty-first century.

The question of grieving – why we feel stricken by grief, why we fail to grieve, and how this failure is socially shaped – has a long trajectory. In an interview with Udi Aloni, Butler gives a short reconstruction of her interest in the conditions under which we fail to grieve for others. From the experience of mourning in the Jewish community in which she was raised, to the postwar generation of German culprits' inability to mourn (as proposed in Mitscherlich and Mitscherlich's widely read study from 1975) to which Butler was drawn as a student, to the unacknowledged emotional loss and stigmatisation of dying and grief for the gay and lesbian communities decimated by AIDS – it is the question of grievability that links early queer politics with war and violence, including her approach to Israel–Palestine (Aloni 2010). In addition, the concept of grievability allowed her to theoretically move away from the inherent singularity of bodies, to lives that can be figured in terms of groups or even populations. Take an example from the era of the AIDS epidemic. Random individuals infected with HIV turned into a strangely coherent population marked as a contagious embodiment of evil, a vampiric sexuality collapsing into something 'sexually exotic, alien, unnatural, oral, anal, compulsive, violent, protean, polymorphic, polyvocal, polysemous, invisible, soulless, transient, superhumanly mobile, infectious, murderous, suicidal, and a threat to wife, children, home, and phallus' (Hanson 1991: 325; on another level of reality, these same people appeared, as Hanson strongly put it, in a 'portrait of a lover as pallbearer' [ibid.: 334]). The AIDS crisis revealed that some lives are worth sustaining, while others are utterly worthless. Similarly, in an armed conflict, there are many lives that do not get to even be pallbearers, or indeed corpses that deserve burial. The logic of distinction between abundant and destructible or superfluous life (Cooper 2008) is embedded in different class, racial and gendered histories of devalued and unrecognised labour all over the world. Soaring inequalities establish lives as valuing, and thus mattering, differently.

Butler has begun to address these issues as directly biopolitical in her latest works, because they are similarly organised around the norm dividing lives into those that need to be protected and mourned, and those effectively dispensable and thus ungrievable. Her work on these issues was prompted, however, by the violent attack on the United States in 2001 and the subsequent 'war on terror', which raised the questions of violence, vulnerability and loss – to some extent already operative in Butler's vocabulary – to a different level. The term '9/11', a shorthand for a string of events that shaped international politics of the early twenty-first century, presented grief, loss and mourning in an entirely new light, giving them entirely new political meaning.

Faced with vulnerability, with injurability, with being wounded or losing our loved ones, how do we respond? Do we retaliate? Should we be ready to – in the name of loss and wound – quickly create new, *insignificant* losses, propping up ungrievability as a value? Should we have the (almost national) duty to recuperate harm done to us, stoking fantasies of invulnerability and impermeability? Or else, do we try to work against such 'horrid masculinism' (Stauffer 2003), attempting instead to become responsive to the shared conditions of life, and politically reimagine the possibility of community on the basis of vulnerability and loss (PL: 20)?

> The question that preoccupies me in the light of recent global violence is, Who counts as human? Whose lives count as lives? And, finally, What *makes for a grievable life*? Despite our differences in location and history, my guess is that it is possible to appeal to a 'we', for all of us have some notion of what is to have lost somebody. Loss has made a tenuous 'we' of us all. (PL: 20)

Because we are socially constituted, loss and vulnerability appear as resources for building a political community. We are 'attached to others, at risk of losing those attachments, exposed to others, at risk of violence by virtue of that exposure' (PL: 20). The primary 'aliena- tion in sociality' (PLP: 28) diagnosed in *The Psychic Life of Power*, from *Precarious Life* onward starts to function as an equalising feature of lives. The capacity to grieve – or, rather, readiness to give ourselves over to grief – to acknowledge the losses of the other, any other, assumes that we apprehend our belonging to the basic com- munity of beings whose only reality is a social one.

It seems that in the works written after 2001, sociality started to have a different valence for Butler, and the notion of grievability contributed immensely to this change. If up to that point Butler was mainly concerned with how certain bodies never really measure up to the social norm, the social now began to appear as a resource rather than an obstacle. The fact that sociality is constitutive for the bonds we share, regardless of our will and predisposition, appears as the contingent foundation for a peculiar social ontology Butler is offering. This move helped her to further hone a position of radical egalitarianism. The profound inequality diagnosed by the theory of performativity transformed into a call for radical equality. Not all lives are grievable, although all are precarious, always and from the start given over to the world. To politically reimagine the social world has to entail the possibility of equal grievability, of lives mattering equally.

Mourning Otherwise

An encounter with grief, which is in a sense an encounter with the loss of relation, shows, above all, that in relations we are always 'beyond ourselves'. This is much more than to say that we are relational beings. It is about an ecstatic quality of humans – of not being our own, being given over to the other without at the same time being owned by them (UG: 149). The other, the relation, is constitutive of who we are. Thus, being beyond ourselves means becoming other than what we are by way of the other, forever incapable of returning to a previous state when the other was not there (GAO: 27). But we are not constitutively beyond ourselves only due to the encounters with the particular 'you's to whom the 'I' is given over. We are thus because we are continuously given over to the world, to sociality. It is the body that makes us the centre of relations due to its 'socially ecstatic structure' (FoW: 33), that is, to being exposed to the willed and unwilled proximity of others, and the circumstances that go beyond our intentions and the power to control them. (This is a recurring thought in Butler. We find it as early as 1986: 'This *ek-static* reality of human beings is, however, a corporeal experience; the body is not a lifeless fact of existence, but a mode of becoming' [Butler 1986: 38].)

Butler believes that grief, a response to loss and vulnerability, can urge us to politically reimagine the possibility of a different community. Our being 'for' and 'by virtue' of another (PL: 24) is particularly acute when we are beyond or beside ourselves with desire or grief. Both are forms of dispossession; they also open us to the apprehension that, being conditioned by relations, we are in fact continuously dispossessed. In grieving, as much as in desiring, it becomes apparent how partial our autonomy is and how our control over life is of necessity compromised by possible losses that are an integral part of life, of an 'I' conditioned and sustained by others, in relations and reciprocity. Loss has the power to deconstitute, but perhaps also reconstitute us, to recompose us anew.

Many have read this attempt at political reimagination of community as problematic, either because it relies too much on melancholic subjectivity derived from a rereading of Freud's account of mourning and melancholia (Freud 1917; McIvor 2012), or because it does not move farther than the 'sofa', where we go to be recomposed in our private losses (Ruti 2017), or else because ethical sensitivity, procured by the ideas of vulnerability, exposure and grief, gets purchased at the cost of the denial of politics (Dean 2008: 109; cf. Honig 2010). What Butler calls a 'you', a someone who matters very much to me, whose loss may completely defragment me and without whom my life would make much less sense, is my very private, ungeneralisable 'you'. If a politics does emerge out of the loss of someone dear, it most often assumes retaliation, creating new losses and more grief. Butler, however, points us in a completely different direction. The many, innumerable 'you's expand into the structure of sociality itself. Opposing the idea that grief is privatising and thus depoliticising, Butler claims that it 'furnishes a sense of political community of a complex order, and it does this first of all by bringing to the fore the relational ties' (PL: 22). It furnishes us at the same time with a sense of fundamental dependency on others, but also on a liveable world. Relationality is thus not conceived 'only as a descriptive or historical fact of our formation, but also as an ongoing normative dimension of our social and political lives, one in which we are compelled to take stock of our interdependence' (PL: 47).

This is where the complex idea of interdependence makes its first appearance. We will return to it at the very end of the next chapter, when other concepts around which it has been built are also introduced. In the Preface to *Precarious Life*, interdependence appears 'inevitable' and as the very 'basis for global political community'; but at the time, Butler confesses to still not knowing how to theorise it (PL: xii–xiii). Interdependence will have immense significance in shaping her understanding of social ontology, organised around the opposition to 'liberal versions of human ontology' (PL: 25). Significantly, however, it was first conceptualised through an encounter with the monstrosities of war. As we shall see, this is also the reason why nonviolence goes hand in hand with interdependence.

Wars are not only legitimised modes of manufacturing death, but also modes of violating relations. The presupposition of any war is the existence of destructible lives, whose loss need not and cannot be grieved. They therefore rest upon a differentiation of lives, on the production of a restricted notion of the human. All wars function as the operationalisation of the unjustifiable right to restrict relations, whereby 'our' relations have value and significance, while others are declared expendable or insignificant, inexistent although they exist. In a vicious cycle of violent retaliation, wars have the force to ultimately annul relations altogether.

Facing the nation at war after 9/11 urged Butler to think of the possibilities of a creation of some 'we' different from and larger than 'us' who share national intimacy. Interdependence and vulnerability would be imagined as the basis for global political community, in contrast to sovereign independence and desired invulnerability of a nation in war. Independence and invulnerability seem to rest upon an enormously exaggerated fantasy of invincibility and inviolability, and the production of grievable and ungrievable losses, based on a unilateral proclamation of what is rational and affective, sensible and memorable. The severe censorship of any kind of critical approach to the power relations that created this political subjectivity sustains the disavowal of responsibility and justifies retaliatory violence. In an atmosphere in which any critique becomes identified with high treason, the erasure of loss is encouraged by the rapidly foreclosed mourning and ensured by the production of new losses through vengeful wounding of others.

This description certainly does not apply only to the 'war on terror'. The so-called Yugoslav wars are but one example, already past recollection in the long line of armed conflicts. In her brilliant study of the political dissidence of the Women in Black, the Belgrade-based group that became the symbol of 'agonistic mourning', Athena Athanasiou shows how war works within a differential distribution of grief. To be a 'we', a kind of aggrandised political individual through whom the nation speaks, we are allowed to mourn only 'our own', only the relations that are lost to us and only those through whom we became exposed to loss. Any form of dissent from national intimacy turns into a transgression, a betrayal. Essentially, however, this betrayal works against the produced restriction of humanness – against 'us' being the exemplary humans, and 'them' less-than-human. The 'betrayal' of Women in Black was a form of collective resistance that arose from loss. It was an attempt to endure and account for loss by creating alternative ties of belonging and maintaining its structural possibility as 'affirmation of the political, from which to resist sovereignty' (Athanasiou 2017: 39, 67). The group's gathering in Belgrade's central square, clad in black and in performative silence, from the autumn of 1991 until today, is an assembly of plural bodies that perform agency in concert (NT: 9). It is also, importantly, a living archive, an embodied counter-memory, an uncanny afterlife of wars that stands bodily in the way of normative forgetfulness and of continual recreation of violence that became institutionalised, both in war and in its aftermath. This 'spatial poetics of self-estrangement' (Athanasiou 2017: 173), of improper mourning in the heart of the city, politicises affectivity, reclaiming both the *polis* and the courage belonging not to a heroic warrior, but to a 'situated performative ethos of collective endurance, resistance, and political engagement' (ibid.: 242).

Returning to the events inaugurated by 9/11, Başak Ertür reconstructs what happens when the idea of a political community based on loss and vulnerability fails to take root. Violence acquires performative and symbolic autonomy, becoming something of a culture and institution unto itself. The limits to dissenting public discourses were used to legitimise violence. Later, they will not only become institutionalised through law, but also governmentalised through radicalisation discourses that create varieties of 'terrorists' all over the world – among them, groups like 'Academics for Peace' who support a peaceful solution to the Kurdish-Turkish conflict. Vulnerability was not understood as an ineliminable part of sociality that invites us to accommodate it in our critical imaginaries of our unchosen cohabitation. Instead, it began to have an increasingly institutionalised political life of its own. Such is the case, for example, with 'vulnerability to radicalisation', which becomes a problem addressed through risk management and resilience-building, shoring up a paternalist, securitarian and ever more interventionist state (Ertür 2017: 69–72; cf. Butler, Gambetti and Sabsay 2016). In retrospect, the hegemonic discourse produced by the long-lasting 'war on terror' started to shape the spaces and conditions of thought 'partially because it thrives on war: the more prolonged the military war, the more its autonomously generative formations play havoc with the viability and audibility of critical registers in which historicities and temporalities of violence may be understood' (Ertür 2017:73).

Notes

1. In an applied politics sense, this can be, of course, a very disorienting direction, if a direction at all. This brings us back to the question of

political agency. However, in the spirit of the performative theory of agency, we can say that the performative insurrection has its own direct political forms. 'If resistance is to enact the very principles of democracy for which it struggles, then resistance has to be *plural* and it has to be *embodied*. It will also entail the gathering of the ungrievable in public space, marking their existence and their demand for livable lives, the demand to live a life *prior* to death, simply put' (NT: 216).

2. Let us stay with women for a moment longer, and consider the confounding phrase 'women's human rights'. What this doubling of women and humans – at first glance paradoxical – seems to convey is that 'human' was somehow too narrow to encompass women as well. As if glued on, 'women' here appear as a necessary correction of the human. A demand for women's human rights transforms the idea of what the human is and what human rights may be, highlighting that the value of 'human' is not equally distributed among humans. However, if 'women' then starts to work as an identity, based on the internal boundaries of the idea of 'woman', it may become yet another site of differentiation among humans. When it too starts to produce exclusions, its role ceases to be socially transformative. On the contrary, it becomes conservative, remaining steadfast only in the demand for expansion of space within the existing order, standing in the way of possibilities it initially opened up in the limited and limiting notion of the human.

3. Butler is here clearly referring to *The Human Condition*, and we can suppose that she had the ancient *polis* in mind. However, this claim largely applies to the contemporary neoliberal *homo economicus* as well. In *Undoing the Demos*, published in the same year as *Notes Toward a Performative Theory of Assembly*, Wendy Brown develops this point in detail, arguing that women, being the main provisioners of care in households, schools and workplaces, remain 'the invisible structure for all developing, mature, and worn-out human capital – children, adults, disabled, elderly' (2015: 105). This responsibility is still formulated as an effect of nature, not of power. In truth, unlike in the times of the Athenian *polis*, those positioned as women in the sexual division of labour which neoliberal order continues to reproduce, today have a choice: either they themselves also become *homo economicus*, 'in which case the world becomes uninhabitable, or women's activities and bearing as *femina domestica* remain the unavowed glue for a world whose governing principle cannot hold it together, in which case women occupy their old place as unacknowledged props and supplements to masculinist liberal subjects' (ibid.: 104–5).

Chapter 5

Nonviolence

Politics and Ethics of Nonviolence

A long paragraph towards the end of the first chapter of *Undoing Gender* gathers together several important political conclusions of the first phase of Butler's work:

> We must ask [. . .] what humans require in order to maintain and repro-
> duce the conditions of their own livability? And what are our politics
> such that we are, in whatever way is possible, both conceptualizing the
> possibility of the livable life, and arranging for its institutional support?
> There will always be disagreement about what this means, and those
> who claim that a single political direction is necessitated by virtue of this
> commitment will be mistaken. But this is only because to live is to live
> a life politically, in relation to power, in relation to others, in the act of
> assuming responsibility for a collective future. To assume responsibility
> for a future, however, is not to know its direction fully in advance, since
> the future, especially the future with and for others, requires a certain
> openness and unknowingness; it implies becoming part of a process the
> outcome of which no one subject can surely predict. It also implies that
> a certain agonism and contestation over the course of direction will and
> must be in play [. . .] It may also be that life itself becomes foreclosed
> when the right way is decided in advance, when we impose what is right
> for everyone and without finding a way to enter into community, and to
> discover there the 'right' in the midst of cultural translation. (UG: 39)

Nearly all key notions are here: life in relation to power, in relation
to others, liveable life as human life, conditions of liveability (liveable world), unknowingness, the political *in medias res*, futurity,
radical democracy and cultural translation. To be sure, some hesitation is also discernible, chiefly in regard to the nature of the 'new'
that opens when we act in concert and in plurality, but these seem to
belong to all collective struggles starting with equality. Missing from
this note on political performativity is an answer to the question: on
what ground is equality maintained within the agonistic, plural and
embodied voices that demand translation and, through translation,

access to the universal and its limitless extension? The answer requires the introduction of the notion that all lives are precarious and need to be grievable: the existential, structural trait common to all socially conditioned beings, and the normative, political ideal of equality.

As the quote underscores, one political direction – what road do we take towards the liveable life? – is neither sufficient, nor possible in a radically democratic contestation. There is no single normative sketch of the good life, a single methodology that could abolish all bad forms of life. In line with this, there is no single politically pertinent way to reach and maintain the radical aim of equality. Collective struggles which continue their life translated into certain global obligations belong to one plane of the political. The other plane refers to a decisive repudiation of violence, something that has the potential to transform the political here and now. *The Force of Nonviolence: Ethico-Political Bind* can be understood as the most direct exposition of this idea. As suggested by its subtitle, the book has a strong ethical aspect, missing in overt form from the paragraph quoted above.

Needless to say, the debate on Butler's 'ethical turn' produced a wide array of reactions, but two main lines are easy to detect: one locates her interest in ethics as a newer development, the other sees it as a continuation of her thought (Loizidou 2007; Mills 2007; Chambers and Carver 2008; Thiem 2008; Honig 2010; Rushing 2010; Murphy 2011; Stark 2014; Lloyd 2015; Karhu 2016). The debate centres around the issue of what happens to the political with the sudden onrush of 'ethical' categories, such as grievability, vulnerability, responsibility, grief and precariousness. For many, the 'ethical turn' meant the abandonment of action in favour of the vulnerable body and a strong departure from subversive politics.

At first, Butler demonstrated a certain hesitancy towards ethics, discernible in her texts and interviews published at the turn of the century. For example, the edited volume *The Turn to Ethics* features Butler's contribution entitled 'Ethical Ambivalence' (2000). Roughly at the same time, in a conversation with William Connolly, she 'confesses to worrying about the turn to ethics', as she tends to think 'that ethics displaces from politics, and I suppose for me the use of power as a point of departure for a critical analysis is substantially different from an ethical framework' (Butler and Connolly 2000). Reading Antigone through Hegel's rendering of the figure in the *Phenomenology of Spirit* section on 'The Ethical Life' (where

Antigone ends up being defined as the 'irony of community'), Butler sees her as an impossibly ethical character who is, precisely for this reason, political, laying 'claim to a rageful agency within the public sphere' (AC: 31, 35). Two relevant texts also appeared in 2001: a reading of Foucault's understanding of critique as virtue, and a prelude to her 'first extended study of moral philosophy'. In the latter, she attempts a grounding of personal or social responsibility, despite working with a theory of a subject that is not self-grounding (Butler 2001b: 22). Both the text on Foucault and her early version of 'Giving an Account of Oneself' investigate the possibility of ethics within the horizon of norms (GAO: 25). We may claim, however, that all these texts retain a level of ambivalence.

It seems that Butler was ready to explore some kind of vague ethical position, the need for which appeared from the moment persistence in alterity – in sociality – came to be understood as the precondition of persistence in one's own being (PLP: 28; Barbec 2017). The ethical was never meant to replace the political, or to take its privileged place. It has been part and parcel of Butler's understanding of the social which both constitutes and dispossesses us, making us continuously vulnerable to terms we did not make, but for which, in a very performative way, we may well be responsible. Although we can claim that this is what Butler's philosophy has been about from the very start, it becomes explicit from the moment when she begins to underscore sociality as constitutive for the bonds we share. The experience of war and the call for a global political community also engendered another very important question: what does it mean to share a violent bond, one that does violence, a bond through which we act and are acted upon violently? However, it needs to be mentioned that from the very introduction of ethical issues, 'an ethics of non-violence' (Butler 2000) appeared as a crucial.

I propose we take up nonviolence as the point where performativity and precarity meet. I take my cue here from *The Force of Nonviolence*, which I will be following in this chapter, claiming that nonviolence is a way of acknowledging social relation (FN: 9). This critical extension might seem peculiar, but in fact follows from the elaboration of social reality or the social world detailed in the previous chapters. If performativity is about the relation between bodies and norms, if transformative agency is about possibilities to remake this relation, and if liveable life requires a liveable world, then nonviolence also appears in the midst of this relation, albeit with an ethico-political twist. Nonviolence translates into doing something with the fact that persistence in sociality is a condition of persistence in one's own being.

There is a relation between the body and the world that needs to be acknowledged in order for anyone to persist in the world. The meaning of the word 'acknowledgement' is not univocal here. It assumes action; it assumes working through ethical obligations that appear together with others being thrown into the world, with us and just like us; it also assumes a critique of what counts as reality, and acceptance of a certain unknowingness as the point of departure of agency. 'When the world presents as a force field of violence, the task of nonviolence is to find ways of living and acting in *that world*' (FN: 10, italics mine). Living is, thus, already acting when presented with a task 'such that violence is checked or ameliorated, or its direction turned, precisely at moments when it seems to saturate the world and offer no way out' (FN: 15).

Nonviolence does not rest on sympathy, love or identification with some or even all people, but on an assumption of a common world, built by those like us who we do not and cannot know. At this juncture, 'moral and political philosophy meet, with consequences for both how we end up doing politics, and what world we seek to help bring into being' (FN: 7). A specific 'bringing world into being', nonviolent performativity is thus based on ethical and political obligations we have simply by virtue of being part of the world.

Trajectory of Violence

To say that violence is a newer theme in Butler's work would require yet more 'careful reading'. As I claimed at the very beginning, we would not be wrong in saying that her entire oeuvre can be read as a philosophical struggle for the reduction of violence. That said, as Emma Ingala insightfully shows (2019: 192), violence appears under many names: as material, categorical, normative, textual, social, epistemic, ethical, legal and state violence, and is understood as a physical, linguistic, emotional, institutional and economic phenomenon – but is rarely defined (cf. Ingala 2021). In this section, which seeks to provide the trajectory of the performative movement of the notion of violence, I rely on Ingala's division into two phases of Butler's work. In the first, the notion of violence appears mostly under the name of normative violence, 'inherent to the normalization involved in the process of subjectivation and, in particular, of gender norms' (ibid.). From *Precarious Life* onwards, violence is much more related to vulnerability and the fundamental precariousness of bodily life. What, according to Ingala, connects the two phases is the understanding of violence as 'the stabilisation or petrification of a particular worldview that is thereafter represented as natural and definitive. Non-violence, on the contrary, is conceived as the interruption or suspension of this stabilization, as an opening to other possible worlds' (ibid.).

When related to how gender norms work, violence is termed normative (GT: xix–xx). We become our gender through performing the possibilities available to us. If those are circumscribed, our performances will be too. But the constraint to perform in line with what possibilities there are, to become a man or woman (although one is not born one), goes together with certain violence. Recall that performances are never self-referential and unconditioned, but take place within rigid, regulatory frames. The girl-subject becomes a girl because she grows into a maze of symbolic demands, taboos, sanctions, injunctions, prohibitions, idealisations and threats: as a girl, you ought not behave in this way; girls are such and such; this is how you too must be; in order to be a real girl, you have to do such and such; if you behave like this, you are not a real girl, and so on. Because embedded in structures that shape our body and psyche long before we are capable of judgement or decision, normative violence does not appear as violence at all. It is not something we (consciously) give consent to; it is, rather, something that builds on the sphere of the unconsenting. Denaturalisation of norms – probably the main task of both *Gender Trouble* and *Bodies That Matter* – shows that what we experience and understand as real, as given and beyond our action, is in fact very much enacted and established as real. The process of establishment involves the constraint to enact precisely those possibilities as real. Denaturalisation of norms, the removal of the veil of naturalness from something so fundamentally social, disrupts 'the ideal morphological constraints upon the human', lifting the sentence of death within life from 'those who fail to approximate the norm' (GT: xx). Such a fate – known well to Antigone, unwilling to submit to the norms of the *polis* and gender order on which the *polis* is dependent – is essentially violent.

But the physical side of violence of the norm can never be underestimated. Under Wittig's influence, Butler insisted long ago that violence enacted against people turned into 'sexed' objects can be understood as a violent enforcement of a category. Enforcement – the crimes against people reduced to their 'sex' – can be seen as the violent social action of the category/norm itself (GT: 225; cf. Karhu 2016). Normative violence *'enables* the typical physical violence that we routinely recognise and simultaneously *erases* such violence from our ordinary view' (Chambers and Carver 2008: 76). A physical blow or strike is neither the only nor even a privileged form of violence; it belongs to broader structures of normative violence. Importantly, however, the threat, the harm and injury are embodied (FN: 137). Lest we forget, Antigone dies rather than succumb to the norm.

Bodies become gendered through their involvement in everyday performances of gender ideals. These ideals are real – but their reality resides neither in the Platonic world of ideas nor in the natural configuration of the body. They are real on condition of their social performativity. The norm does not exist in itself: it is continually embodied and acted out under constraint (itself an effect of sedimentation of acts) and through social practices that re-idealise and re-institute it 'in and through the daily social rituals of bodily life' (UG: 48). Re-idealisation and re-institution of the norm confirm certain possibilities as real and suspend others as unreal. This suspension is violent because it rests upon exclusions we all perform daily, thus contributing to the ossification of certain possibilities. In a binary-configured reality (rather than a plural one), there are bodies that remain unaccounted and uncounted.

What is the exact nature of normative violence? If it is central to the petrification of the real, can it be said to have an ontological status? Catherine Mills and Ann Murphy offered such an argument, in an attempt to account for what they see as the rift between the articulations of normative and ethical violence. I agree with Mills that Butler was from the beginning 'dedicated to developing a critical ontology of embodied subjectivity and an account of the possibilities of political transformation' (Mills 2007: 135). But her ontology entails that the subject who wishes to be ethical and advocate for a nonviolent ethics is constrained by the norms and dependent on their constitutive violence (ibid.: 148). Similarly, for Murphy, the very possibility of non-violent ethics is compromised by the profound difference between ontological, transcendental violence and ethical violence that properly belongs to the domain of moral philosophy (Murphy 2011: 199). Is normative violence ontological? Is bodily reality violent, and is it necessarily thus? Butler dismisses this argument (Butler 2007a): ontologisation of norms not only ontologises violence, but also bodily performances that govern themselves according to supposedly transcendental norms. The ontological status of violence reintroduces determinism, leaving even less room for agency, and thus for reality to be re-enacted differently and – what is particularly important to Butler – less violently (GT: xxiii).

The hypothesis of the ontological status of normative violence overlooks the importance of the double movement of performativity: the interrelatedness of norms and bodies, and the processual character of reality. The double movement – acting and being acted upon – is captured well by the notions of materialisation/embodiment (of the norm and the body itself). Norms become material, real in and through bodies that materialise them; bodies become material and mattering by materialising the norm. Reality does not consist of transcendental norms and static bits of matter, but of reiterative processes of embodiment. Materialisation is a 'kind of citationality, the acquisition of being through the citing of power, a citing that establishes an originary complicity with power in the formation of the "I"' (BTM: xxiii). The process of becoming something, materialising into an embodied self, becoming an 'I', assumes a compliance with that which procures being. With each repetition, the 'I' affirms that the acquisition of being has taken place in precisely that way. And if what procures being is restrictive, constraining and violent, then materialisation will also contain an element of violence. Nonetheless, as shown in the chapter on agency, citationality contains within itself the possibility of its own deconstitution. There is no necessity in the way processes of materialisation are structured: even if violence is constitutive in established reality – as it is, by becoming differently, we open up possibilities of nonviolence. Constraint is not the same as necessity – 'even if norms originated in violence, it would not follow that the fate of norms is only and always to reiterate the violence at their origin. And it would also still be possible that if norms continued to exercise violence, they do not always exercise it in the same way' (Butler 2007a: 183).

Contrary to Mills and Murphy, I suggest we understand normative violence in terms of effects the constraint has on bodies. Violence of norms appears as a restricted set of possibilities within the real established by repetition. Those bodies that do not materialise the norm (due to a lack of appropriate possibilities in the given real) appear as impossible, and are thus harmed by the norm or are more open to harm and injury. If what is established through repetition is a relation between the body and the world, then some bodies are violently foreclosed from a relation, while others are part of a harmful and violent relation.

The possibility of social transformation – but also, significantly, of nonviolence – appears only within the real and in the midst of repetition, but through displacement or the rerouting of violent effects of the norms. This is at the heart of agency: although our actions might be conditioned towards enacting or producing violence, there is nothing that completely predetermines us to act in a given way. The possibility of doing otherwise is contained in the acting itself, allowing us also to reject the restrictive norms and their violent effects, as well as appeal to 'a norm of nonviolence' (UG: 220). From the perspective of established reality, such an appeal may seem insurrectionary, or indeed subversive. But it is certainly possible (as a possibility in the relation between the body and the world), and even necessary if we wish to advocate for equality: because norms do not only refer to 'the regulatory or normalizing function of power, but from another perspective, norms are precisely what binds individuals together, forming the basis of their ethical and political claims' (UG: 219).

With life and liveability, normative violence moves into the background. Of course, this shift in focus needs to be taken with caution, because, for example, normative violence appears in *Frames of War* as 'the norms of gender through which I come to understand myself or my survivability' (FoW: 53), while in *The Force of Nonviolence* we find it again under the name of racial, gender and sexual violence. With liveable life and the concomitant issues, new types of questions emerge. The ethical query is how to allow the human to be something that does not already exist in the sphere of the accepted and established. How is it possible to allow its rearticulation 'in the name of a more capacious and, finally, less violent world, not knowing in advance what precise form our humanness does and will take' (UG: 35)?

The generalisation of this issue – how to think of a world where all lives are liveable? – began to strongly foreground another perspective on norms. In it, norms are binding and the basis of ethical and political claims. An appeal to a norm of nonviolence is, as is self-evident, an appeal to a norm, one which is, so to say, already present, provided by the relation between the body and the world. The question then is, how to think of a world in which violence is not what socially configures us to fit into an established social reality. A possible suggestion, if we follow Butler, is to generalise the idea of vulnerability.

Therefore, violence of (gender) norms foregrounds humans who are particularly exposed to the violence of exclusion, (non-) appearance, lack of recognition. Normative violence limits plurality, producing and maintaining narrowed possibilities, which renders certain bodies particularly vulnerable. Many of these people are today lumped together under an administrative label of 'vulnerable groups'. However, in the second phase of Butler's work, the implied dyad – the vulnerables and the invulnerables – is problematised differently. 'When vulnerability is owned as an exclusive predicate of one subject and invulnerability attributed to another, a different kind of disavowal takes place' (Butler, Gambetti and Sabsay 2016: 4). Vulnerability belongs to the configuration of the body, but the body is always living only in the (social) world; it is given over to sociality. Although inextricable from our embodiedness and, in that sense, an existential condition, vulnerability is, at the same time, materialised differently by different bodies. Seen as living sets of relations, bodies are also socially and politically conditioned into being, which makes them more or less exposed to precarity and dispossession.

If an appeal to the norm of nonviolence emerges in *Undoing Gender*, *Precarious Life* announces the necessity of a non-violent ethics based on the understanding of the ease with which human life is annulled (PL: xxvii). Normative violence already assumes that the human functions as a differential norm. Lives that are less real or unreal, condemned to unliveability, are seen, felt and thought of as lacking a human face. They can therefore be erased, expunged, deleted, obliterated or destroyed – ef*face*d. Violence dehumanises and thus derealises. It turns one into something unreal, it negates one's reality, it suspends it in a point where one is neither dead nor alive (UG: 25; PL: 33). In that sense, Butler's critique of normative violence already contained the seed of a critique that would develop into an explicit anti-war and antimilitarist stance. Butler has spoken of peace only on rare occasions, describing it once as 'active and difficult resistance to the temptation of war [. . .] something that has to be vigilantly maintained [. . .] a commitment to living with certain kind of vulnerability to others and susceptibility to being wounded that actually gives our individual lives meaning' (Stauffer 2003). This understanding of peace is, I believe, what has engendered the notion of nonviolence as an active struggle against violence.

An insurrection at the level of ontology leads us to question what is real, whose lives are real and whose derealised, and whether violence takes place due to that unreality. But, importantly, it also urges us to think how reality might be remade (PL: 33). This remaking has as its goal a reality that will accommodate more real lives, and less violence that circumscribes the real. This goal is, however, not remote, located in a far-away future when we will have become better humans. If our reality becomes established through our own acting, and if one is consistent in rejecting the fantasy of full sovereignty and transcendence of power, then within the given circumstances, *in medias res*, we can open up to a transformation of what we are and become different(ly). Nonviolence – or, rather, consequent, vigilant and active rejection of violence – becomes a political form of rearticulation and displacement of violent norms: acting that opens up to that which is new, yet is already present, 'within the terms of performance'.

Again, two extreme poles of interpretation emerge from a discussion of (non)violence. On the one hand, violence in Butler is read as ontological, fundamental to reality itself. For this reason, it cannot be eliminated or diminished, making the call to nonviolence meaningless because impossible. The other direction remains dissatisfied with the ostensibly low transformative stake of the ethical demands of nonviolence. Since the theory of performativity is stubbornly silent on the reality that emerges 'after' normative violence, and since it does not insist on this or that (type of gendered) world as best, nor rest on a prescription to 'subvert gender in the way I say, and life will be good' (GT: xxi) – it appears too indeterminate, politically translating into a seeming lack of combativeness, even passivity.

It appears that both interpretative poles remain entrenched in the already existing alternatives: there is either no possibility of change and all struggle is a priori meaningless, or a struggle is indeed possible, but requires normative foundations, a predetermined subject of struggle, a plan of action and elaborate description of what is to be achieved by this action and, possibly, yes, a certain 'ultimate violence'. What Butler proposes is forging another path, which would itself be non-violent: reject the violent unchangeability and search for modes of action in the present, without recourse to ultimate violence that promises to abolish violence altogether. I propose we heed these profoundly feminist words:

> Women know this question well [. . .] There is the possibility of appearing impermeable, of repudiating vulnerability itself. Nothing about being socially constituted as women restrains us from simply becoming violent ourselves. And then there is the other age-old option, the possibility of wishing for death or becoming dead, as a vain effort to preempt or deflect

the next blow. But perhaps there is some other way to live such that one becomes neither affectively dead nor mimetically violent, a way out of the circle of violence altogether. This possibility has to do with *demanding a world* in which bodily vulnerability is protected without therefore being eradicated. (PL: 42, italics mine)

It is precisely from a certain kind of feminist perspective that Butler draws a demand for a liveable world, for a non-violent relation between the body and the world. This perspective shapes a critique of a presumptively masculine idea of a self-sufficient and a-social subject, embedded in liberal versions of ontology. 'Surely the critique of the idea that any of us can exist outside a condition of dependency is an important, enduring contribution of feminist theory and politics' (Antonello and Farneti 2009). From such critique springs the need, itself ethical and political, for a world in which vulnerability would not figure as weakness that needs hiding or protection, but a demand for conditions that make the liveable life more plausible for more living beings (Butler 2018: 249). A demand for such conditions can be decidedly normative, such as in the form of global obligations, whereby we gather to formulate and demand whatever needs to be taken into account for a liveable life to be possible. But it can also be performative, whereby we seek in our 'action to sustain a world without which life itself is imperilled [. . .] which allows us to understand performativity as part of an ethical philosophy, if not a form of social praxis' (ibid.).

A Relation between the Body and the World

At the beginning of this chapter, nonviolence was described as a way of acknowledging a social relation. Although social relation could be considered the main subject of this book, the last pages will be specifically devoted to the closer elaboration of four key concepts directly related to it: vulnerability, interdependence, plurality and cohabitation. These concepts cover different, but overlapping, dimensions of life in and of the body. These dimensions are emphatically unchosen, but are in play by the mere fact that we are embodied in the world.

Recall that Butler was engaged in a 'specifically philosophical exercise in exposing and tracing the installation and operation of false universals' (Butler 1993b: 30), that may as well be understood as the metaphysical foundations of thinking and acting. This exercise appeared in *Gender Trouble* under the name of 'genealogy of gender ontology' (GT: 45). As I have hinted throughout the book, in the texts written after 2001, something that could be called alternative ontology began to be articulated, in many ways surpassing the framework of gender ontology. However, shifting the focus from gender as such was by no means the removal of focus from that which is gendered. At the heart of this alternative ontology – different to metaphysical, humanist, liberal versions of ontology – are bodies. If 'we are to make broader social and political claims about rights to protection and entitlements to persistence and flourishing, we will first have to be supported by a new bodily ontology' (FoW: 2). Given that bodily reality is social, a reference to ontology would not presume a description of structures that are distinct from how these structures are organised and maintained socially and politically: their enactment is part of their ontology (NT: 61). Bodies are in their very being 'given over to others, to norms, to social and political organisations that have developed historically in order to maximize precariousness for some and minimize precariousness for others' (FoW: 2–3). Thus, the ontology of the body is a social ontology, which turns its subject 'less [into] a discrete substance than an active and transitive set of interrelations' (FoW: 147). In effect, this means that we cannot extract bodies from their constituting relations. Our constitutive vulnerability should not be considered as a subjective state, pertaining to the vulnerability of the body alone, but as a feature of our interdependent lives (FN: 45). Bodies are vulnerable to history, to culture, to economic arrangements in which they desire to persist (NT: 148).

This exposure that is vulnerability can be understood either as exposure to lack and loss, or as an opening to possibility of relation (Devenney 2020: 75). Either way, it signals a certain form of relationality, a dependence on relation. Bodies are undeniably spatial and this spatiality is precisely part of their exposure. As bodies, we take up place. And regardless of our being singular, we do not take up place alone. We are thus exposed and vulnerable to an unchosen plurality of others, on whom we depend in various ways. As bodies in the world we are dependent on a relation. Neither body nor world are pure existentials, however. The world into which we are born and in which we live is a social one. Yet it is the same world in which plurality can be articulated or restricted (binarised) – in it, the relation on which one depends can be given or foreclosed – indeed, in which our exposure makes us differently vulnerable to relations or their lack.

The corporeal facts of vulnerability, interdependence, plurality and cohabitation are fundamentally unchosen. They are constitutive for our existence, but we can make no decisions about them as such. We can try to make certain decisions in order to lessen vulnerability or even out its distribution, but no one can ever decide to be invulnerable. Or, consider our dependency on infrastructure. If there is no road, we could decide to make one (no easy task, since no one builds a road on their own). But in order to move, in the most basic sense, freely and safely, we depend on the existence of roads. There is no prior decision for this dependency. It, rather, motivates decisions, it urges to work and organise with others, for a road we will all use and make part of our common good. Interdependence – my dependence on infrastructure, on other people, on political decisions, on social norms (for example, that I, as a woman, will be free and safe to move on that road alone) – is a heteronomous condition of autonomy.

Our existence on Earth is largely a matter of coincidence: no one chooses to be born, nor indeed where, in what body, nor the way one is raised – the content of the first administrative paper that stamps our existence lies beyond our will. We are thrown into the world and become part of it, along with all others who are here equally coincidentally. The 'we' is plural and cohabiting, space-sharing. I can survive – but also the notion of plurality can survive – on condition that the basic postulate of our common thrownness in the world is acknowledged: whoever is here already, has a right to be here.

This alternative, social, bodily ontology is premised on the following: there is an undeniable plurality of bodies that seek protection and sustenance; bodies are dependent on the world that sustains their survival or threatens it, and they occupy space together in an unchosen cohabitation. The body and the world are indeed neither separated nor separable, as the bond between them comes about through our acting, as much as the acting is itself conditioned by it. The ethical and political question is how to demand radical equality based on these premises, and how to struggle against violence that in such circumstances always presents itself as a viable, even desirable option.

Does an Individual Have a Body?

The alternative ontology Butler claims to offer is developed in opposition to its 'liberal versions' (PL: 25), or against 'ontology of individualism' (FoW: 19). The emphasis on the *social* status may lead us to conclude that *socius* is missing from the liberal version of the story about the real, the story that begins and often ends with the individual. The emphatic stress on the body may as well lead us to presume that in the dominant versions of the story on reality, body has a peripheral, less significant position. Finally, some of the basic categories of this alternative ontology invite an understanding which in a certain way recomposes the entities it operates with, considering them not just as traits or episodic dispositions of a discrete unit, but rather as 'a mode of relationality that time and again calls some aspect of that discreteness into question' (NT: 130). What remains of an individual when put through this sieve?

First and foremost, the individual is not an expected concept in Butler's opus. The characters of her stories are 'I', the self, 'you',[1] 'we'. Before *The Force of Nonviolence*, the individual is not given any substantial attention, and appears only in passing (e.g., PLP: 10–11). In *Precarious Life* it surfaces together with sovereign autonomy and grief, when Butler suggests that grief displays relationality in ways that challenge the very notion of ourselves as autonomous and in control. It is precisely in this context that the liberal versions of human ontology appear as insufficient to elucidate the disposition of ourselves outside ourselves, something that follows from our being for and by virtue of the other. Autonomy is scrutinised in *Giving an Account of Oneself*, a long response to the critics of poststructuralism, which tries to consider the responsibility of an ecstatic subject (who is again, *stricto sensu*, not an individual). In *Frames of War* and *Parting Ways*, an alternative social ontology is fully developed: its point of departure is a shared reality that differs profoundly from the one inhabited by discrete individuals in liberal ontologies. The subjects of alternative ontology are distinct, but not discrete; in common, but unchosen; in bodies that are at once never fully their own; laying claims of autonomy over one's self, yet never entirely independent of relations and infrastructures, and constitutively exposed to their loss. However, Butler is careful not to name these subjects in any specific way.

There is one significant place in *Frames of War* that invites us to challenge the premise of the dual ontologies, separating the individual, the singular 'one', from the group, in order not to lose the social aspect of their ontology (FoW: 166). The 'group' would later indeed be theorised as the performative assembly, a 'we' that is embodied, plural and acting politically in concert. We are told that concerted action is not a sum of discrete individual acts, in the same way that the 'alliance is not reducible to a collection of individuals, and it is, strictly speaking, not individuals who act' (NT: 84).

Butler takes from Arendt the idea of a self conceived as plurality, as a kind of a 'federated self', a subject inherently relational (D: 122). However, she resists Arendt's elaboration of the basic human condition, in which humans act as singular in a space created between people acting in concert. Instead, Butler will move 'plurality' out of the Arendtian philosophically timeless realm of 'human beings', and into the changing social and political realm (Pulkkinen 2018: 138–9). Nevertheless, the 'we' of alliances and assemblies, borrowed from Arendt but remodelled, still does not seem to tell us more about the individual. What happens to those who act once alliance is disbanded, once the self becomes un-federated? We do not know, because an individual remains in the background, behind Butler's other conceptual tools.

We should recall, however, that the politically performative 'we' is not the only 'we' Butler theorised. There is still a generalisable 'we' that emerges in the context of vulnerability and loss. At the time, this other 'we' appeared too tenuous to Butler to serve as ground for a critique of the individual (PL: 20). But, reading Butler, Adriana Cavarero shows no doubt about the name of the autonomous and sovereign subject that thinks of itself as closed and self-sufficient: 'this is the well-known subject, also called "the individual", that "shores itself up, seeks to reconstitute its imagined wholeness, but only at the price of denying its own vulnerability, its dependency, its exposure"' (Cavarero 2011: 21). For Cavarero, Butler gives sufficient reason for the claim that the well-known figure of the individual cannot be generalised into the 'we' that Butler wished to politically establish. Such a 'we' would take into account our partial discreteness, the fact that we are sustained by our many relations with the world, which are part of the ecstatic nature of the embodied self. Thus, whatever 'we' gets created by the subjects of such an ontology, it seems right to ask whether an individual, the cornerstone of the 'liberal version of ontology', can even remain its integral part.

A 'critique of individualism' finally appears in *The Force of Nonviolence*, as part of the debate on what is real and therefore politically realisable. Butler writes that quite a few of her interlocutors proclaim the advancement of nonviolence as entirely unrealistic; as a provocation, but possibly also to make us think how we conceive of the real, believing that realism is devoid of fictitiousness, she returns to another potent political fiction, that of the state of nature. By doing so, Butler is only joining the long line of those who scrutinised the fictiveness of this (allegedly) paradigmatically pre-political framework. Nevertheless, I suggest we read this differently. Without referencing any specific story from the state of nature, she says that,

> in the state of nature, we are already, for some reason, individuals, and we are in conflict with one another. We are not given to understand how we became individuated, nor are we told precisely why conflict is the first of our passionate relations, rather than dependency or attachment. (FN: 30)

The fact that originary people are depicted as warring is what concerns her primarily, but it turns out that the fabric from which they are produced is also significant.

This frieze sequence outside space and time offers a story of the 'beginning', in which it is precisely the beginning that is problematic: the warring individuals are not entirely formless and faceless, although they lack proper social names and recognisable forms of communication that would later temper their thuggish character. In the state of nature – which is the state of *our* nature – actors, who are individuals, have the following features: they are men, adults, self-sufficient and left to their own resources. When a natural individual encounters another natural individual, they use all available pre-social means of self-defence, which results in a spiral of reciprocal violence, stoppable only by an improbable contractual agreement of truce. This is an 'ontology of unbinding' (Cavarero 2011: 23), of atomised self-preserving 'wolves', bound only later and through contract, the liberal subject's most cherished form of 'relationality'.

Upon reflection, it is highly unusual that one such fiction became something so unobjectionable, to be used as grounds for defence of political realism. The individual is, of course, the most appropriate subject for liberal versions of ontology, the reality of which (after the 'first' contract) consists of self-sufficient monads detached from the world, independent from its relations and one from another. They first live in the world alone, and only subsequently and almost accidentally in relations they choose, shaping them according to their will and best judgement. The individual – the one, the undivided – is not only independent, but owes its self-actualisation solely to itself, and is in complete possession of itself (Zaharijević 2021b). 'Not only has the individual a property in his own person and capacities [. . .] it is this property, this exclusion of others [from them], that makes a man human' (Macpherson 1993: 142). The individual is in control over their place in the world – a rather hazier, changing *mise en scène* than something constitutively related to the individual. As a matter of fact, the sovereignty of the individual lies precisely in a certain invulnerability to the world, which however needs to be further secured by binding contracts.

The reality of the liberal version of ontology, extending the fictionalisation of its remarkable beginnings ad infinitum, after the state of natural war has been placed under unnatural control, differs fundamentally from what Butler suggests. Paraphrasing Simone de Beauvoir, Butler says the story

> begins this way: every individual emerges in the course of the process of individuation. No one is born an individual; if someone becomes an individual over time, he or she does not escape the fundamental conditions of dependency in the course of that process. (FN: 40–1)

Fundamental conditions of dependency are not some subsequent features transferred from the social world into a state of nature. If we care to actually imagine the state of our 'nature', the conditions would include our embodiedness. However one imagines the situation that comes after the 'social transformation of nature', the body continues to exist in its dependent, vulnerable and precarious way. Erasing – or rather denying – those features, one erases and denies that we come as bodies.

To be sure, embodiedness and other non-virile dimensions of existence are not erased *in toto*. One could assume that even in the story of the state of nature there were children, infirm or ailing adults, perchance even some women. These characters, however, have no significance for the warfare plot. The figure of the human emerging onto the world is gendered, 'but not by a social assignment; rather, it is because he is an *individual*' that 'the primary and founding figure of the human is masculine. That comes as no surprise; masculinity is defined by its lack of dependency (and that is not exactly news, but it continues somehow to be quite startling)' (FN: 37). The masculine figure is also, emphatically, not a child, as children are creatures totally consigned to relationship, in a condition of total defencelessness, as Cavarero says (2011: 30–1). This invisibility – or, at best, selective visibility – is integral to the regulative ideal of the liberal version of ontology populated by 'bodiless' beings, where everyone is an individual. The moment one steps onto the scene equipped 'with a body', the 'natural' a priori equality of individuals disappears. Therein lies the paradoxical duality of such a reality, with enormous social and political consequences: the fiction of equality of self-sufficient monads is hard to disentangle from the fantasy of mastery. *Not having a body*, that is, being invulnerable, sovereign and independent, is conventionally shaped around deprivations that place 'bodies' among those who are weaker, defenceless and dependent, open to harm and injury, women being the traditional 'vulnerable group'.[2]

For Butler, 'the body is not, and never was, a self-subsisting kind of being [. . .] the body is given over to others in order to persist' (FN: 49). The fictitiousness of an individual as a self-sufficient and invulnerable being is based on the abstraction of embodiedness. 'Vulnerability is something that is a trait belonging to others – various beings dependent on, and thus subordinated to, the invulnerable individual, invulnerable because he is supposedly not defined by any relations towards others' (Zaharijević 2020b: 9). This fundamental unrelationality is at the core of invulnerability. It is almost Robinsonian in kind, because the individual seems to have an undisputed capacity to survive in any circumstances, without others, beyond society. Such a capacity does not depend only on a firm will, enormous amounts of self-control and skill to adjust to a life on a virgin island, but rather on a fictitious absence of the body. 'Bodilessness' is the essential precondition for invulnerability.

Vulnerability

In recent times we have witnessed a prodigious increase in transdisciplinary research focused on vulnerability. Defining it as sticky and a true boundary concept, Marja-Liisa Honkasalo (2018: 3) points out that it refers to a universal condition, but also to a phenomenon, policy imperative, psychoemotional trait, individual or intersubjective experience, or a political ontology. Vulnerability is most often related to the concepts of relationality, dependency, care, porous boundaries, and recognition. Despite the revival, the concept, as Estelle Ferrarese poignantly shows (2016: 150), continues to come up against considerable reluctance. It is seen as notoriously lacking in virility, being too Christian and conservative in substance, as it insists on conservation of nature, species and life, reducing politics to care and putting too strong a stress on the inescapable mortality of the body that stands in the way of all (emancipatory) politics. This seems to be the point on which thinkers as different as Arendt and Badiou agree.

The undeniable fact is that, with vulnerability, the 'ignoble' body has reappeared (or rather appeared in a new light) in considerations about the world. It can no longer be dispatched (even if only temporarily) to a walled-in 'somewhere', where it will be cared for in its cyclical needs, and from where it later emerges into the public as originator of actions. Our embodied humanity, as Martha Fineman defines it, calls for understanding vulnerability as arising from embodiment. The body 'carries with it the ever-present possibility of harm, injury, and misfortune from mildly adverse to catastrophically devastating events, whether accidental, intentional or otherwise' (2008: 9). Instead of creating an ever-wider array of the vulnerable, we should understand vulnerability as 'a universal, inevitable, enduring aspect of the human condition that must be at the heart of our concept of social and state responsibility' (ibid.: 8). With the body, care also made its breakthrough into politics. Ethics of care, some suggest, needs to become a resource for politics, building on 'values of caring – attentiveness, responsibility, nurturance, compassion, meeting others' needs – traditionally associated with women and traditionally excluded from public consideration' (Tronto 1994: 2–3). In addition, action and morality are intimately related to our ways of thinking and seeing vulnerability (or, rather, ways of not seeing it). Disavowed as belonging to others with whom one needs to disidentify, vulnerability is produced into a highly negative state, and unseen as a shared condition by means of a cultivated ignorance. Erinn Gilson relates this produced ignorance with a pursuit of invulnerability as a desirable form of subjectivity (Gilson 2011: 312). Having penetrated into all pores of our understanding of life, vulnerability ultimately questions the philosophical 'anthropology of the social contract' (Ferrarese 2016: 153), in which the individual appears as the sole owner of oneself, and the sole originator of social relations that come into being through (it seems, of necessity) *his* will. Apparently, the introduction of this notion into thinking transforms many of the fundamental premises about us in the world, working 'to undo the world such as it is' (ibid.: 158).

If hegemonic anthropology of the social contract begins (and ends) with male adults, the story of vulnerability begins with our birth. Instead of arising from our inescapable mortality, vulnerability is in fact an inextricable characteristic of natality, of our original needy appearance in the world. This appearance, birth, rarely problematised in the long history of philosophy, is the alternative, but rather more realistic, story of our beginning, taking place before we turn into wolves or contracting parties. In a psychoanalytic register, the vulnerable states of a grown-up need to be connected to the primary vulnerability of a child, related to the care and support – or lack thereof – of (unchosen, but most intimate) others. 'Babies' and infants' correspondingly near-total dependence on adult care renders them vulnerable to failures, mistakes, indifference, inattention and malice on the part of their care-givers', which is carried into adult life (Stone 2019: 73). In a different register proposed by Cavarero, the infant is a creature fundamentally and structurally consigned to relations, and thus the primary paradigm of vulnerability. This also introduces a major difference between child and adult, as vulnerability and helplessness are not so complete in the latter (Cavarero 2011: 30–1). For Butler too, the subject is not thinkable without this legacy. In order to think and manage violence, one needs to 'return to the "primary helplessness" and think of that in relation to what we might call unmanageable (or unbearable) dependency' of the adult (Martínez Ruiz 2016: 63).

As we have seen in the previous chapter, vulnerability became a very prominent concept with *Precarious Life*. In Butler's fully developed ontology of the body, vulnerability appears as something entirely basic, because the body is 'a social phenomenon [. . .] exposed to others, vulnerable by definition' (FoW: 33). This existential, constitutive vulnerability is, however, inextricable from the one unequally shared, as we embody our humanity in the world differently to one another:

> In a way, we all live with this particular vulnerability, a vulnerability to the other that is part of bodily life, a vulnerability to a sudden address from elsewhere that we cannot preempt. This vulnerability, however, becomes highly exacerbated under certain social and political conditions, especially those in which violence is a way of life and the means to secure self-defence are limited. (PL: 29)

In itself, vulnerability is neither good nor bad: it is 'a basic kind of openness to being affected and affecting in both positive and negative ways' (Gilson 2011: 310). Abstracted from its social life, vulnerability as a category encompasses the states of passivity (something is or can be done to us), affectivity (we are susceptible to affects, impressions, responsiveness), dispossession (being given over to others turns us into dispossessible beings), and exposure (we are always somewhere in the world). Our vulnerability is simply given – so much so that it cannot be annulled without complete annulment of ourselves. However, vulnerability can be abstracted from sociality only for heuristic reasons. Since it always appears only socially shaped and is related to all domains in which power relations operate (subsistence of the body, language, desire, labour, the need for belonging, to name a few), it can *become* bad. When it does, one can certainly desire to become less vulnerable, less injurable in one's inescapable exposure. When we are stricken by our vulnerability, we may wish to be less or not exposed, dispossessible, affected. We may wish to play dead or strike back.

But let us here recall how Butler sought a third path regarding violence, because the same line of reasoning can be applied here. As Gilson rightly underlines, vulner*ability* is a condition of openness and potentiality (ibid.): opening us to love, learning, taking pleasure in relations, as well as to suffering and harm, to loss of the very constitutive relations. Vulnerability and agency are not mutually exclusive terms. On the contrary, Butler invites us to reimagine a community (and act on this reimagination) based on generalisable vulnerability and loss: vulnerability, together with dependency, is part of the performative account of agency (Butler 2016a: 19). Vulnerability presents itself as a limit, but it also enables, it is that which prompts us into being and into being agentic.

Enabling Vulnerability

At the end of the previous chapter I claimed that a major shift took place in Butler's writings after 2001, when sociality turned into a resource, rather than an obstacle. We can trace this shift precisely through the notion of vulnerability, which had made its first appearance in the two books published in 1997. *Excitable Speech* elaborates on our linguistic injurability, which signals not only that we are exposed to harm of the name, but that in our coming to be, we depend on the address of the Other. 'It is by being interpellated within the terms of language that a certain social existence of the body first becomes possible' (ES: 5). As soon as one is born, one is given a name. The name inaugurates one into existence. Language already has names in store, they are already socially sedimented in the language. Since the attributed name is unchosen – the birth name, prosoponym, as well as the pronoun that follows it – one may be injured by it at a certain point in life, when one can claim for oneself to be an 'I'. But before one can even say 'I, Adriana', 'I, Julia', 'I, Jane', Adriana, Julia and Jane have all already been addressed by the other, interpellated into existence, constituted into what will be the posterior position of a subject:

This 'I' that I am is already social, already bound to a social world that exceeds the domain of familiarity, both urgent and largely impersonal. I first become thinkable in the mind of the other, as 'you' or as gendered pronoun, and that phantasmatic ideation gives birth to me as a social creature. (FN: 101)

Linguistic norms can injure. If the body is not congruent with its socially ascribed name or has trouble dealing with the social demands that accompany that name, the norms can produce violent effects on the body. Yet, if there is no other proper name for us, if we are not recognisable, we do not exist in the proper way. For that reason, although the name may be harmful to us, we often conform to it in order to survive: it enables us to live in established social reality.

The Psychic Life of Power, on the other hand, could be understood as a long answer to the question why we respond to the names that misdescribe us, why we abide by norms that have the power to injure us and, ultimately, possibly make our lives unliveable. The longing for a social existence is here defined as longing for subjection (PLP: 20), for remaining constituted or fending off de-constitution. If the subject depends on norms that fall outside the domain of volition, then the 'vulnerability of the subject to a power not of its own making is unavoidable. The vulnerability qualifies the subject as an exploitable kind of being' (PLP: 20). Power relations imprinted on us very early on tend to be those to which we are most stubbornly, most passionately attached. Thus, our primary vulnerability does not disappear once we leave the crib. In order to survive, we remain attached to those possibilities that guarantee our social existence. We attach to the norm that gives us back the sense of who we are, keeping us forever socially mediated, and in a relation to ourselves which is never entirely transparent (Butler 2002b: 17).

We are thus vulnerable to norms and to others, but this vulnerability is enabling – it does not preclude our agency or, as it turns out, our capacity for responsibility (Butler 2001b). However, one needs to admit that the 'enabling' aspects of vulnerability, as it is expounded in *Excitable Speech* and *The Psychic Life of Power*, somehow still seem primarily restrictive. They appear more as obstacle than resource. The strange, almost counter-intuitive formulation 'alienation in sociality' (PLP: 28) testifies to this. We are, it seems, enabled to persist due to being alienated in sociality. But if we are alienated, it remains unclear whether we are then truly enabled – whether our life can ever go beyond largely incapacious survival. Still missing from Butler's account on enabling vulnerability was a certain affirmation of this unwanted, unchosen relationality, through which 'alienation' also acquired a new name. After 2001, when she shifts to using *given over* to the social (rather than alienated in it), enabling vulnerability turns into a pillar of her ethico-political stance. From then on, the desire to persist will of necessity encompass the desire to live in a world that reflects the possibility of that persistence, also reflecting the value of others' lives as much as my own (UG: 235; SS: 65). The notion of interdependency, which assumes that we inhabit the world together and that 'our fates are, as it were, given over to one another' (FN: 51), was yet to be conceived.

Kelly Oliver noticed this paradox early in the sections of *Witnessing* dealing with Butler. If we see ourselves through the lens of alienation in a world not of our own making, if our becoming in the world is marked by a certain loss inflicted upon us by the world, then the only path for us has to be to liberate ourselves from our vulnerability to the world. Agency would then be reduced to a desired de-alienation from sociality, in order to recover from the primary loss. Oliver suggests that we are here faced with an advancement of an idea Butler fiercely argued against, because the desired de-alienation can easily be interpreted as a longing for a self-possessed, independent sovereign subject. Only if one starts from an ideal of the self-possessed autonomous subject can dependence on the other, on relation, appear as alienating, subjugating and violent. What *The Psychic Life of Power* defined as an enabling aspect of vulnerability seems only to secure a life at the expense of violence and death. If dependence on the Other is, as Oliver suggests, taken to be the source of life, as the very possibility of transformation and the point of acknowledgement of transferential relations with others, then we can 'begin to "work through" rather than repeat violence. "Working through" is a profoundly ethical operation insofar as it forces us not only to acknowledge our relations and obligations to others [. . .] but also thereby to transform those relations into more ethical relations' (Oliver 2001: 67–9).

We can say that this is precisely what took place with the introduction of the notion of precarious life, and even more so with the strong emphasis on interdependence. There can be no original dispossession of the subject, if to become a subject is to become in relation (Devenney 2020: 76). Dependence and vulnerability needed to cease to be alienating, becoming truly enabling instead. For that, the self had to be defined through relations, as being bound up with others, being undone by others (PW: 98; PL: 23; FoW: 54). We can be undone by others only because we were first done by and 'composed' of others (Drichel 2013: 15–16). Introducing ethical considerations – a 'you' whom I recognise and respect rather than wish to kill or injure, thereby working through violence without repeating it – does not dilute the importance of the norms through which both 'you' and 'I' appear as recognisable. Vulnerability that enables passionate attachment to one's own existence is given a new valence: 'I' am subordinated to the world that makes me relatable and offers me relations, and although 'I' come to exist in and through 'your' address and 'our' relation, it is the world, that is, social reality that mediates my addressability – my very possibility.

THE OTHER/YOU/FACE: RESPONSIBILITY

Subjects of Desire begins with a discussion of a unified subject who leads a unified philosophical life, itself discrete, unambiguous, easy to locate and name properly, with internally consistent desires. Such a subject serves as a necessary psychological premise and normative ideal in moral philosophies of all philosophers who 'time and again wanted to have a love affair with the good, maintaining that the true philosopher is one who spontaneously and easily desires the good, and just as easily translates those desires into good deeds' (SD: 5). Surely this is not the subject Butler's philosophy of complicated desires provides us with. Let us not, however, be too quick to claim that because it is ungrounded, non-unified, has fuzzy borders, is hard to locate and even harder to name, no moral philosophy follows from a performatively ungrounded subject. Perhaps we should here take note of Elena Loizidou (2007: 46) who, at the beginning of her analysis of Butler's ethics, suggests that a subject can no longer be seen as the ground for ethics, but as its problem. We should certainly draw on Butler herself, who bidding farewell to the subject as the metaphysical ground for morality, did not disavow the claim that a 'moral psychology' assumes a 'moral ontology, a theory about what a being must be like in order to be capable of moral deliberation and action' (SD: 6).

Butler's ethical considerations are particularly concerned with the question of responsibility. In the conversation with Antonello and Farneti (2009), she mentions she wanted to think about responsibility not as a purely individual matter. It always includes a 'you' (even if I call myself to accountability), someone who asks me to take responsibility for my actions. This responsiveness happens in language – which sometimes also necessitates translation – and is therefore always already socially mediated. At first glance, there seems to be nothing complicated about such a claim. However, if a subject is not entirely responsible for its coming to being, if its agency is conditioned and emerges under constraint, if it is dispossessed by relations, incoherent and opaque to itself, how can it be said to be responsible for the other? On another, but related plane, if what motivates the subject (constitutively) is to persist, how will responsibility for the other avoid clashing with the Spinozian desire to be? The question becomes even more acute if we consider that Butler shapes her own ethical position drawing on Levinasian ethics, for which vulnerability of the other is of primary importance.

For Levinas, being exposed to the vulnerability of the other questions my own *conatus essendi*, even suspends my right to self-persistence. My own desire to be is inevitably at variance with the ethical demand of another (Levinas 1999: 69). In an encounter with a 'you' – who to me always appears as a face and carries a single unbearably commanding message, 'Thou shalt not kill' – something has to happen to my constitutive vulnerability. In this situation, my own vulnerability either remains primary, permitting elision of another's vulnerability from my point of view, or else it will recede before the vulnerability of the other. 'An appeal of the face of my fellowman', says Levinas, reminds me of its abandonment, defencelessness and mortality. 'In its ethical urgency, [it] postpones or cancels the obligations the "summoned *I*" has towards itself and in which the concern for the death of the other can be more important to the *I* than its concern as an I for itself' (Levinas 1998: 227). In a relationship with the other, the subject loses its initial place. For Levinas, this is a point of awakening to humanity: and the humanity of the subject is emphatically in responsibility – 'in passivity, in reception, in obligation with regard to the other' (ibid.: 112). According to Levinas, the ethical is possible precisely because we take vulnerability – precariousness and helplessness of the other – as our own *primary* obligation. So, when Butler claims that responsibility is not about cultivating a will but about making use of an unwilled susceptibility as a resource for becoming responsive to the other, she seems to be following in Levinas' wake. The face of the other obligates me, puts an ethical demand on me, 'meaning that I am, as it were, precluded from revenge', whatever the other has done or intends to do, 'by virtue of a relation I never chose' (GAO: 91).

The importance of relations, of many 'you's who present themselves with uncompromising facial demands and 'whose language
is spoken by the shared narrative scene' (Cavarero 2000: 92), seems
unrelatable to the (Spinozan) subject who is always in the field of
passionate attachments. However, following in Levinas' wake seems
to be in contradiction with Spinoza's desire for persistence, crucial
for Butler's understanding of the enabling vulnerability. Worse still,
it is also at variance with a certain Foucauldian legacy in Butler's
understanding of subject constitution. Critique or desubjectivisation in Foucault is not motivated by a desire for recognition, and
the 'you' is not necessarily implicated in the normative scene one
strives to desubjectivate oneself from. Foucault's 'question effectively
remains "Who can I be, given the regime of truth that determines
ontology for me?"' (GAO: 25), and is important for Butler, in that
it foregrounds the normative frame in which the desire to persist
takes place. However, Foucault 'does not ask the question "Who are
you?"' (GAO: 25), the question that initiates an encounter with the
other, and implicates me in a relation of responsibility (GAO: 88).

Butler spun a moral philosophy from sources not easily inter-
woven. Therefore, the 'moral ontology' that she offers is a peculiar
blend of the 'I', 'you' and the world. All of those are implicated in any
action of the 'I': ecstatic, opaque, stubbornly attached, only later and
on occasion critical of regimes of truth that determine its ontology,
regardless of its will. My constitutive vulnerability (to norms or
regimes of truth; to language; to care when helpless; to various kinds
of dispossession; to the other in the guise of institutions or infrastructure that prop me up; to a 'you' without whom my life would cease
to be what it is, without whom I would be but a cracked, splintered
'i', deprived of relation that gave my life content and meaning) is
vulnerability to a relation, or to its possible absence, withdrawal or
disappearance. It is the same vulnerability – to our being alienated in
sociality, given over to the world – as the one that in *Precarious Life*
appears under the name of 'common human vulnerability' (PL: 30).
For an 'I' to be, and to be recognised by a 'you', there needs to be a
world that provides a relation, that mediates relationality. What is
'mine' is hardly ever disentangled from what appears as a bond, a
tension, a knot with the world, from which one cannot free oneself
(SS: 67).

This is the basis of *Giving an Account of Oneself*, the paradigmatically 'ethics' book of Butler's opus. Each of our attempts to be
accountable and provide an account of oneself, to tell one's story,

perhaps an autobiography, to commence with the 'I', assumes three crucial points. First, my story is always told to someone else, someone who addressed me, who approaches me with a question – such as 'who are you?' – to which I respond by saying, '*I* am. . . this is *my* account of *myself*'. In a world inhabited by one human only, one would not have a name, a pronoun, a history to tell. Such a world would not be a stage, because no others would be there to sustain a scene of address. There would be no occasion to respond to someone and claim an 'I' for myself. In effect, the relation to the other is 'a more primary ethical relation than a reflexive effort to give an account of oneself' (GAO: 21). Second, the terms we give when accounting for ourselves, 'by which we make ourselves intelligible to ourselves and to others, are not of our making. They are social in character, and they establish social norms, a domain of unfreedom and substitut-ability within which our "singular" stories are told' (GAO: 21). Telling one's story, even when one reveals dizzily intimate, untold thoughts and feelings, that up to that point maybe never appeared in one's own words, is an act of language. This linguistic shoring up gives us something and at the same time takes it away from us: I can hand over something that is 'mine', but the mode of transfer is never mine alone, and this residuum is felt in situations when language fails us, when we are left speechless. Third, however exhaustive and painstakingly attentive to detail I might be in trying to respond to the query 'who are you?', my account is destined to remain flawed and incomplete. There is a chasm in the relation between language and the body that remains inscribed in my speech. My singular body is mine, but it is also ineffable, escaping me at some point. The story of my body is a story of a body also not mine: it is immersed in my formative histories that are unavailable until retrieved from someone else's memories, recited as someone else's recollections (of someone who possibly remembers the day I first answered a call, turned my head to the name given to me, or when I reacted to a social address that constituted me, for the first time, as a girl-subject). As the subject of my own account, 'I' am always, at least to some extent, opaque to myself. 'My narrative begins *in medias res*, when many things have already taken place to make me and my story possible in language' (GAO: 39).

Such an 'I' has nothing to do with philosophies that want to have easy love affairs with the good, utterly failing to provide an ethical subject defined by self-reflexivity, the capacity for acting on prin-ciples, rational accountability for one's actions and the ability to project into the future – of the kind Seyla Benhabib wanted to protect from postmodernist incursion. Not given in advance, not constituted once and for all, fundamentally not discrete and self-transparent, not capable of taking itself as its own source of normativity, continuously faltering in biographising itself, this subject appears ethical only on condition of a certain unknowingness and an implication of the other in its formation – making it foreign to itself (GAO: 84).

An ethics Butler proposes begins with heterogeneous forms of vulnerability that strongly encourage one's desire to persist. But in this ethics, the other is also present from the start, and precisely this binding relationality (towards the 'you', towards the norm) becomes a resource for ethics. Importantly, the ethical appears also within the region of unwilled and from the limits of self-knowledge. Butler's subject does not first know and then act ethically towards the other. To the contrary: the subject is opaque to itself by virtue of its relations to others. Similarly, the exposure to the other is not only a result of an autonomous decision of the subject. In Butler, the unwilled susceptibility is what is at once exposing to violence and demanding a certain practice of nonviolence (GAO: 64; Drichel 2013: 18).

The dilemma about what is more primary – vulnerability of the other or my own vulnerability – ultimately appears not to be a real dilemma, because there is no I without you/s. That continuous state of being mired, given over ('even the word "dependency" cannot do the job here' [Butler 2001b: 37]) and acted upon is what gives place, provides a position in language and enables or restricts my own acting. The unwilled, unchosen passivity – impressionability and susceptibility – appears as a condition of possibility of any responsiveness; it gives a possibility to respond and re-act, thus constituting the I who speaks and acts. Depending on the address and shared narrative scene, the subject is susceptible to unreciprocated action. Susceptibility fundamentally involves the other in the constitution of the 'I'. This relation is beyond my will. Yet, the unwilled – that the other is already implicated in the 'I' (for whom I am always a 'you' or a 'she') – is an ethical resource too (GAO: 100). An acknowledgement of this primary relation to otherness – in effect, more primary than the relation to the self – is what keeps narcissistic desire at bay. 'This primary susceptibility to the action and the face of the other, the full ambivalence of an unwanted address, is what constitutes our exposure to injury *and* our responsibility for the Other' (GAO: 91). Responsibility is drawn from an ability to respond, in the now, and not from a posterior, self-reflective position when one decides whose vulnerability is primary and whose secondary. We cannot examine the question of responsibility in isolation from the other, because this would mean taking ourselves out of the mode of address that frames the very question of responsibility (Butler 2001b: 38). Responding to a face, a vulnerable 'you', who may in return wound (the vulnerable) me, is what opens me to responsibility and a practice of nonviolence in an emphatically non-reciprocal way, 'as an experiment to living otherwise' (Butler 2001b: 39; GAO: 100).

Therefore, to respond to the face commanding us not to kill means 'to be awake to what is precarious in another life or, rather, the precariousness of life itself' (PL: 134). Responding to a face certainly requires us to bid farewell to an egoistic individual, without relinquishing our desire to persist. In Butler's interpretation of Spinoza's 'ethics under pressure' (SS: 85), this desire always assumes a world that allows for the possibility of persistence, possible only if it reflects the value of our common human vulnerability, a common physicality, a common risk. Ethics, so to say, requires politics, and they merge in the notion of interdependence.

But, before we finally turn to interdependence, there is one more important question to be answered. Is ethics of nonviolence a passive, non-agentic stance, or does it, conversely, imply any form of action – or any form of autonomy? Recall that no one is born an individual, but only becomes one, and in this becoming, one is never entirely removed from the conditions of its dependency, never attaining the level of invulnerability. To reach for violence can be seen as seeking to reassert mastery, independence and unity (GAO: 64). To refrain from violence seems to mean to do otherwise, to reject mastery, independence and unity, or, in other words, to remain passive in one's dependency, disunity and subjection. This is, however, not what Butler proposes. To refrain from violence is a form of doing, a kind of action against such a reassertion, which consents to one's dependency, disunity and subjection. They become enabling aspects of our critical agency and responsibility towards the other(s). Also, a certain autonomy is required for such an action: there is some kind of decision involved in our active refraining from violence. Whatever we choose to name it, it is not 'sovereign autonomy', 'a state of individuation, taken as self-persisting prior to and apart from any relations of dependency on the world of others' (UG: 32).

There is no sovereign autonomy, so long as we are dispossessed and undone by the social conditions that constitute us. The social world functions as 'a sign of our constitutive heteronomy' (UG: 100). The alterations of the world come from an 'increment of acts, collective and diffuse, belonging to no single subject, and yet one effect of these alterations is to make acting like a subject possible' (UG: 100–1). Thus, as Amber Knight reminds us (contrary to Ruti [2017] and Cyfer [2019]), 'while being entirely self-knowing and self-determining is not possible, it is within our reach to have some limited ability to form and act on our choices' (Knight 2021: 184). This limited ability appears within the field not of our own making, which is, at the same time, also performatively of our own making, through our own agentic acts, through repeating, or acting otherwise. This agentic heteronomous autonomy appears in the form of critique of the social reality that determines ontology for us, possibly even depriving us of a right to ontology, stripping us of the name of the human. It also manifests as ethical action, in which we risk ourselves, at the moment of our unknowingness, 'when what conditions us and what lies before us diverge from one another, when our willingness to become undone constitutes our chance of becoming human' (GAO: 80).

INTERDEPENDENCE AND OBLIGATIONS

Although a 'you' has a central role in the constitution of an 'I', Butler is not solely devoted to a dyadic relation of the face and the one who, through that face, gets constituted as an ethical subject. Common human vulnerability emerges as common and human only in the social world in which we all live, in a world that makes us bound to one another and conditions our coming out as human. Responsibility, in that sense, involves more than a relation of a vulnerable I to a vulnerable you. It involves more than a dyadic encounter. Responsibility is also about our common accountability for a social relation, through which any of our encounters may happen. This is where the ethico-political notion of interdependence comes in.

The key point of interdependence is that 'the subject that I am is bound to the subject that I am not' (FoW: 43). Significantly, this subject that I am not but to whom I am still bound, this 'you' without whom 'I' stops making sense, is not only chosen. It is also unchosen, an unknown subject with whom I nevertheless share a bond. Sometimes, a position which is particularly poignant in situations of war, I am also bound to the subject I find threatening, abject, unintelligible, a face without a proper face, thus not defenceless, but dangerous to all that I am. In *Frames of War* Butler puts this plainly: 'we each have the power to destroy and to be destroyed, and [. . .] we are bound to one another in this power and this precariousness' (FoW: 43). In the same place, she insists that interdependency has to be avowed, and that it has to be instituted though binding multilateral and global agreements. Wars in fact only feed on the disavowal of our shared precariousness and the refusal to institute it, denying 'the ongoing and irrefutable ways in which we are all subject to one another, vulnerable to destruction by the other' (FoW: 43).

What does it mean to avow interdependency? For Butler, this entails a recognition of a generalised condition of precariousness (FoW: 48):

> Precariousness has to be grasped not simply as a feature of *this* or *that* life, but as a generalized condition whose very generality can be denied only by denying precariousness itself. And the injunction to think precariousness in terms of equality emerges precisely from the irrefutable generalizability of this condition. (FoW: 22)

Since we are social beings, we neither survive nor live as isolated, bounded beings, but our boundaries expose us to others. To avow interdependency assumes that we are able and willing to apprehend that 'the life of the other, the life that is not our own, is also our life, since what ever sense "our" life has is derived precisely from this sociality, this being already, and from the start, dependent on a world of others, constituted in and by a social world' (NT: 108). The avowal of interdependency rests upon a demand for social relation that is not based on destruction and eradication. It is, in other words, a demand for a liveable world.

In various places, Butler insists that the demand for a liveable world can be drawn from the lessons on fundamental equality and potential eradication of two self-consciousnesses. Let us, therefore, one last time, bring Hegel into the discussion. The creation of the master and the bondsman ends equality between these entities (bodies, as Butler insists early on), also putting an end to the radical violence that might have otherwise led to their total annihilation. Domination, 'the relation that replaces the urge to kill [. . .] [becomes] the effort to annihilate within the context of life' (SD: 52). At first glance, it seems that there is no way out of this violent situation in which one is either eradicated or dominated. 'According to Hegel, there is no subject without violence. Being a subject [. . .] means dealing with violence as something that determines our way

211

of being' (Illetterati 2022: 36). Butler, however, reads Hegel differently. The desire for recognition makes this an encounter of equals, creating a bond between them, establishing them as constitutively relational (UG: 149–50) and conscious of their fundamental vulnerability to the other. So, 'prior to any calculation [to subdue and dominate], we are already constituted through ties that bind and unbind in specific and consequential ways' (FoW: 182). 'The mere possibility of our connection to others (which does not presume an actual encounter) is central to our sense of self and our existence as a subject [and] this relational structure is beyond individual choice' (Stark 2014: 92). For Butler, this has major consequences for how we deal with (this unchosen) relationality. Domination, solely a continuation of annihilation in the context of life, is not a counterpoint to annihilation. The only true counterpoint to annihilation is the transformation of the social relation that rests upon this false dichotomy. Transformation relies on the avowal of two very basic assumptions: that we acknowledge our reciprocal destructiveness; and that we acknowledge that an endless, indeterminable eradication (until death or in life) annihilates not only particular lives, but also the relation between them. If eradication and domination are not the only possibilities the constitutive relationality offers – as they both, in the final instance, annihilate it – what remains is the acknowledgement of the relation existing between my life and the life of another. Recognition of the interdependent bond is not a philosophical or a poetic embellishment of an ugly world, but a formidable and binding ethico-political demand that obligates us to safeguard the relation on which our lives depend (Butler 2019b).

Butler's understanding of the social bond derives not only from a peculiar reformulation of Hegel, but also from certain inversions of Kleinian psychoanalytic positions (FN: 96), particularly important for the articulation of nonviolence as a way of acknowledging a relation. Interfering with the psychic life of the social bond is necessary in order to show that social bond does not arise out of expediency, interest, sympathy or calculation. For Melanie Klein, the ego attempts to preserve objects that threaten and provoke aggression in it (Klein 1935: 148). Aggression and destructiveness are integral parts of one's psychic life, but must be transformed in order for the ego to survive (ibid.: 154). It is at the basis of this elementary vulnerability, out of a need to forestall the possibility to become (psychically) destroyed, that morality develops, implying that desire to preserve the other is entangled with a desire for self-preservation. This double movement of aggression and preservation is important for Butler, although she readily confesses to have used Klein in un-Kleinian ways (FoW: 44–5). Butler seeks to show that, if my being is never entirely 'mine', if my dependence on the world can be annihilated only by self-annihilation, the endeavour to preserve the life of the other is something broader than the striving to survive and persist in my own self-subsistence. The endeavour to survive becomes equal to the endeavour to preserve a relation that constitutes me, 'because who "I" am is nothing without your life, and life itself has to be rethought as this complex, passionate, antagonistic, and necessary set of relations to others' (FoW: 44). To give consent to the world in which annihilation of lives is a norm means that we consent to an unliveable world. Responsibility for the other, any other, means support of the liveable world, one in which annihilation stops being an option.

As necessary as it is, avowal of interdependency is not sufficient. Across various places, Butler insists that interdependency also needs to be instituted though binding, multilateral and global agreements, which presuppose a persistent work through institutions. In that sense, the notion of interdependency is very often accompanied by the idea of obligatoriness. Prior to 2001, when Butler began to think of violence in terms of total destruction, her work was not marked by obligation. I would claim that the introduction of Levinas into her thought inaugurated particularly strong obligations, so characteristic of his ethical positions. Although Butler did not follow Levinas blindly in terms of the content of ethical obligations, what remains permanently Levinasian in her thought is the search for an obligative form of interdependence. In a more recent interview, she says:

> The ethical and the political converge at the problem of violence and non-violence, since at such junctures, we have to ask what kind of obligations we owe to one another. If we seek to derive such obligations from the social bonds that we have, then we are elaborating ethical principles from, and about, a socio-political situation. What we call a 'bond' is not ethical at the exclusion of the social or political. I know that some Levinasians would have it that way, but I am more interested in the nexus of interdependency and potential violence that characterizes social bonds [. . .] It is only because we are already implicated in the lives of others, and so part of an ongoing political existence, that we develop obligations that we can call 'ethical'. (Ingala 2017: 27–8)

Obligations rest upon recognition that lives – all lives – are precarious. Precariousness arises from our interdependence, from the entanglement of my life with other lives. We can abhor this fact, reject it with indignation or stubbornly argue against it, but this will not stop the social bond from being shaped as nurturing or threatening to our fundamentally social being.

The obligation towards other lives is ethical, but it voices itself also as a political demand for the creation of conditions for lives to be liveable. The stakes of one such demand are very high. First, the obligation towards other lives must become the basis for global solutions (FN: 44; cf. Barbec 2017). Then, 'the fact that our lives are dependent on others can become the basis of claims for nonmilitaristic political solutions, one which we cannot will away, one which we must attend to, even abide by' (UG: 22–3; cf. Stauffer 2003). Wars, however, only make transparent how fragile and destructible our existences are. In reality as we know it, there are differential modes of protection of humans from destruction and harm. Some bodies are perceived as virtually uninjurable, others as injurable, and yet others as almost continually injured. This perception has everything to do with the fantasy of mastery and the unequal distribution of vulnerability. The fantasy of mastery implies the existence of invulnerables (and their duty to protect – their own – vulnerables), as well as the existence of disposable populations whose lives do not count as lives. Such stratification enormously affects how we make our way through the world, whether the body we inhabit is understood, seen and felt as threatening or socially dead. It is also worth considering to what extent the boundaries of the self are entangled in the relation between the world and the body. To be born a black person in a country with a legacy of slavery, segregation and deeply unequal institutional structures means that however strong one's will to survive, it is entirely possible to die pinned down under the knee of a white police officer, managing only to utter 'I can't breathe'.

For this reason, the politics of interdependence assumes a rejection not only of militarism, but also of nationalism and racism, as they depend on a 'racial schema', a frame or norm that produces some lives as already ungrievable, 'snuffed out, because, from the start, such a life did not register as a life, a life worth safeguarding' (FN: 121). Ethical obligations are not enough. 'The moral precept that prohibits killing has to be expanded to a political principle that seeks to safeguard lives through institutional and economic means' without distinguishing between grievable and ungrievable populations (FN: 100). Politics of interdependency stands against political formations that justify and promote the unequal distribution of vulnerability (Butler, Gambetti and Sabsay 2016: 5; cf. Salmon 2016), sometimes also presenting it as a natural state of things (return to the 'natural roles' between sexes in the worldwide struggles against 'gender ideology' is indeed a return to the fiction of the state of nature in which all dependent forms of life remain in the invisible background, foregrounding only male, adult, white, independent sovereign warriors). Finally, the politics of interdependency takes stock of the damaged life, a life without a sense of futurity. In this era of accelerating inequality, there is an obligation to struggle against precarity, against acclimatising whole populations to insecurity, which is today the commonest form of abuse of our precariousness (D: 43; Butler in Lorey 2015: viii; Pagès and Trachman 2012: 2; Kania 2013).

Cohabitation

> What does it mean then to live with one another? It can be unhappy, it can be wretched, it can be ambivalent, it can even be full of antagonism, but all of that can play out in the political sphere without recourse to expulsion or genocide. And that is our obligation, to stay in the sphere with whatever murderous rage we have, without acting on it. (Filar 2014)

If performativity is about acting, and acting takes place as a relation of the body and the world, then our acting does something to this relation, we act on it as much as we are acted upon by it. This is the double movement of performativity. In that sense, we can understand politics of interdependency as a call for a different performativity, for acting differently in order to enact a different relation between bodies and the world. In the world in which there are so many destructive forms of relations – not only allowed, but pursued with vigour – the annihilation of the social relation gets reproduced and is, time and again, performatively affirmed, recited, reiterated. An act of violence is, in that sense, a paradigmatic performative act. In terms of social ontology, it is the act that violates the bond of our basic interdependence.

However, it is not only that our particular persistances are bound up with one another, but we are bound up because we are proximate, adjacent, up against one another, because we – an undetermined plurality of bodies – take space at the same time. Therefore, to accept our *common* condition of interdependence implies a prior acceptance of our *convergent* condition of cohabitation (PW: 130). No body exists without existing somewhere, without being in some 'there' (FoW: 53), materialising those possibilities present. And as no body lives alone in the world, bodies inhabit and co-inhabit this 'thereness'. To acknowledge the world in which bodies live as plural, where they are together because bound by proximity and sharing the world, precisely due to which no one is deprived of relations one fundamentally depends on – forms the basis of a strong ethico-political stance. However, this position is also shaped by a fundamental quandary regarding violence: we either have the right to choose with whom we cohabit on the Earth, or such a right does not belong to us, at any time, in any circumstances.

This dramatic dilemma becomes particularly prominent in *Parting Ways*, a critical endeavour to recreate a pre-Zionist and non-Zionist political Jewish subject who rejects violence against Palestinians, which is itself performative of 'a possibility to be part of the Jewish people while criticizing Zionism as their only political realization' (Rozmarin 2021: 36, 29). Here, as elsewhere, the dilemma is articulated primarily through Arendtian conceptual tools. This can hardly come as a surprise: Arendt tried to imagine a polity different than the nation-state, statelessness being its recurrent predicament. This imagination was followed by a 'political obligation to analyse and oppose deportations, population transfers and statelessness in ways that refused a nationalist ethos' (Butler 2007b). However, it was Arendt's idea that the *conditio humana* is predicated on plurality that had the most important role in Butler's formulations on cohabitation. *The Human Condition* opens with the claim 'that men, not Man, live on the earth and inhabit the world' (Arendt 1998: 7), plurality thus appearing as an ontological precondition not only of all political life, but also of the political itself.

Humans occupy space. They are contiguous, bordering and touching one another in their precarious tenancy of a single space and time. Such a state can clearly be quite undesirable, antagonistic, wretched, especially if one adjacent to me, whose bodily boundaries rub against mine, is not to my liking or jeopardises me, or when this very closeness acts as a potential threat. And although we can surely do something to shape this given plurality and manage cohabitation – political life serves precisely this purpose – the very givenness of plurality precedes our will and is outside the sphere of the chosen. The ontological dimension of unchosenness is also part of our vulnerability and interdependence: we do not simply choose to be vulnerable or depend on a relation. But the unchosen dimension of plurality and cohabitation is what gives meaning to vulnerability and dependence: in an imaginary

world inhabited by one person, the fact of one's vulnerability (to relation) ceases to be meaningful. That we are 'here', thrown in the world
with others, is our being here together. The fundamental impossibility to decide upon this convergence of 'me' and 'we' being here,
reflects our primary belonging to the world. If cohabitation – a shared
thrownness into the world – can be at all considered in causal terms, it
is a consequence of the mere fact of birth. We are born into the world
that contains and contained others. (Primary plurality could be taken
to be a contingent foundation of the theory of performativity: the fact
of one's birth is the only thing that is outside the sphere of acting and
is, at the same time, a condition of possibility of any acting. Natality –
the fact that all of us appear in the world by virtue of birth – assumes
that our unprecedented appearance takes place in a world with others
already present. On this point, through contingent but factual births,
Simone de Beauvoir and Hannah Arendt meet in a peculiar way in
Butler's theory.)

Both that others are already there, and that belonging to this
'there' is less than mastery and ownership, can be 'a source of a great
range of emotional consequences from desire to hostility or, indeed,
some combination of the two' (PW: 176). But, although 'we might
sometimes choose where to live, and who to live by or with [. . .]
we cannot choose with whom to cohabit the earth' (PW: 125). This
fundamental lack of choice can produce antagonism and wretchedness, but it nonetheless demands an active preservation and affirmation 'of the unchosen character of inclusive and plural cohabitation'
(PW: 25). This demand may seem counter-intuitive, especially within
the liberal version of human ontology and its attendant anthropology
of the social contract. Reality inhabited by self-sufficient individuals for whom all relationality arises from various kinds of contracts
entered into with full knowledge of one's intentions, makes no room
for relations that precede volitional acts, deliberation and choice
(PW: 23, 129–30). A 'world' that functions only as an agglomerate of
individuals, whose ties are artificial, chosen and posterior, who form
a 'together' merely as an arithmetic sum composed of independent
units, is paradoxically both the world of laissez-faire individuals who
buzz around the world, living and letting others live, on condition
that the basic prohibition of encroachment of one's self-sufficiency is
respected; and a world in which the right to mastery can be invoked
at any time when the real or perceived trespasses take place.

When primary relationality provided to us by the world is not
taken into account, the right to mastery translates into a decision

on who has the right to be thrown into the world. In her report on the banality of evil, Hannah Arendt wrote about the exemplary enactment of the right to annul plurality (Arendt 2006). The report, composed during Eichmann's trial in Jerusalem, famously exposed her to public opprobrium and produced a number of controversies, many of which were related to Arendt's observations on Eichmann himself. Instead of the embodiment of radical evil, Arendt describes Eichmann as a not particularly intelligent man, lacking the strong emotions required to become a fanatic supporter of an ideology. Nor were there any traces of a mental disorder; he did not display any particular sense of responsibility; he demonstrated no capacity to expose his motives for participation in atrocities; the word 'duty', to which he so often referred, remained mired in clichés and stock phrases. No diabolical or demonic profundity could have been extracted from Eichmann. Upon reflection, Arendt tells us that she was struck 'by a manifest shallowness in the doer that made it impossible to trace the uncontestable evil of his deeds to any deeper level of roots or motives. The deeds were monstrous, but the doer [. . .] was quite ordinary, commonplace [. . .] [characterised not by] stupidity but *thoughtlessness*' (Arendt 1981: 4). This emphasised thoughtlessness led Arendt to ultimately characterise the unthinkable evil produced by this terrifying machinery as 'banal'. Nevertheless, Arendt did consider him guilty of a crime that requires no demonic layer. As Eichmann supported and carried out a 'policy of not wanting to share the earth with the Jewish people and the people of a number of other nations', acting 'as though' he and his superiors had a right to decide who should and who should not inhabit the world, 'we find that no one [. . .] can be expected to share the earth with you' (Arendt 2006: 279). The decision that Eichmann and his superiors made goes directly against the unchosen character of earthly cohabitation. The 'we', the conjectured plurality through which Arendt expressed herself – not from the position of judge, but in an operation of judgement nonetheless, directly opposite to thoughtlessness – practically and performatively enacts the 'recognition of equality that follows from her conception of human plurality' (Butler 2011b: 294–5). Anyone born has the right to be here.

Although we can and often do choose with whom we share a bed, a flat or a neighbourhood, 'we cannot choose with whom to share the earth without engaging in genocide' (D: 122). It is the unchosen character of cohabitation that produces a normative demand to refuse genocide. This refusal cannot be partial: we either concede to the invocation of a 'genocidal prerogative' (Butler 2011b: 292; PW: 166) or we do whatever must be done to accept and preserve an unchosen condition of lives on earth. 'We cannot understand cohabitation without understanding that a generalized precarity obliges us to oppose genocide and to sustain life on egalitarian terms' (NT: 119). Tacit acceptance of lives that do not count as life, that are not worth preserving or grieving because they are already lost or losable, belongs to the 'very definition of genocidal epistemology' (FN: 112).

If we do not choose with whom we inhabit the earth, we need to actively keep – sustain and preserve – the unchosen character of our plurality. The modes of support will differ but will have to take into account the performative power of our acting. Antiracist struggle teaches how to build on a dream: from the moment Martin Luther King Jr first put into words the hopes of many previous generations for sons of former slaves and sons of former slave owners to sit together at the table of brotherhood, to today's enactment of racial justice in the form of the Black Lives Matter movement. In this dream, we appear in an already given world, one with an already given history of actions, which prevent us from disregarding what came before our appearance. These actions, however, do not determine our present, nor the performative possibilities of sustaining plurality. There is thus an 'obligation not to destroy any part of the human population or to make lives unlivable' (PW: 24). This obligation urges us to 'devise institutions and policies that actively preserve and affirm the unchosen character of open-ended and plural cohabitation' (NT: 112–13; Birulés 2009; Sarra 2012), because it is an obligation no one can have alone, an obligation that can never belong to any one in particular. It can always and only be realised on a wider plane, through different forms of collective action (NT: 171–2; D: 67; FN: 46–7).

Notes

1. The question of 'you' in Butler is most often related to her encounter with Levinas. Although that is certainly not incorrect, I wish to draw attention to Adriana Cavarero's mediation of that encounter, which then also of necessity involves Arendt and, on another register, Fanon. The rehabilitation of the 'you' as the core of politics (Cavarero 2000), which Butler never fails to attribute directly to Cavarero (UG: 35; GAO: 30–5; SS: 197; Antonello and Farneti 2009), was extremely important in the articulation of both Butler's idea of the relation (PL), and the idea of the narrative, the biography, the account we give of ourselves (GAO), in

which the other, the 'you' is always already implied. Here is Butler very early on: 'For her, the question most central to recognition is a direct one; and it is addressed to the Other: "who are you?" This question assumes that there is an Other before us, one we do not know, whom we cannot fully apprehend, one whose uniqueness and nonsubstitutability sets a limit to the model of reciprocal recognition offered within the Hegelian scheme [. . .] Cavarero argues that we are beings who are, of necessity, *exposed* to one another, and that our political situation consists in part in learning how best to handle this constant and necessary exposure. In a sense, this theory of the "outside" to the subject radicalizes the ecstatic trend in the Hegelian position [. . .] In her view, one can only tell an autobiography, one can only reference an "I" in relation to a "you": without the "you", my own story becomes impossible' (Butler 2001b: 24). The exchange between Butler and Cavarero is profound and in many ways exemplary of feminist acknowledgement and solidarity in struggle (cf. Cavarero 2011, 2016; Pulkkinen 2020).

2. On the one hand, selective dependency, fragility and imperilment serve as justification for domination, and on the other, make the protection of what is 'our own' – possessions, women, family, children, nation, culture, and so on – particularly urgent. The fantasy of mastery, which rests upon total impermeability, total invulnerability, is a guiding fantasy for many forms of nationalism and militarism (Zimmer, Heidingsfelder and Adler 2010). After 2001, the US government set out to create the representation of the country as sovereign, impermeable, invulnerable, because it was unacceptable that its frontiers had been breached. This representation depended on an image of efficacious, militarised man, whose body and will are indestructible – the image of 'pure action and pure aggression' (Birulés 2009; cf. Stauffer 2003). This fantasy had been created in the United States, but also elsewhere and on many occasions, through political, military and media strategical alliances. This explains Butler's interest in the power of media, frames and images, most discernible in *Frames of War*.

Our Place

'My' place is that which I occupy as an embodied being. Yet, by my very embodied nature, I am an ecstatic being, outside of myself, given over to others. 'My' place is thus not entirely mine, because we, as bodies, cohabitate, we are and we have together. In a world in which to have means to be the sole possessor, having something together often means not having it; we are taught that we must do all in our power to reclaim what belongs to us and reject the state of dispossession into which our bodies put us:

> To say that 'my' place is already the place of another is to say that place is never singularly possessed and that this question of cohabitation in the same place is unavoidable. It is in light of this question of cohabitation that the question of violence emerges. (PW: 62)

Violence appears as a reclamation of my own being and a rejection of the shared world that dispossesses me.

Reclamation and rejection shape the relation between the body and the world, which in its radical form can turn into an annihilation of others constitutive of the relation, and thus an annihilation of the relation itself. The 'quandary' – whether someone (an individual, a group or a nation) has the right to reclaim their own place for oneself, which in the final instance may lead to purging the place of others – requires an unambiguous affirmation *or* rejection of violence. From 2001, when she suggested that responsibility involves 'an experiment to living otherwise' (Butler 2001b: 39), opening us towards a practice of nonviolence in an emphatically non-reciprocal way, Judith Butler's answer to this question is an unambiguous *no*.

Nonviolence thus appears as an active form of perseverance in cohabitation. To persevere in cohabitation – a having that is not having, a having that is sharing – is to claim responsibility for the liveable world and commitment to the equality of lives. To persevere is to sustain an affirmation of the social relation in the force field of violence, because nonviolence only becomes possible at the moment

221

when to strike or strike back appears an obvious or desirable reaction. We act non-violently not only when we refrain from violence, but when this refraining is an active struggle against violence, 'a way of rerouting aggression' (FN: 27). Rerouting is an important word, reminiscent of rearticulation and resignification, referring to repeating otherwise. We struggle with(in) ourselves against our own anger or rage, and we do it in order not to annihilate the other, preventing the eradication of the relation that constitutes us both. Rerouting – taking responsibility for the social relation – happens only in the fray, only 'within the terms of the performance' (Butler 1998: 526). Cohabitation does not provide the opportunity to pause being vulnerable and exposed 'for a while, to pull the curtain down, and let it rise only if one can have a say in the production of the play itself' (Benhabib 1995a: 21). To take responsibility for the world that gives us social relation is possible only from within the world itself, and *in medias res* of violence.

The practice of nonviolence is a critical and ethical *no* to doing violence, a decisive rejection of acting violently, of repeating violently. Nonviolence is resistance to the activation of the sedimented layers of the past uses of violence, because 'when any of us commit acts of violence, we are, in and through those acts, building a more violent world' (FN: 19). There is, however, also a political obligation to jointly think of ways to conserve cohabitation without violence, securing conditions under which this remains a viable possibility. For that we urgently need 'institutions and policies that actively preserve and affirm the unchosen character of open-ended and plural cohabitation' (NT: 112–13). Bearing in mind the double movement of performativity, this dimension is crucial: in our acting, we 'do' the world, but we are at the same time thrown into the world which is not of our making alone. The practice of nonviolence includes both our own acts, rerouted from doing violence, *and* norms and institutions that allow for a world in which violence is not the first – or second – option. If there are no institutional obligations and no institutions that seek to preserve our interdependency, individual non-violent acts – necessary as they are – will remain isolated heroic deeds. To practise nonviolence in an unheroic way, nonviolence has to be an instituted and enabled social norm.

To be sure, from a viewpoint of our 'reality', nonviolence as a social norm looks simply unreal. Nevertheless, if we follow Judith Butler, there is a philosophical obligation to resolutely espouse the unrealistic, that which under existing conditions has the status of the impossible. Due to its contingent and contextual character that can never be predicted at the level of theory, 'in politics, sometimes the thing that "will never happen" actually starts to happen' (Bell 1999: 166). 'And maybe one of the jobs of theory or philosophy is to elevate principles that seem impossible [. . .] to stand by them and will them' in the name of possible life (Filar 2014). Surely, pondering reality is one of the oldest jobs of philosophy, and perhaps a 'critique of what counts as reality' (FN: 10) does not go too far from the description of what an idealist political philosophy does. 'Perhaps nonviolence requires a certain leave-taking from reality as it is currently constituted, laying open the possibilities that belong to a newer political imaginary' (FN: 10–11).

Now, perhaps it is surprising to hear Judith Butler espousing what seems like idealism. Was Butler not both celebrated and vilified for her all too subversive approach to all that seemed solid? At the very end of this book, after many attempts throughout to show that Butler sought the possibilities of change, with cohabitation we arrived at the opposite of social transformation: conservation. Similarly, how can the task now, at the last, seem to be to stand by and will the impossible? There are, further, two important questions arising from such leave-taking of reality. First, if we need to imagine and will a world in which peaceful cohabitation functions as the basis of ethics and politics, are we speaking of some other, newer and better world – perhaps utopian? Second, if nonviolence is our pathway there, does this mean that such a world would be populated with beautiful souls, beings entirely lacking violent impulses who acquiesce to ceding their place?; that is to say, are we speaking of an utterly different people?

To answer these questions, we need to revisit, once again, what has, throughout this book, been understood as reality or the world. To that end, I propose we look back at the lines that give shape to this book: the paragraph on the insurrection at the level of ontology (PL: 33). The insurrection takes place when we pose critical questions about the world, such as 'whose life is real?' and 'how can reality be remade?'. These questions were, significantly, accompanied by those on violence: what was the relation between violence and lives considered 'unreal'? How does violence effect (un)reality? What is the perspective of the human if violence of derealisation always remains possible?

Insurrection at the level of ontology does not entail stepping outside the real; rather, it means saying *no* to such reality, taking leave of it, yet without searching for some new, non-place reality, for some *utopos*. Quite the contrary, insurrection requires us to stay in what is our only real place, into which we have been thrown in a plural, unchosen way. Since 'our' place makes many of us unreal, the insurrection says 'no' to derealisation and ascription of layers of reality that allows expendable and ungrievable lives to exist. To rebel means to desire and will a place in 'our real' where no lives are unreal; it means to demand that here, in the midst of the relation between the body and the world, there can be no lives whose reality is violently abolished. The insurrection at the level of ontology is a demand for *our place* without the violence that renders some lives unreal. In the last instance, the insurrection at the level of ontology is an insurrection against violence committed against anyone who is part of this, our 'ownly' world.

True, Judith Butler speaks of an alternative ontology, and it stands to reason that an alternative reality begins when the insurrection comes to an end. Some other, new world appears in the midst of reality as it is. If the various denials and selective formations that produce inequality among lives were indeed to be abolished, another, new world would appear in the midst of reality. With unconditional consent to cohabitation, something new *is* on the horizon, which at the present moment belongs to the domain of the unknown. This 'new' will be an effect of social transformation: a world that conserves and enhances social relations, in which norms do not develop differential recognisability, vulnerability, dependency, precarity, grievability; a world where the question 'who counts as human?' stops making sense.

In persevering in putting forth seemingly impossible principles – one of which is that bodies are formative of social relations and that they need protection from harm! – we encourage this 'new' to appear and keep it in circulation. Presenting 'impossibility' as possible begets possibility. Thus, we are not talking about some other place and world, but about possibilities that have to be opened and kept open here, in our shared place, which can only then be truly ours. The insurrection at the level of ontology can happen only within reality itself and against existing formations of the social relation that produce and perpetuate inequality in the midst of equality.

In this equation, nonviolence functions as an insurrection against violence integral to the established social relations. Nonviolence is a practice that – *right now* – stopping a violent act or process, enables us to remain in our only place. It is what can be done *in medias res*, in a world that has not banished aggression from life and politics. Nonviolence does not come about in a fairy-tale world populated by beautiful souls (or if it did, given such a world, it would not be important). As a practice, nonviolence is crucial precisely in conditions that produce us through violence. Agency appears when our acting turns away from what keeps us bound (and subjected) to these norms. To rebel against the reality that constitutes us (a critical gesture) assumes neither its destruction nor transcendence, but a performative turn or rerouting of violent norms. Its purpose is to acknowledge social relation (an ethical gesture), beyond which there is no other reality. The turn that demands the transformation of our own production must take place in the midst of violence, rerouting it, contesting 'the determining power of that production; in other words, [making] good use of the iterability of those norms and, hence, their fragility and transformability' (Butler 2007a: 185).

How would reality look if it were remade on the basis of radical egalitarianism? What would our reality be if our ontology, based on precariousness, plurality and interdependence, were also politically sustained and protected? We do not know yet. It is a matter for the future. Although not part of the world in which we presently live, equality is to be politically advanced. This presupposes that we think and act in the now, as if able to acknowledge our ontological equality. What kind of reality would emerge from those political struggles is still as unpredictable and contingent as the imaginary of those who might inhabit it. We remain unknowing of a world without the possibility of annihilation of the social bond. What would reality look like if all lives were possible? How would the human look if its possibilities were not violently established?

> To safeguard the future of life is not to impose the form that such a life will take, the path that such a life will follow: it is a way of holding open the contingent and unpredictable forms that lives may take. (FN: 146)

To tend politically to the future cannot happen from a programmatic point already situated in an alleged future.

We tend to the future by doing in the now. This can also be taken to be an answer to the question about the beautiful souls, people who would presumably live in a good or at least better world. A world in which annihilation is not an allowed form of a social relation, in which no one can invoke the genocidal prerogative, in which no human is expendable, would indeed be a world inhabited by beautiful souls. We do not know such a world yet. But a fairy-tale description of the world is not what Judith Butler supplies. Rather, however foreclosed such a possibility may appear in our given frames, her political philosophy is an injunction to think radical equality here and now.

Bibliography

Texts by Judith Butler

Asad, T., W. Brown, J. Butler and S. Mahmood. 2009. *Is Critique Secular? Blasphemy, Injury, and Free Speech.* Berkeley: University of California Press.

Beck-Gernsheim, E., J. Butler and L. Puigvert. 2003. *Women and Social Transformation.* New York: Peter Lang.

Benhabib, S., J. Butler, D. Cornell and N. Fraser. 1995. *Feminist Contentions: A Philosophical Exchange.* New York: Routledge.

Butler, J. 1985. 'Variations on Sex and Gender: Beauvoir, Wittig, and Foucault'. *Praxis International* 4: 505–16.

Butler, J. 1986. 'Sex and Gender in Simone de Beauvoir's *Second Sex*'. *Yale French Studies* 72: 35–49.

Butler, J. 1987. *Subjects of Desire: Hegelian Reflections in Twentieth-Century France.* New York: Columbia University Press.

Butler, J. 1988. 'Performative Acts and Gender Constitution: An Essay in Phenomenology and Feminist Theory'. *Theatre Journal* 40 (4): 519–31.

Butler, J. 1989. 'Sexual Ideology and Phenomenological Description: A Feminist Critique of Merleau-Ponty's *Phenomenology of Perception*'. In *The Thinking Muse*, edited by J. Allen and I. M. Young, 85–100. Bloomington and Indianapolis: Indiana University Press.

Butler, J. 1991. 'Imitation and Gender Insubordination'. In *Inside/Out. Lesbian Theories, Gay Theories*, edited by D. Fuss, 13–31. New York and London: Routledge.

Butler, J. 1993a. 'Gender as Performance'. In *A Critical Sense: Interviews with Intellectuals*, edited by P. Osborne, 109–25. London and New York: Routledge.

Butler, J. 1993b. 'Critically Queer'. *GLQ* 1: 17–32.

Butler, J. 1993c. 'Endangered/Endangering: Schematic Racism and White Paranoia'. In *Reading Rodney King: Reading Urban Uprising*, edited by R. Gooding-Williams, 15–22. New York: Routledge.

Butler, J. 1994. 'Against Proper Objects: Introduction'. *differences* 6 (2&3): 1–26.

Butler, J. 1995a. 'Contingent Foundations'. In *Feminist Contentions*, edited by S. Benhabib et al., 35–58. New York: Routledge.

Butler, J. 1995b. 'For a Careful Reading'. In *Feminist Contentions*, edited by S. Benhabib et al., 127–44. New York: Routledge.

Butler, J. 1996. 'Universality in Culture'. In *For the Love of the Country*, edited by M. Nussbaum, 45–52. Boston, MA: Beacon Press.

Butler, J. 1997a. *Excitable Speech: A Politics of the Performative*. New York and London: Routledge.

Butler, J. 1997b. *The Psychic Life of Power: Theories in Subjection*. Stanford, CA: Stanford University Press.

Butler, J. 1997c. 'Further Reflections on Conversations of Our Times'. *Diacritics* 27 (1): 13–15.

Butler, J. 1998. 'Merely Cultural'. *New Left Review* 1 (227): 33–44.

Butler, J. 1999 [1990]. *Gender Trouble: Feminism and the Subversion of Identity*. New York and London: Routledge.

Butler, J. 2000. 'Ethical Ambivalence'. In *The Turn to Ethics*, edited by M. Garber, B. Hanssen and R. L. Walkowitz, 15–28. New York and London: Routledge. https://www.diaphanes.net/titel/ethical-ambivalence-2222

Butler, J. 2001a. 'What is Critique? An Essay on Foucault's Virtue'. Available at https://transversal.at/transversal/0806/butler/en (accessed 8 December 2022).

Butler, J. 2001b. 'Giving an Account of Oneself'. *Diacritics* 31 (4): 22–40.

Butler, J. 2002a. *Antigone's Claim: Kinship Between Life and Death*. New York: Columbia University Press.

Butler, J. 2002b. 'Bodies and Power, Revisited'. *Radical Philosophy* 114: 13–19.

Butler, J. 2004a. *Precarious Life: The Powers of Mourning and Violence*. London and New York: Verso.

Butler, J. 2004b. *Undoing Gender*. New York and London: Routledge.

Butler, J. 2005. *Giving an Account of Oneself*. New York: Fordham University Press.

Butler, J. 2007a. 'Reply from Judith Butler to Mills and Jenkins'. *differences* 18 (2): 180–95.

Butler, J. 2007b. 'I Merely Belong to Them'. *London Review of Books* 29 (9). Available at https://www.lrb.co.uk/the-paper/v29/n09/judith-butler/i-merely-belong-to-them.

Butler, J. 2009a. *Frames of War: When Is Life Grievable?* London and New York: Verso.

Butler, J. 2009b. 'Performativity, Precarity and Sexual Politics'. *AIBR. Revista de Antropologia Iberoamericana* 4 (3): i–xiii.

Butler, J. 2009c. 'Critique, Dissent, Disciplinarity'. *Critical Inquiry* 35: 773–95.

Butler, J. 2010. 'Performative Agency'. *Journal of Cultural Economy* 3 (2): 147–61.

Butler, J. 2011a [1993]. *Bodies That Matter: On the Discursive Limits of 'Sex'*. New York and London: Routledge.

Butler, J. 2011b. 'Hannah Arendt's Death Sentences'. *Comparative Literature Studies* 48 (3): 280–95.

Butler, J. 2012. *Parting Ways: Jewishness and the Critique of Violence*. New York: Columbia University Press.

Butler, J. 2015a. 'Laclau, Marx, and the Performative Power of Negation'. Verso blog. Available at https://www.versobooks.com/blogs/5238-judith -butler-laclau-marx-and-the-performative-power-of-negation?utm_sour ce=facebook&utm_medium=social&utm_campaign=verso_blog&fbcli d=IwAR26_HK9DKrQoaL8uCrBtk_Z7oj5S-N_n0kPMaMg4DhI1oOt 1cuSqw-jGo8 (accessed 8 December 2022).

Butler, J. 2015b. *Notes Toward a Performative Theory of Assembly*. Cambridge, MA and London: Harvard University Press.

Butler, J. 2015c. *Senses of the Subject*. New York: Fordham University Press.

Butler, J. 2016a. 'Rethinking Vulnerability and Resistance'. In *Vulnerability in Resistance*, edited by J. Butler, Z. Gambetti and L. Sabsay, 12–27. Durham, NC: Duke University Press.

Butler, J. 2016b. 'Uprising'. In *Uprisings*, edited by G. Didi-Huberman, 23–36. Paris: Gallimard, Jeu de Paume.

Butler, J. 2018. 'Reply from Judith Butler'. *Philosophy and Phenomenological Research* XCVI (1): 243–9.

Butler, J. 2019a. 'Gender in Translation: Beyond Monolingualism'. *philoSOPHIA* 9 (1): 1–25.

Butler, J. 2019b. 'Hegel for Our Times'. The Institute of Art and Ideas. Available at https://iai.tv/articles/hegel-for-our-times-judith-butler-auid -1273 (accessed 8 December 2022).

Butler, J. 2020. *The Force of Nonviolence: An Ethico-Political Bind*. London and New York: Verso.

Butler, J. 2021. 'Why is the Idea of "Gender" Provoking Backlash the World Over?' *The Guardian*, 23 October. Available at https://www.theguardi an.com/us-news/commentisfree/2021/oct/23/judith-butler-gender-ideolo gy-backlash (accessed 8 December 2022).

Butler, J. and A. Athanasiou. 2013. *Dispossession: The Performative in the Political*. Cambridge: Polity.

Butler, J., Z. Gambetti and L. Sabsay. 2016. 'Introduction'. In *Vulnerability in Resistance*, edited by J. Butler, Z. Gambetti and L. Sabsay, 1–11. Durham, NC: Duke University Press.

Butler, J., J. Habermas, C. Taylor and C. West. 2011. *The Power of Religion in the Public Sphere*. New York: Columbia University Press.

Butler, J., E. Laclau and R. Laddaga. 1997. 'The Uses of Equality'. *Diacritics* 27 (1): 2–12.

Butler J., E. Laclau and S. Žižek. 2000. *Contingency, Hegemony, Universality*. London and New York: Verso.

Butler, J. and G. C. Spivak. 2007. *Who Sings the Nation-State? Language, Politics, Belonging*. London, New York, Calcutta: Seagull.

Butler, J. and S. Taylor. 2008. *Examined Life*. Available at https://www.yo utube.com/watch?v=k0HZaPkF6qE&ab_channel=%E9%BB%83%E5 %B0%8F%E7%AB%B9 (accessed 8 December 2022).

Butler, J. and E. Weed. 2011. 'Introduction'. In *The Question of Gender: Joan W. Scott's Critical Feminism*, edited by J. Butler and E. Weed, 1–10. Bloomington and Indianapolis: Indiana University Press.

Interviews with Judith Butler

Aloni, U. 2010. 'Judith Butler: As a Jew, I Was Taught It Was Ethically Imperative to Speak Up'. *Haaretz*, 24 February. Available at https://www .haaretz.com/1.5052023 (accessed 8 December 2022).

Antonello, P. and R. Farneti. 2009. 'Antigone's Claim: A Conversation with Judith Butler'. *Theory & Event* 12 (1). DOI: 10.1353/tae.0.0048.

Avramopolou, E. 2014. 'Crisis, Critique and the Possibilities of the Political'. *The Cyprus Review* 26 (1): 195–203.

Barbec, S. 2017. 'An Interview with Judith Butler'. Verso blog. Available at https://www.versobooks.com/blogs/3304-an-interview-with-judith-but ler (accessed 8 December 2022).

Bell, V. 1999. 'On Speech, Race and Melancholia: An Interview with Judith Butler'. *Theory, Culture & Society* 16 (2): 163–75.

Bella, K. 2011. 'Bodies in Alliance: Gender Theorist Judith Butler on the Occupy and SlutWalk Movements'. *Truthout*, 15 December. Available at https://truthout.org/articles/bodies-in-alliance-gender-theorist-judith -butler-on-the-occupy-and-slutwalk-movements/ (accessed 8 December 2022).

Birulés, F. 2009. 'Interview with Judith Butler: Gender is Extramoral'. *Mronline*. Available at https://mronline.org/2009/05/16/interview-with -judith-butler-gender-is-extramoral/ (accessed 8 December 2022).

Blumenfeld, W. J. and M. S, Breen. 2005. '"There is a person here": An Interview with Judith Butler'. In *Butler Matters: Judith Butler's Impact on Feminist and Queer Studies*, edited by M. S. Breen and W. J. Blumenfeld, 7–24. Aldershot: Ashgate.

Butler, J. and W. E. Connolly. 2000. 'Politics, Power and Ethics'. *Theory & Event* 4 (2). muse.jhu.edu/article/32589.

Butler, J. 2007c. 'Gender Trouble: Still Revolutionary of Obsolete?' Interview for Bang Bang, Belgium weekly Queer radio magazine. Available at http:// www.fahamu.org/mbbc/wp-content/uploads/2011/09/BangBang2007In terviewwithJudithButler.pdf (accessed 8 December 2022).

Danbolt, M. 2015. 'In the Hands of the Social: An Interview with Judith

Butler'. http://www.f-r-a-n-k.org/conversations/01/pdfs/150518_FRA NK_conversations_Butler.pdf.

Filar, R. 2014. 'Willing the Impossible: An Interview with Judith Butler'. *Open Democracy*. Available at https://www.opendemocracy.net/en/trans formation/willing-impossible-interview-with-judith-butler/ (accessed 8 December 2022).

Heckert, J. 2011. 'On Anarchism: An Interview with Judith Butler'. In *Anarchism and Sexuality: Ethics, Relationships and Power*, edited by J. Heckert and R. Cleminson, 93–100. New York: Routledge.

Ingala, E. 2017. 'Judith Butler: A Living Engagement with Politics'. *Isegoria* 56: 21–37.

Kania, E. 2013. 'Exercising Politics. Interview with Judith Butler'. *R.Evolutions* 1(1): 32–41.

Kotz, L. 1992. 'The Body You Want'. *Artforum*, 82–9.

Martínez Ruiz, R. 2016. 'A Conversation with Judith Butler'. *The Undecidable Unconsciousness* 3: 51–65.

McCann, M. 2011. 'Whose Lives Matter? An Interview with Judith Butler'. Available at https://www.dailyxtra.com/whose-lives-matter-an-intervi ew-with-judith-butler-34248 (accessed 9 January 2023).

Meijer, I. C. and B. Prins. 1998. 'How Bodies Come to Matter: An Interview with Judith Butler'. *Signs* 23 (2): 275–86.

O'Hana, S. 2017. 'Judith Butler on the Poetry of Guantanamo: "In some ways, literature and the arts help to make the world bearable"'. *Literary Hub*, 7 July. Available at https://lithub.com/judith-butler-on-the-poetry -of-guantanamo/ (accessed 8 December 2022).

Olson, G. A. and L. Worsham. 2000. 'Changing the Subject: Judith Butler's Politics of Radical Resignification'. *JAC* 20 (4): 727–65.

Pagès, C. and M. Trachman. 2012. 'Analytics of Power. An Interview with Judith Butler'. *Books and Ideas*. Available at https://booksandideas.net /IMG/pdf/20121129_an_analytics_of_power.pdf (accessed 8 December 2022).

Phelps, J. 2013. 'Judith Butler on Performativity and Performance'. *Counterpulse*. Available at http://counterpulse.org/judith-butler-gender -performativity/ (accessed 8 December 2022).

Pheng C. and E. Grosz. 1998. 'The Future of Sexual Difference: An Interview with Judith Butler and Drucilla Cornell'. *Diacritics* 28 (1): 19–42.

Power, N. 2009. 'The Books interview: Judith Butler'. *The New Statesman*. https://www.newstatesman.com/2009/08/media-death-frames-war -obama.

Reddy, V. and J. Butler. 2004. 'Troubling Genders, Subverting Identities: Interview with Judith Butler'. *Agenda: Empowering Women for Gender Equity*, African Feminisms 62 (2,1): 115–23.

Salmon, C. 2016. 'Trump, Fascism and the Construction of "the People"'.

Verso blog, 29 December. Available at https://www.versobooks.com/bl ogs/3025-trump-fascism-and-the-construction-of-the-people-an-intervi ew-with-judith-butler (accessed 8 December 2022).

Sarra, S. 2012. 'Solidarity in the Streets. An Interview with Judith Butler'. *Rabble*, 23 May. Available at https://rabble.ca/news/2012/05/solidarity -streets-interview-judith-butler (accessed 8 December 2022).

Schneider, N. and J. Butler. 2010. 'A Carefully Crafted F**k You'. *Guernica Mag*. Available at https://www.guernicamag.com/a_carefully_crafted_fk _you/ (accessed 8 December 2022).

Seeliger, M. and P.-I. Villa Braslavsky. 2022. 'Reflections on the Contemporary Public Sphere: An Interview with Judith Butler'. *Theory, Culture & Society*, 20 January. Available at https://journals.sagepub.com /doi/full/10.1177/02632764211066260 (accessed 8 December 2022).

Stauffer, J. 2003. 'Peace is a Resistance to the Terrible Satisfactions of War'. *The Believer*, 1 May. Available at https://believermag.com/an-interview -with-judith-butler/ (accessed 8 December 2022).

Tohidi, N. 2017. 'An Interview on Feminist Ethics and Theory with Judith Butler'. *Journal of Middle East Women's Studies* 13 (3): 461–8.

Uzelac, M. 2000. 'Reći ću da sam žena politički i javno'. *Zarez* 39. Available at http://www.womenngo.org.rs/sajt/sajt/saopstenja/razgovori/batler.htm (accessed 8 December 2022).

Willig, R. 2012. 'Recognition and Critique: An Interview with Judith Butler'. *Distinktion: Scandinavian Journal of Social Theory* 13 (1): 139–44.

Yancy, G. and J. Butler. 2015. 'What's Wrong with "All Lives Matter"?' *New York Times*, 12 January. Available at http://opinionator.blogs .nytimes.com/2015/01/12/whats-wrong-with-all-lives-matter/?_r=0 (accessed 8 December 2022).

Zaharijević, A. and J. Butler. 2016. 'In Conversation with Judith Butler: Binds Yet to Be Settled'. *Filozofija i društvo* 27 (1): 105–14.

Zimmer, U., M. Heidingsfelder and S. Adler. 2010. 'AVIVA-Interview with Judith Butler'. Available at https://www.aviva-berlin.de/aviva/content_In terviews.php?id=1427323 (accessed 8 December 2022).

Other Works

Abbagnano, N. 2020. 'Existentialism as Philosophy of the Possible'. *Journal of Continental Philosophy* 1 (2): 260–76.

Abrams, K. 2011. 'Performing Interdependence: Judith Butler and Sunaura Taylor in the Examined Life'. *Columbia Journal of Gender & Law* 21 (2): 72–89.

Adorno, T. 1951. *Minima Moralia. Reflexionen aus dem beschädigten Leben*. Berlin und Frankfurt am Mein: Suhrkamp Verlag.

Agamben, G. 1998. *Homo Sacer: Sovereign Power and Bare Life*. Stanford, CA: Stanford University Press.

Ahmed, S. 2007. 'A Phenomenology of Whiteness'. *Feminist Theory* 8 (2): 149–68.

Alamo, S. and S. Hekman. 2008. 'Introduction: Emerging Models of Materiality in Feminist Theory'. In *Material Feminisms*, edited by S. Alamo and S. Hekman, 1–22. Bloomington: Indiana University Press.

Allen, A. 1998. 'Power Trouble: Performativity as Critical Theory'. *Constellations* 5 (4): 456–71.

Allen, A. and R. Goddard. 2014. 'The Domestication of Foucault. Government, Critique, War'. *History of the Human Sciences* 27 (5): 26–53.

Antić, M. and I. Radačić. 2020. 'The Evolving Understanding of Gender in International Law and "Gender Ideology" Pushback 25 Years since the Beijing Conference on Women'. *Women's Studies International Forum* 83.

Arendt, H. 1962. *The Origins of Totalitarianism*. Cleveland and New York: Meridian Books.

Arendt, H. 1981. *The Life of the Mind*. New York: Harcourt Brace Jovanovich.

Arendt, H. 1990. *On Revolution*. London: Penguin.

Arendt, H. 1998. *The Human Condition*. Chicago: University of Chicago Press.

Arendt, H. 2005. 'Socrates'. In *The Promise of Politics*, edited by J. Kohn, 5–39. New York: Schocken Books.

Arendt, H. 2006. *Eichmann in Jerusalem: A Report on the Banality of Evil*. New York: Penguin.

Aristotle. 1991a. *Metaphysics. Complete Works*. Princeton, NJ: Princeton University Press.

Aristotle. 1991b. *Generation of Animals. Complete Works*. Princeton, NJ: Princeton University Press.

Aristotle. 1991c. *Politics. Complete Works*. Princeton, NJ: Princeton University Press.

Arruzza, C. 2015. 'Gender as Social Temporality: Butler and Marx'. *Historical Materialism* 23 (1): 28–52.

Ashenden, S. and D. Owen (eds). 1999. *Foucault Contra Habermas*. London: Sage.

Athanasiou, A. 2017. *Agonistic Mourning: Political Dissidence and the Women in Black*. Edinburgh: Edinburgh University Press.

Athanasiou, A. and E. Tzelepis. 2010. 'Mourning (as) Woman: Event, Catachresis, and "That Other Face of Discourse"'. In *Rewriting Difference: Luce Irigaray and the 'Greeks'*, edited by E. Tzelepis and A. Athanasiou, 105–18. New York: SUNY Press.

Austin, J. 1962. *How to Do Things with Words*. Oxford: Clarendon Press.

Barad, K. 2007. *Meeting the Universe Halfway: Quantum Physics and the Entanglement of Matter and Meaning*. Durham, NC and London: Duke University Press.

Beauvoir, S de. 1956. *The Second Sex*. London: Jonathan Cape.

Benhabib, S. 1995a. 'Feminism and Postmodernism'. In *Feminist Contentions: A Philosophical Exchange*, edited by S. Benhabib et al., 17–34. New York and London: Routledge.

Benhabib, S. 1995b. 'Subjectivity, Historiography, and Politics'. In *Feminist Contentions: A Philosophical Exchange*, edited by S. Benhabib et al., 107–26. New York and London: Routledge.

Benjamin, W. 1977. 'The Task of the Translator'. *Illuminations*. Fontana/ Collins.

Benjamin, W. 2004. 'Critique of Violence'. In *Selected Writings, Vol. 1*, edited by M. Bullock and M. W. Jennings, 236–52. Cambridge, MA. and London: The Belknap Press.

Berger, A. E. 2014. *The Queer Turn in Feminism: Identities, Sexualities, and the Theater of Gender*. New York: Fordham University Press.

Bhabha, H. 1994. *The Location of Culture*. London and New York: Routledge.

Bojanić, P. 2019. '"Leben und Gewalt" or "Gewalt und Leben". A Commentary on Paragraph 18 of Walter Benjamin's "Towards the Critique of Violence"'. *Critical Times* 2 (2): 320–9.

Boucher, G. 2006. 'The Politics of Performativity: A Critique of Judith Butler'. *Parrhesia* 1: 112–41.

Bourke, J. 2013. *What It Means to Be a Human?* London: Virago.

Braidotti, R. 1994. *Nomadic Subjects: Embodiment and Sexual Difference in Contemporary Feminist Theory*. New York: Columbia University Press.

Braidotti, R. and J. Butler. 1994. 'Feminism by Any Other Name'. *differences* 6 (2–3): 27–61.

Brown, W. 2001. *Politics Out of History*. Princeton, NJ and Oxford: Princeton University Press.

Brown, W. 2015. *Undoing the Demos: Neoliberalism's Stealth Revolution*. New York: Zone Books.

Cabrera, E. 2018. 'From Subjection to Dispossession: Butler's Recent Performative Thought on Foucault's Latest Work'. *CLCWeb: Comparative Literature and Culture* 20(4).

Campbell, K. 2002. 'The Politics of Kinship'. *Economy and Society* 31 (4): 642–50.

Canovan, M. 1990. 'Socrates or Heidegger? Hannah Arendt's Reflections on Philosophy and Politics'. *Social Research* 57 (1): 135–65.

Cavarero, A. 2000. *Relating Narratives: Storytelling and Selfhood*. London and New York: Routledge.

Cavarero, A. 2011. *Horrorism: Naming Contemporary Violence*. New York: Columbia University Press.

Cavarero, A. 2016. *Inclinations*. Stanford, CA: Stanford University Press.

Cavarero, A. 2021. 'Rethinking Radical Democracy with Butler'. In *Bodies That Still Matter: Resonances of Work of Judith Butler*, edited by A.

Halsema, K. Kwastek and R. van der Ooever, 141–54. Amsterdam: Amsterdam University Press.

Chambers, S. and T. Carver. 2008. *Judith Butler and Political Theory: Troubling Politics*. London and New York: Routledge.

Charpentier, A. 2019. 'On Judith Butler's "Ontological Turn"'. *Raisons politiques* 76 (4): 43–54.

Clare, S. 2009. 'Agency, Signification, and Temporality'. *Hypatia* 24 (2): 50–62.

Cooper, M. 2008. *Life as Surplus: Biotechnology and Capitalism in the Neoliberal Era*. Seattle and London: University of Washington Press.

Crenshaw, K. W. 2020. 'The Unmattering of Black Lives'. *The New Republic*, 21 May. Available at https://newrepublic.com/article/157769/unmattering-black-lives (accessed 8 December 2022).

Cyfer, I. 2019. 'What's the Trouble with Humanity? A Feminist Critique of Judith Butler's Ethics of Vulnerability'. *Digitum* 23: 1–15.

Dean, J. 2008. 'Change of Address: Butler's Ethics at Sovereignty's Deadlock'. In *Judith Butler's Precarious Politics*, edited by T. Carver and S. A. Chambers, 109–26. London and New York: Routledge.

Delphi, C. 1995. 'The Invention of French Feminism: An Essential Move'. *Yale French Studies* 87: 190–221.

Derrida, J. 1988. *Limited Inc*. Evanston, IL: Northwestern University Press.

Deutscher, P. 1997. *Yielding Gender: Feminism, Deconstruction and the History of Philosophy*. London: Routledge.

Deutscher, P. 2017. *Foucault's Futures: A Critique of Reproductive Reason*. New York: Columbia University Press.

Devenney, M. 2020. *Towards an Improper Politics*. Edinburgh: Edinburgh University Press.

Diels, H. 1960. *Die Fragmente der Vorsokratiker*. Berlin: Weidmannsche Verlagbuchhandlung.

Disch, L. 1999. 'Judith Butler and the Politics of the Performative'. *Political Theory* 27 (4): 545–59.

Drichel, S. 2013. 'Reframing Vulnerability: "So obviously the problem. . ."?' *SubStance* 42 (3): 3–27.

Duden, B. 1993. 'Die Frau ohne Unterleib: Zu Judith Butlers Entkörperung'. *Feministische Studien* 2: 24–33.

Duggan, L. 1998. 'The Theory Wars, or, Who's Afraid of Judith Butler?' *Journal of Women's History* 10 (1): 9–19.

Ebert, T. 1993. 'Ludic Feminism, the Body, Performance, and Labor: Bringing "Materialism" Back into Feminist Cultural Studies'. *Cultural Critique* 23: 5–50.

Ertür, B. 2017. 'The Onus of Thought in the War on Terror'. *Theory & Event* 20 (1): 66–75.

Fanon, F. 1986. *Black Skins, White Masks*. London: Pluto Classic.

Fausto-Sterling, A. 2000. *Sexing the Body: Gender Politics and the Construction of Sexuality*. New York: Basic Books.

Feola, M. 2014. 'Norms, Vision and Violence: Judith Butler on the Politics of Legibility'. *Contemporary Political Theory* 13 (2): 130–48.

Ferguson, A., I. Philipson, I. Diamond, L. Quinby, C. Vance and A. Barr Snitow. 1984. 'Forum: The Feminist Sexuality Debates'. *Signs* 10 (1): 106–35.

Ferrarese, E. 2011. 'Judith Butler's "Not Particularly Postmodern Insight" of Recognition'. *Philosophy and Social Criticism* 37 (7): 759–73.

Ferrarese, E. 2016. 'Vulnerability: A Concept with Which to Undo the World as It Is?' *Critical Horizons* 17 (2): 149–59.

Fineman, M. A. 2008. 'The Vulnerable Subject: Anchoring Equality in the Human Condition'. *Yale Journal of Law and Feminism* 20 (1): 1–23.

Foucault, M. 1978. *The History of Sexuality. Volume I: An Introduction*. New York: Pantheon.

Foucault, M. 1980a. 'Prison Talk'. In *Power/Knowledge*, edited by C. Gordon, 55–62. New York: Pantheon.

Foucault, M. 1980b. 'The Confessions of the Flesh'. In *Power/Knowledge*, edited by C. Gordon, 194–228. New York: Pantheon.

Foucault, M. 1996a. 'From Torture to Cellblock'. In *Foucault Live*, edited by S. Lotringer, 207–13. New York: Semiotext(e).

Foucault, M. 1996b. 'Space, Power and Knowledge'. In *Foucault Live*, edited by S. Lotringer, 335–48. New York: Semiotext(e).

Foucault, M. 1997a. *Il faut défendre la société*. EHESS, Gallimard, Seuil.

Foucault, M. 1997b. 'The Ethics of Concern for Self as a Practice of Freedom'. In *Ethics: Subjectivity and Truth*, edited by P. Rabinow, 280–302. New York: The New Press.

Foucault, M. 1997c. 'The Masked Philosopher'. In *Ethics: Subjectivity and Truth*, ed. P. Rabinow, 321–8. New York: The New Press.

Foucault, M. 2000. 'Preface'. In G. Deleuze and F. Guattari, *Anti-Oedipus*. Minneapolis: University of Minnesota Press.

Foucault, M. 2002a. *The Order of Things*. London and New York: Routledge.

Foucault, M. 2002b. 'The Subject and Power'. In *Power: The Essential Works of Michel Foucault 1954–1984*, edited by J. D. Faubion, 326–48. London: Penguin.

Foucault, M. 2003. *Society Must Be Defended*. New York: Picador.

Foucault, M. 2007a. 'What is Critique?' In *The Politics of Truth*, edited by S. Lotringer, 41–82. New York: Semiotext(e).

Foucault, M. 2007b. 'What is Enlightenment?' In *The Politics of Truth*, edited by S. Lotringer, 97–120. New York: Semiotext(e).

Foucault, M. 2012. 'The Mesh of Power'. *Viewpoint Magazine*, 12 September. Available at https://viewpointmag.com/2012/09/12/the-mesh-of-power/ (accessed 8 December 2022).

Foucault, M. 2014. 'Interview with Hean François and John De Wit'. In *Wrong-Doing, Truth-Telling*, edited by F. Brion and B. Harcourt, 253–70. Chicago: University of Chicago Press and UCL.

Foucault, M. 2018. 'Interview with Farès Sassine: There Can't Be Societies Without Uprisings'. *Foucault Studies* 25: 324–50.

Foultier, A. P. 2013. 'Language and the Gendered Body: Butler's Early Reading of Merleau-Ponty'. *Hypatia* 28 (4): 767–83.

Fraser, N. 1995. 'False Antitheses: A Response to Seyla Benhabib and Judith Butler'. In *Feminist Contentions: A Philosophical Exchange*, edited by S. Benhabib et al., 59–74. New York and London: Routledge.

Fraser, N. 1996.' Michel Foucault: A "Young Conservative"'. In *Feminist Interpretations of Michel Foucault*, edited by S. J. Hekman, 15–38. University Park: Pennsylvania State University Press.

Freud, S. 1912. 'On the Universal Tendency to Debasement in the Sphere of Love'. In *The Standard Edition of the Complete Psychological Works of Sigmund Freud, Vol. 11*, 177–90. London: The Hogarth Press and the Institute of Psycho-Analysis [1957].

Freud, S. 1917. 'Mourning and Melancholia'. In *The Standard Edition of the Complete Psychological Works of Sigmund Freud, Vol. 14*, 243–58. London: The Hogarth Press and the Institute of Psycho-Analysis [1957].

Geddes, P. and A. Thomson. 1889. *The Evolution of Sex*. London: Walter Scott.

Germon, J. 2009. *Gender: A Genealogy of an Idea*. New York: Palgrave Macmillan.

Gilson, E. 2011. 'Vulnerability, Ignorance, and Oppression'. *Hypatia* 26 (2): 308–32.

Girard, F. 2007. 'Negotiating Sexual Rights and Sexual Orientation at the UN'. *SexPolitics: Reports from the Frontlines*. Available at http://www.sxpolitics.net/frontlines/book/pdf/capitulo9_united_nations.pdf (accessed 8 December 2022).

Glick, E. 2000. 'Sex Positive: Feminism, Queer Theory, and the Politics of Transgression'. *Feminist Review* 64: 19–45.

Goffman, E. 1956. *The Presentation of Self in Everyday Life*. Edinburgh: University of Edinburgh.

Graff, A. and E. Korolczuk. 2022. *Anti-Gender Politics in the Populist Moment*. London and New York: Routledge.

Habermas, J. 1982. 'The Entwinement of Myth and Enlightenment: Re-Reading *Dialectic of Enlightenment*'. *New German Critique* 26: 13–30.

Hanson, E. 1991. 'Undead'. In *Inside/Out. Lesbian Theories, Gay Theories*, edited by D. Fuss, 324–40. New York and London: Routledge.

Hark, S. 2001. 'Disputed Territory: Feminist Studies in Germany and Its Queer Discontents'. *Amerikastudien/American Studies* 46 (1): 87–103.

Hartsock, N. 1997. 'Comment on Hekman's "Truth and Method: Feminist Standpoint Theory Revisited": Truth or Justice?' *Signs* 22 (2): 367–74.

Hegel, G. W. F. 1977. *The Phenomenology of Spirit*. Oxford: Oxford University Press.

Hemmings, C. 2005. 'Telling Feminist Stories'. *Feminist Theory* 6 (2): 115–39.

Hennessy, R. 2000. *Profit and Pleasure: Sexual Identities in Late Capitalism*. New York and London: Routledge.

Hobbes, T. 1965. *Leviathan*. Oxford: Clarendon Press.

Holusha, J. 2006. 'Bush Says Anthem Should Be in English'. *The New York Times*, 28 April. Available at https://www.nytimes.com/2006/04/28/us/bush-says-anthem-should-be-in-english.html (accessed 8 December 2022).

Honig, B. 2009. *Emergency Politics: Paradox, Law, Democracy*. Princeton, NJ: Princeton University Press.

Honig, B. 2010. 'Antigone's Two Laws: Greek Tragedy and the Politics of Humanism'. *New Literary History* 41 (1): 1–33.

Honkasalo, M.-L. 2018. 'Vulnerability and Inquiring into Relationality'. *Suomen Antropologi* 43 (3): 1–21.

Honneth, A. 2008. *Reification: A New Look at an Old Idea*. Oxford: Oxford University Press.

Hood-Williams, J. and W. C. Harrison. 1998. 'Trouble with Gender'. *The Sociological Review* 46 (1): 73–94.

hooks, b. 1981. *Ain't I a Woman?* Boston, MA: South End Press.

Hunter, W. A. 1803. *A Systematic and Historical Exposition of Roman Law in the Order of a Code*. London: Sweet & Maxwell.

Illetterati, L. 2022. 'Subjectivity and Violence: A Hegelian Perspective'. In *Violence and Reflexivity. The Place of Critique in the Reality of Domination*, edited by M. Ivković, Adriana Zaharijević and G. Pudar Draško, 33-52. Lanham and Boulder: Lexington Books.

Ingala, E. 2018a. 'Catachresis and Mis-Being in Judith Butler and Étienne Balibar: Contemporary Refigurations of the Human as a Face Drawn in the Sand'. *Literature and Theology* 32 (2): 142–60.

Ingala, E. 2018b. 'From Hannah Arendt to Judith Butler: The Conditions of the Political'. In *Subjectivity and the Political*, edited by G. Rae and E. Ingala, 35–54. New York and London: Routledge.

Ingala, E. 2019. 'Judith Butler: From a Normative Violence to an Ethics of Non-violence'. In *The Meanings of Violence: From Critical Theory to Biopolitics*, edited by G. Rae and E. Ingala, 191–208. New York: Routledge.

Ingala, E. 2021. 'Contemporary Declinations of Violence: Thinking Extreme Violence and Vulnerability with Étienne Balibar and Judith Butler'. In *Rethinking Vulnerability and Exclusion*, edited by B. Rodríguez, N. Sánchez Madrid and A. Zaharijević, 117–34. Cham: Palgrave Macmillan.

Jagger, G. 2008. *Judith Butler: Sexual Politics, Social Change and the Power of the Performative*. Abingdon and New York: Routledge.

Jaspers, K. 1956. *Philosophie II. Existenzerhellung.* Berlin: Springer-Verlag.

Käll, L. F. 2015. 'A Path Between Voluntarism and Determinism. Tracing Elements of Phenomenology in Judith Butler's Account of Performativity'. *Lamba nordica* 2–3: 23–48.

Karhu, S. 2016. 'Judith Butler's Critique of Violence and the Legacy of Monique Wittig'. *Hypatia* 31 (4): 827–43.

Kessler, S. and W. McKenna. 1978. *Gender: An Ethnomethodological Approach.* Chicago: University of Chicago Press.

Kim, D. K. 2007. *Melancholic Freedom: Agency and the Spirit of Politics.* Oxford and New York: Oxford University Press.

Kirby, V. 2006. *Judith Butler: Live Theory.* London and New York: Continuum.

Kitzinger, C. and S. Wilkinson. 1994. 'Virgins and Queers: Rehabilitating Heterosexuality?' *Gender and Society* 8 (3): 444–62.

Klein, M. 1935. 'A Contribution to the Psychogenesis of Manic-Depressive States'. *The International Journal of Psychoanalysis* 16: 145–74.

Knight, A. 2021. 'Feminist Vulnerability Politics: Judith Butler on Autonomy and the Pursuit of a "Livable Life"'. *Feminist Formations* 33 (3): 175–98.

Kołakowski, L. 2010. 'Kapłan i Błazen. Rozważania o teologicznym dziedzictwie współczesnego myślenia'. In *Nasza wesoła apokalipsa. Wybór najważniejszych esejów*, edited by Z. Mentzel, 49–82. Kraków: Znak.

Kramer, S. 2015. 'Judith Butler's "New Humanism": A Thing or Not a Thing, and So What?' *philoSOPHIA* 5 (1): 25–40.

Kristeva, J. 1982. *Powers of Horror: An Essay on Abjection.* New York: Columbia University Press.

Lacan, J. 1977. *Écrits: A Selection.* New York: Norton.

Laclau, E. and C. Mouffe. 2001. *Hegemony and Socialist Strategy: Towards a Radical Democratic Politics.* London: Verso.

Laqueur, T. 2003. *Making Sex: Body and Gender from Greeks to Freud.* Cambridge, MA and London: Harvard University Press.

Levinas, E. 1998. *Entre Nous. On Thinking-of-the-Other.* New York: Columbia University Press.

Levinas, E. 1999. *Alterity and Transcendence.* New York: Columbia University Press.

Lloyd, G. 1983. 'Masters, Slaves and Others'. *Radical Philosophy* 34: 1–9.

Lloyd, M. 1999. 'Performativity, Parody, Politics'. *Theory, Culture & Society* 16 (2): 195–213.

Lloyd, M. 2007. *Judith Butler: From Norms to Politics.* Cambridge: Polity.

Lloyd, M. 2008. 'Towards a Cultural Politics of Vulnerability: Precarious Lives and Ungrievable Deaths'. In *Judith Butler's Precarious Politics*, edited by T. Carver and S. A. Chambers, 93–105. London and New York: Routledge.

Lloyd, M. 2009. 'Performing Radical Politics'. In *The Politics of Radical*

Democracy, edited by A. Little and M. Lloyd, 33–51. Edinburgh: Edinburgh University Press.

Lloyd, M. (ed.). 2015. *Judith Butler and Ethics*. Edinburgh: Edinburgh University Press.

Loidolt, S. 2018. *Phenomenology of Plurality: Hannah Arendt on Political Intersubjectivity*. New York and London: Routledge.

Loizidou, E. 2007. *Judith Butler: Ethics, Law, Politics*. Abingdon and New York: Routledge Cavendish.

Loizidou, E. 2008. 'Butler and Life: Law, Sovereignty, Power'. In *Judith Butler's Precarious Politics*, edited by T. Carver and S. A. Chambers, 145–56. Abingdon: Routledge.

Lorey, I. 2015. *State of Insecurity: Government of the Precarious*, with a Foreword by J. Butler. London and New York: Verso.

Lovibond, S. 1996. 'Meaning What We Say: Feminist Ethics and the Critique of Humanism'. *New Left Review* 1 (220): 98–115.

Lundgren-Gothlin, E. 1996. *Sex and Existence: Simone de Beauvoir's* The Second Sex. Hanover, NH: Wesleyan University Press/University Press of New England.

Lynteris, C. 2013. 'The State as a Social Relation: An Anthropological Critique'. *Anthropology & Materialism. A Journal of Social Research* 1. DOI: 10.4000/am.291.

Macpherson, C. B. 1993. *The Theory of Possessive Individualism*. Oxford: Oxford University Press.

Magnus, K. Dow. 2006. 'The Unaccountable Subject: Judith Butler and the Social Conditions of Intersubjective Agency'. *Hypatia* 21 (2): 81–103.

Mahmood, S. 2001. 'Feminist Theory, Embodiment, and the Docile Agent: Some Reflections on the Egyptian Islamic Revival'. *Cultural Anthropology* 16 (2): 202–36.

Marx, K. 1972. *The Eighteenth Brumaire of Louis Bonaparte*. Moscow: Progress Publishers.

McIvor, D. 2012. 'Bringing Ourselves to Grief: Judith Butler and the Politics of Mourning'. *Political Theory* 40 (4): 409–36.

McNay, L. 1999. 'Subject, Psyche and Agency: The Work of Judith Butler'. *Theory, Culture & Society* 16 (2): 175–93.

McNeilly, K. 2015. 'From the Right to Life to the Right to Livability: Radically Reapproaching "Life" in Human Rights Politics'. *Australian Feminist Law Journal* 41 (1): 141–59.

McWhorter, L. 2013. 'Post-Liberation Feminism and Practices of Freedom'. *Foucault Studies* 16: 54–73.

Merleau-Ponty, M. 1962. *The Phenomenology of Perception*. Boston, MA: Routledge & Kegan Paul.

Millett, K. 1970. *Sexual Politics*. New York: Doubleday.

Mills, C. 2007. 'Normative Violence, Vulnerability, and Responsibility'. *differences* 18 (2): 133–56.

Mitscherlich, A. and M. Mitscherlich. 1975. *An Inability to Mourn: Principles of Collective Behavior.* New York: Grove Press.

Mohanty, C. T. 1988. 'Under Western Eyes: Feminist Scholarship and Colonial Discourses'. *Feminist Review* 30 (1): 61–88.

Moi, T. 1999. *What is a Woman? And Other Essays.* Oxford: Oxford University Press.

Moraga, C. and G. Anzaldúa. 2015. *This Bridge Called My Back: Writings by Radical Women of Color.* New York: SUNY Press.

Mort, F. and R. Peters. 2005 [1979]. 'Foucault Recalled: Interview with Michel Foucault'. *New Formations* 55: 9–22.

Möser, C. 2019. 'Gender Travelling across France, Germany and the US: The Feminist Gender Debates as Cultural Translations'. In *Feminist Translation Studies: Local and Transnational Perspectives*, edited by O. Castro and E. Ergun, 80–92. London and New York: Routledge.

Murphy, A. 2011. 'The Remainder: Between Symbolic and Material Violence'. In *Philosophy and the Return of Violence*, edited by N. Eckstrand and C. S. Yates, 189–201. New York: Continuum.

Nelson, L. 1999. 'Bodies (and Spaces) Do Matter: The Limits of Performativity'. *Gender, Place & Culture* 6 (4): 331–53.

Newton, E. 1979. *Mother Camp: Female Impersonators in America.* Chicago: University of Chicago Press.

Nicholson, L. 1995. 'Introduction'. In *Feminist Contentions*, edited by S. Benhabib et al., 1–16. London: Routledge.

Nietzsche, F. 1989. *On the Genealogy of Morals: Ecce Homo.* New York: Vintage.

Nietzsche, F. 2006. *Daybreak.* Cambridge: Cambridge University Press.

Nussbaum, M. 1999. 'The Professor of Parody'. *The New Republic*, 22 February. Available at https://newrepublic.com/article/150687/professor -parody (accessed 9 December 2022).

Oliver, K. 2001. *Witnessing: Beyond Recognition.* Minneapolis and London: University of Minnesota Press.

Oosterveld, V. 2005. 'The Definition of "Gender" in the Rome Statute of the International Criminal Court: A Step Forward or Back for International Criminal Justice?' *Harvard Human Rights Journal* 18: 55–84.

Phillips Simpson, P. 1998. *A Philosophical Commentary on the* Politics *of Aristotle.* Chapel Hill: University of North Carolina Press.

Probyn, E. 1995. 'Lesbians in Space: Gender, Sex and the Structure of Missing'. *Gender, Place & Culture* 2 (1): 77–84.

Prosser, J. 1998. *Second Skins: The Body Narratives of Transsexuality.* New York: Columbia University Press.

Pulkkinen, T. 2018. 'Judith Butler's Politics of Philosophy in *Notes Toward a Performative Theory of Assembly* – Arendt, Cavarero, and Human "Appearing" and "Plurality"'. *Redescriptions* 21 (2): 128–47.

Pulkkinen, T. 2020. 'Vulnerability and the Human in Judith Butler's and

Adriana Cavarero's Feminist Thought: A Politics of Philosophy Point of View'. *Redescriptions* 23 (2): 151–64.

Purvis, J. 2003. 'Hegelian Dimensions of *The Second Sex*: A Feminist Consideration'. *Journal of French and Francophone Philosophy* 13 (1): 128–56.

Redecker, E. von. 2016. 'Exodus by Dispossession? Butler and Landauer on Fundamental Collectivity'. Lecture at the Institute for Philosophy and Social Theory, 18 October 2016. Available at https://www.youtube.com /watch?v=_xzcHexaP6E (accessed 9 December 2022).

Redecker, E. von. 2017. 'Gender Parody'. In *Gender: Laughter*, edited by B. Papenburg, 279–92. New York: Palgrave Macmillan.

Richard, L. 2019. 'Is Ontological Thinking a Dead End for Emancipatory Politics? Radical Democracy, Embodiment, and Judith Butler's "Ontological Turn"'. *Raisons politiques* 76 (4): 55–75.

Riley, D. 1988. *Am I That Name?* Minneapolis: University of Minnesota Press.

Rothschild, C. 2005. *Written Out: How Sexuality Is Used to Attack Women's Organizing*. New York and New Brunswick: International Gay and Lesbian Human Rights Commission and Center for Women's Global Leadership.

Rozmarin, M. 2021. 'Critical Belonging: Cohabitation, Plurality, and Critique in Butler's *Parting Ways*'. *Redescriptions* 24 (1): 27–41.

Rubin, G. 1992 [1984]. 'Thinking Sex: Notes for a Radical Theory of Politics of Sexuality'. In *Pleasure and Danger: Exploring Female Sexuality*, edited by C. S. Vance, 267–93. London: Pandora.

Rubin, G. 1997 [1975]. 'The Traffic in Women: Notes on the "Political Economy" of Sex'. In *The Second Wave: A Reader in Feminist Theory*, edited by L. Nicholson, 27–62. New York and London: Routledge.

Rubin, G. and J. Butler. 1994. 'Sexual Traffic. Interview'. *differences* 6 (2+3): 62–99.

Rushing, S. 2010. 'Preparing for Politics: Judith Butler's Ethical Dispositions'. *Contemporary Political Theory* 9 (3): 284–303.

Ruti, M. 2017. 'The Ethics of Precarity: Judith Butler's Reluctant Universalism'. In *Remains of the Social*, edited by M. van Bever Donker, R. Truscott, G. Minkley, P. Lalu, 92–116. Johannesburg: Wits University Press.

Sabsay, L. 2016. *The Political Imaginary of Sexual Freedom: Subjectivity and Power in the New Sexual Democratic Turn*. London: Palgrave Macmillan.

Safatle, V. 2016. *Grand Hotel Abyss: Desire, Recognition and Restoration of the Subject*. Leuven: Leuven University Press.

Salih, S. 2002. *Judith Butler*. London and New York: Routledge.

Sartre, J.-P. 2007. *Existentialism Is a Humanism*. New Haven, CT and London: Yale University Press.

Sawicki, J. 2005. 'Queering Foucault and the Subject of Feminism'. In *The Cambridge Companion to Michel Foucault*, edited by G. Gutting, 379–400. Cambridge: Cambridge University Press.

Schippers, B. 2014. *The Political Philosophy of Judith Butler*. London and New York: Routledge.

Schweppenhäuser, G. 2004. 'Adorno's Negative Moral Philosophy'. In *The Cambridge Companion to Adorno*, edited by T. Huhn, 328–53. Cambridge: Cambridge University Press.

Scott, J. 1986. 'Gender: A Useful Category of Historical Analysis'. *The American Historical Review* 91 (5): 1053–75.

Scott, J. 1992. 'Experience'. In *Feminists Theorize the Political*, edited by J. Butler and J. W. Scott, 22–40. New York and London: Routledge.

Sedgwick, E. K. 1994. *Tendencies*. New York and London: Routledge.

Sedgwick, E. K. 2003. *Touching Feeling*. Durham, NC and London: Duke University Press.

Solana, M. 2017. *La noción de subversión en Judith Butler*. Buenos Aires: Teseopress.

Sophocles. 2003. *Antigone*. Oxford: Oxford University Press.

Spinoza, B. 1901. *The Chief Works of Benedict of Spinoza, Vol. II*. London: George Bell and Sons.

Spivak, G. C. 1988. 'Can the Subaltern Speak?' In *Marxism and the Interpretation of Culture*, edited by C. Nelson and L. Grossberg, 271–313. Basingstoke: Macmillan.

Spivak, G. C. 1993. 'The Politics of Translation'. In *Outside in the Teaching Machine*, 179–200. New York: Routledge.

Stark, H. 2014. 'Judith Butler's Post-Hegelian Ethics and the Problem with Recognition'. *Feminist Theory* 15 (1): 89–100.

Stoller, S. 2010. 'Expressivity and Performativity: Merleau-Ponty and Butler'. *Continental Philosophy Review* 43 (1): 97–110.

Stone, A. 2005. 'Towards a Genealogical Feminism: A Reading of Judith Butler's Political Thought'. *Contemporary Political Theory* 4: 4–24.

Stone, A. 2019. *Being Born: Birth and Philosophy*. Oxford: Oxford University Press.

Taylor, C. 1992. 'The Politics of Recognition'. In *Multiculturalism: Examining the Politics of Recognition*, edited by A. Gutmann, 25–73. Princeton, NJ: Princeton University Press.

Thiem, A. 2008. *Unbecoming Subjects: Judith Butler, Moral Philosophy, and Critical Responsibility*. New York: Fordham University Press.

Tortora, P. and S. Keiser. 2013. *The Fairchild Books Dictionary of Fashion*. London: Bloomsbury.

Tronto, J. C. 1994. *Moral Boundaries: A Political Argument for and Ethic of Care*. New York: Routledge.

Vogelmann, F. 2017. 'Measuring, Disrupting, Emancipating: Three Pictures of Critique'. *Constellations* 24 (1): 101–12.

Wapner, P. 1989. 'What's Left: Marx, Foucault and Contemporary Problems of Social Change'. *Praxis International* 1–2: 88–111.

Wehrle, M. 2020. 'Bodily Performativity: Enacting Norms'. In *Phenomenology as Performative Exercise*, edited by L. Guidi and T. Rentsch, 120–39. Leiden: Brill.

West, C. and D. H. Zimmerman. 1987. 'Doing Gender'. *Gender and Society* 1 (2): 125–51.

White, S. 1999. 'As the World Turns: Ontology and Politics in Judith Butler'. *Polity* 32 (2): 155–77.

Wittig, M. 2002 [1981]. 'One is Not Born a Woman'. In *The Straight Mind and Other Essays*, 9–20. Boston, MA: Beacon Press.

Zaharijević, A. 2014. *Ko je pojedinac? Genealoško propitivanje ideje građanina*. Loznica: Karpos.

Zaharijević, A. 2020a. 'Social Ontology: Butler via Arendt via Loidolt'. *Filozofija i društvo* 31 (2): 146–54.

Zaharijević, A. 2020b. 'Becoming a Master of an Island Again: On the Desire to be Bodiless.' *Redescriptions* 23 (2): 1–13.

Zaharijević, A. 2021a. 'On Butler's Theory of Agency'. In *Bodies That Still Matter: Resonances of Work of Judith Butler*, edited by A. Halsema, K. Kwastek and R. van der Ooever, 21–30. Amsterdam: Amsterdam University Press.

Zaharijević, A. 2021b. 'Independent and Invulnerable: Politics of an Individual'. In *Rethinking Vulnerability and Exclusion*, edited by B. Rodríguez, N. Sánchez Madrid and A. Zaharijević, 83–100. Cham: Palgrave Macmillan.

Zaharijević, A. 2022. 'Equal Bodies: The Notion of the Precarious in Judith Butler's Work'. *European Journal of Women's Studies*. DOI: 10.1177/13505068221137695.

Zaharijević, A. and S. Bojanić. 2017. 'The Trajectories of the Concept of Life in Judith Butler's Thought'. *Isegoria* 56: 169–85.

Zaharijević, A. and P. Krstić. 2018. 'U čemu je vrlina kritike?' In *Šta je kritika? Mišel Fuko i Džudit Batler*, edited by A. Zaharijević and P. Krstić, 9–34. Novi Sad and Belgrade: Akademska knjiga and Institut za filozofiju i društvenu teoriju.

Ziarek, E. P. 2008. 'Bare Life on Strike: Notes on the Biopolitics of Race and Gender'. *South Atlantic Quarterly* 107 (1): 89–105.

Zinn, H. 2009. *The Zinn Reader: Writings on Disobedience and Democracy*. New York: Seven Stories Press.

Zylinska, J. 2004. 'The Universal Acts. Judith Butler and the Biopolitics of Immigration'. *Cultural Studies* 18 (4): 523–37.

Index

EU representative:
Easy Access System Europe
Mustamäe tee 50, 10621 Tallinn, Estonia
Gpsr.requests@easproject.com

www.ingramcontent.com/pod-product-compliance
Lightning Source LLC
Chambersburg PA
CBHW070843300326

41935CB00039B/1394